BIG
TROUT

BIG TROUT

How and Where to Target Trophies

Bernie Taylor

Illustrations by Ian Forbes
Foreword by John Randolph

THE LYONS PRESS
Guilford, Connecticut
An imprint of The Globe Pequot Press
www.lyonspress.com

The Lyons Press is an imprint of The Globe Pequot Press

Printed in

10 9 8 7 6 5 4 3 2 1

Design by Compset, Inc.

Library of Congress Cataloging-in-Publication data is available on file.

This book is dedicated to wild trout,
without which it would not have been possible.

CONTENTS

Contents

ACKNOWLEDGMENTS

This book was written over a two-year period; however, it encompasses years of laboratory research and time on the water. Not just my time, but also that of the guides, fellow anglers, and scientists whose work contributed to this book. My guiding angel on this project was Ron Newman, who provided a lifetime of fishing research and organized much of the statistical data in this book. I could not have developed the feeding rhythms hypothesis without his assistance. I also owe my gratitude to four other scientists/anglers. They are Caleb Zurstadt from the U.S. Forest Service, Brad Kerr from Spring Creek Aquatic Concepts, Dr. Robert Behnke from Colorado State University, and Bob Richards, who edited drafts of this book and kept me focused on supporting my observations with hard data.

There were many other individuals from the scientific community who read through draft chapters and offered suggestions or answered important questions. These include Gil Bergen from the Connetquot River State Park, Dr. Norman Anderson from Oregon State University, Dr. Eric Moodie from the University of Winnipeg, Dr. John Palmer from the University of Massachusetts at Amherst, Dr. Gerard Tarling and his associates from the Scottish Association of Marine Science, Dr. Thierry Boujard from INRA Hydrobiologie, Dr. Ronald Douglas from the City University London, Dr. Russ Sardo, Dr. J. Malcolm Elliott from the The Windermere Laboratory, Brian Chan, Rob Dollighan and Jack Leggit from the Fisheries Branch of the British Columbia Ministry of the Environment, Paul Johnson, Dr. Z. Maciej Gliwicz from the University of Warsaw, Dr. Johnathan Jahnke, Dr. Arthur Popper from the University of Maryland, Steve Fajfer from the Wisconsin Dept. of Natural Resources, Dr. David Ross from the Wood's Hole Institute, Roger Schneider from the Utah Department of Wildlife Resources, Dr. James Rose and Dr. William Gern from the University of Wyoming, Dr. Winfried Lampert from the Max Planck Institute, Dr. Wayne Wurtsbaugh from Utah State University, Rhine Messmer, Keith Braun and Steve Marx from the Oregon Department of Fish and Wildlife, Dr. Dick Ryder, Dr. John Sweka from West Virginia University, John Stark, Tom Bly and Darrell Bowman from the Arkansas Game and Fish Commission, Pat Byroth from the Montana Department of Fish, Wildlife and Parks, Dr. Thomas Northcote from the University of British Columbia, Dr. Verdun King from the University of Cambridge, Dr. James Diana from the University of Michigan, Mike Young from the U.S. Forest Service, Dan Dunaway from the Alaska Department of Fish and Game, Jeff Dillon and Dick Oswald from the Idaho Department of Fish and Game, John Viar from the New Hampshire Fish and Game Department, Ira Newbreast from the Blackfeet Fish and Game Department, Roger Greil from Lake Superior State University, Bob Lange from the New York State Department of Environmental Conservation, Dr. Bill Hanneman, and Thomas Waters. There are so many other contributors whose years of research has appeared in the primary literature and is available to us all; their names and contributions are listed in the bibliography.

Thanks to all of the manufacturers and product wholesalers who gave me their support, especially Jim Teeny from Jim Teeny Incorporated, Bruce Holt and Phil Oliva from G. Loomis, Kellie Hawkins from Cabela's, John Mazurkiewicz from Scientific Anglers/Catalyst Marketing Services, Terry Pillan, Dan Foote, Chuck Mize and John Prochnow with Pure Fishing, Dave Hall with Umpqua Feather Merchants, Mark Rogers from Okuma, and the people at Computrol.

There was also a great deal of support from the angling world. My first and foremost thanks are to John Randolph for giving me a chance before I had paid my dues and for writing the foreword to this book. To all of the guides who took me out on the water and/or shared their information in interviews—Bob Gaviglio from the Sun River Fly Shop, Denny Rickards, Bill Kremers, Steve Hickoff, Quille Farnham, Dale Williams from Screaming Reel Fly and Tackle, Carlos Tallent from Gone Fishing with Carlos, Doug Brautigan from Caribou Fly and Tackle, Rick Typher from the Denver Angler, Charlie White, Mark Sosin, Ross Purnell and Greg McDermid from the Virtual Flyshop, Andy Burke and Terry Barron from the Reno Fly Shop, Ed Miranda Sr., Ron Thienes from Wild Billy Lake, Les Jacober and Brett Chaffin from Katmai Lodge, Pete Raynor from Kulik Lodge, Scott Chafe and Ian Gall from Sea Run Outfitters, Paul Smith, Steve Hilbert from Lonesome Duck, Pete Adams and Jeff Lewis from Osprey Lake Lodge, Trapper Rudd from Cutthroat Anglers,

Craig Mathews from Blue Ribbon Flies, Steve Jennings from the Kamloops Fly Shop, Ed Dickson from Diamond Charters, Pete Carlson from Elysia Resort, Tim Heng from the Taylor Creek Fly Shop, Rod Cesario from Dragonfly Anglers, Dale Fulton and Ed Daly from Blue Ribbon Flies/Fulton's Lodge, Rick Kustich from the Oak Orchard Fly Shop, Karl Bruhn, Jerry Kustich, Frank van Neer from East Shore Charters, and Bill Beardsley from Grindstone Lakes.

Thanks to Kit Richards and my angling friends Bob Jones, Dr. Russ Sardo, and Hank Hosfield who edited portions of this draft, and Kenny Austin who assisted me with some of the tests. To Oregon State University, which allowed me to utilize their library and without whom this would have been a very different book. To Ian Forbes, who brought this dry text to life with his captivating illustrations. And finally, to my wife who was supportive throughout this process.

FOREWORD

When I began my childhood fishing on a small mountain trout stream in the Berkshire Mountains of Massachusetts, I thought that a six-inch brook trout was a trophy. It did not occur to me until later that there were bigger trout to be caught downstream in the big river. I was hooked when I caught my first foot-long trout, then a fourteen-incher, and later a sixteen-inch beauty kept me on the path of the leviathan that surely lay in wait over the next hill.

I was becoming a trophy hunter, but my learning curve was relatively flat: Like all those fishers who had preceded me, I learned hit or miss from my mistakes. I found that small beaver ponds grew bigger trout and certain eastern lakes held lakers up to twenty pounds. I read a lot about those lakes and those dream fish, and I spent long days in summer trolling everything from piano wire and streamers to downriggers and "cowbells." In those days I averaged about twenty hours hunched over a sonar for each trout hooked and captured. It did not occur to me that what the scientists call oligotrophic lakes don't have many large fish, and the ones that do live there are the ancient survivors of many lean years.

I finally began to travel and fish widely with my job (Editor of *Fly Fisherman* magazine) and the scales of ignorance fell from my eyes. On the Blackfeet Indian Reservation in Montana I caught my first eight-pound trout, a porcine rainbow; on the Big Horn River I hooked, and lost, a brown that broke 3X; in Alaska I fished over egg-eating 'bows that lay like gray submarines in the ranks of spawning sockeyes. I met Jim Teeny and fished by his side, catching large trout, steelhead, and salmon. I felt heavy trout bump my legs during the evening chironomid rise on the Grindstone Ranch lakes in Oregon and caught them. I fished Monster Lake in Wyoming and hauled in hogs. I sat in the evening hush of Anne

Marie and Minipi Lakes in Labrador and cast No. 6 dries to brookies and landlocked char that averaged five pounds. It was as though Heaven had descended to earth.

During all those years I kept current with the scientific and sporting literature on "aquatic ecosystems." I followed the writings of Al and Ron Lindner, the founders of *In-Fisherman* magazine, and their success with show-and-tell bass and walleye. They wrote about their research on lake water temperature, oxygen content, salinity, and structure and their effect on fish behavior. In spite of all that reading and all that fishing, I could not find the one book that brought all the information together in a synthesis that was understandable to a dedicated trophy trout hunter.

Bernie Taylor followed a similar path as a hunter of trophy trout. I first met him on the Connetquot River on Long Island in 1990. The river is spring creeklike with its own hatchery that spawns brookies, browns, and rainbows, fish that grow to over ten pounds before returning to fresh water from the salt. Now a New York state park, the property had been home to wealthy landowners who wished to fish over large trout in small surroundings and who hosted Ernest Hemingway and other notables among their guests.

I had never seen so many submarine trout in one small, clear stream. To Bernie, who grew up just a few miles away, it was home water, nothing to get excited about. A little later he headed west in search of the country life and we both in our own ways continued searching the world for big trout.

Bernie found them, in many of the same places that I did—out West and up north—but he pursued them in waters that were unknown to most fly fishers. He sought out the fisheries researchers and read their scientific tomes and, gradually, put together the picture of how, when, and where to find the largest wild trout in the world.

It took Taylor more than a decade to research this book and two years to write it. It took me a month to read and understand it all. I read the text and illustrations critically, for I had spent over four decades reading bits and pieces of the scientific and sporting literature piecemeal, and I had spent the same time testing theories from John Alden Knight's solunar tables to George Harvey's night-fishing techniques for trophy trout. I felt I knew something about fishing for large trout in streams, ponds, lakes, and rivers.

What I found in this book is the synthesis of knowledge and fishing that I have been searching for and, more importantly, that I have experienced. For example, in the 1970s I went searching exclusively for large brown trout on Vermont's Battenkill River. During those years, before the downturn in the 'Kill's trout populations, there were abundant large browns (three-pound plus fish) in its West Arlington stretches. I discovered that those large browns would feed actively (on sculpin, their primary food) only in low light, especially in early morning when there was no fishing pressure and the cool night air had dropped the water temperature by about five degrees.

Knight's solunar tables gave me no help in that onstream research. I learned from fishing experience that large trout, especially browns, are low-light feeders. When I came to Taylor's explanation of low-light feeding, in streams and stillwaters, I found confirmation of my fishing experience and the explanations of why large trout feed in low light. The research Taylor cites, and the fishing experiences that he explains, confirm what I have learned about the behavior of large trout over four decades of fishing the water types that he describes. There is important information in this book for aspiring fishers of all kinds.

When I taught my grandson how to fish last summer, he caught bluegills and was excited. But at the end of the day he asked me: "Grandpa, when are we going to catch Big Charlie?"

If you want to catch Big Charlie, you should study this book and take to heart every lesson that it holds, for it can teach you where Big Charlie lives, why he lives there, what he probably eats, and when and where he eats it. You must learn your own waters by studying them for their secrets, their fish, and how the big ones survive. You can get help from fly shops and from veteran anglers who have paid their dues on those streams, lakes, and ponds. But you must also pay your dues. And what you will learn, after reading this book—and fishing, fishing, fishing—is that trophy trout are rare, even on the best trophy waters that Bernie Taylor describes. They are the old soldiers at the top of the survival food chain. With patience, and by following the instructions set forth here, you can catch, and hopefully release, the Big Charlie trout.

There are many important lessons in *Big Trout,* but I like these three: 1) Successful fishing happens only when you have your fly in the water. 2) You can find success by eliminating the variables. Simplicity in your flies, gear, and technique is the golden key to catching trout, especially large ones. 3) If you fish in the places where the big fish are, when they are actively feeding, you will catch them.

Bernie Taylor has trodden on many angling shibboleths and confirmed some others. He has written a new trophy-fishing *vade mecum.* It will help many anglers follow their Yellow Brick Road to the great trout who wait out there for our offerings.

John D. Randolph
Editor/Publisher
Fly Fisherman magazine

INTRODUCTION

It is the fate of all truths that they begin as heresies.
Cardinal Richelieu

I once decided to take a trip to the Rocky Mountain states to catch big trout. My journey began at the local bookstore, where I purchased a few fishing guides about the region. They were books that contained information about rivers and stillwaters that held "big" and "trophy" fish. I returned home and scanned the guides from cover to cover to learn where and how I was going to catch my big trout. It only took me a few minutes to discover that, although most of them discussed "big" and "trophy" trout, none gave me their standards for such fish. They also didn't tell me what time of year I had my greatest chance of hooking into one or how they were really being caught. I had been thinking "trout as long as my leg." My visions of fish body characteristics suddenly changed to colorful and stocky.

Many of the guidebooks had good maps and described the beauty of the waters, hatches, required equipment, guide services, motels, and side trips for my spouse. Some even keyed me in on the unique local flora and fauna to keep an eye out for. These guides were all well-written and valuable books. There must have been countless hours of research, and these places had what I discerned to be nice fish, although not what I was looking for. There have been a few other books about big trout. Most focused on the home water of the angler and did not cover a wide geographic area and different types of waters.

I have not been alone in targeting big trout or in searching for resources that can lead me to them. Perhaps the second most frequently asked question by anglers about any body of water after "Are there any fish in there?" is "Are there any big fish?" My answer: "It all depends on how you qualify a big fish." For the purpose of this book, big trout are browns and rainbows eight pounds and over, cutthroats five pounds and up, and brook trout exceeding four pounds. Someone once showed me a photo of a 7½-pound brown trout and asked me if I thought the fish was big. My answer was yes. Inversely, Labrador anglers would not consider a four-pound brook trout to be out of the ordinary and an eight-pound brown from the Lake Ontario tributaries would be the smallest size you could catch. When I go on the hunt for big trout I am thinking a great deal larger than these standards. (Note that big trout are measured in pounds, not inches.)

To some anglers fish this size may seem really big, almost unimaginably so. As I give slide shows around the country, I often run across anglers who have never caught or even seen a live trout over three pounds. They tend to think that all of the big trout pictures in magazines were shot with either a super-wide-angle lens or involved someone holding the fish too close to the camera. Perhaps there are a few distorted images in print, but big trout are swimming in many of our waters and some anglers are catching them. In this text, I have listed over 85 stillwaters, tailwaters, and migratory trout rivers in North America with big trout that meet my standard. Many of them have larger trophy trout.

My standard does not diminish the worthiness of a three-pound brown trout from a spring creek in Pennsylvania. It is a nice fish, worthy of admiration and due a few snapshots. It just isn't a big trout on a national level. There are other waters where some big trout have been caught, infrequently or in years past, that you won't find in this book. I count the Beaverkill and Willowemoc in the Catskills as two of these. They are legendary for their history and for the contributions of anglers who learned their secrets and laid the groundwork for American fly fishing as we now know it. The big browns are said to hold in the deeper pools, waiting for someone dedicated enough to fish every night over a summer to hook into one.

There are countless other waters that may have some big trout, but the probability of hooking into one, with a fly or otherwise, is slim. And there are other rivers, such as Oregon's Wood River, that seasonally hold big migratory rainbows. However, due to their small numbers and limited public access, they were not included here. Ponds where big trout are planted or fed were eliminated, as well.

Many famous waters that were not included will raise the eyebrows of a few anglers. The Green River, the Beaverhead, the Miracle Mile of the South Platte, the San Juan River at

Navaho Dam, the Colorado River at Lees Ferry, and the Kootenai River are some notable omissions. These and other waters hold large numbers of good-sized trout in the low 20-inch range that are as fat as footballs, including a few fish that meet my big trout standard. However, there are not enough to say that you have a good chance of catching one on a two-day trip. All of the big trout waters covered in this book fit this exacting criteria, shaped with information from regional fisheries biologists and top outfitters.

I have fished for trout in many rivers and stillwaters across our nation and in other countries. Some of my favorite places are those that have unsurpassed scenic beauty and fish significantly shorter than my leg. The Deschutes is one such river that stands out. It takes both tricky wading and casting to set a fly in the trout's lair under the overhanging brush, and they fight no less vigorously than some of the bigger fish I have taken elsewhere. The river's swift currents enable the one-pound "redside" rainbow trout to bend my rod with an arch more characteristic of fish ten times their weight. And, yes, you can enjoy the solitude of a wilderness adventure with a fishing buddy or loved one as much as hauling in huge fish.

But this book was designed to explain why some trout grow larger than others, how anglers can target the right places and times to catch them, and explain some of the science behind big trout behavior and how you can apply this information to catch them. Additionally, some of the principles, techniques, and philosophies described in this book will apply not only to the big trout destinations listed, but will also translate well for anglers seeking to catch the biggest trout in their home water. You may not catch a big trout on your first outing, but your odds will definitely be increased, and if you read this book in its entirety, you will also become a more knowledgeable angler.

I grew up using dry flies and floating fly lines on the East Coast of the United States. This was fishing to me. My concept of fishing was based on what I had experienced on my little stream. I would like to say that my views were provincial, but that excuse wouldn't even qualify, as the stream was only a few miles long. Later travels opened my eyes to other forms of fly fishing, in both fresh, salt, and brackish waters. Some anglers only fish nymphs and others primarily troll bucktails. Some patiently watch a strike indicator on stillwaters. A few will only cast dries or don't fish at all.

I found that there are as many approaches to fishing as there are flies on the shelves of an Orvis shop. For some, fishing is a form of relaxation. For others, a quest, or perhaps an obsession. Some anglers will do whatever it takes to catch big trout, often leaving traditions behind. They have modified their techniques to the varied conditions to which the trout have adapted. Some of these techniques may be deemed extreme by some, perhaps not even fly fishing.

Nevertheless, this book is about how anglers catch big trout on a fly rod, single-action fly reel, fly lines as defined by Scientific Anglers and Cortland, and flies that are either on, or could be on, the pages of an Umpqua catalog. Although the equipment that I describe is related only to fly fishing, the majority of this book is really about big trout, and anglers who use other forms of tackle can benefit from it, as well. My definition of fly fishing is in line with the National Freshwater Fishing Hall of Fame world record books, and with the exception of trolling, adheres to the International Game Fish Association's (IGFA) "Rules for Fly Fishing." You may not buy into some of the ideas presented here, but if you open your mind you may find techniques and tactics that enable you to fish big trout waters that were previously considered unfishable.

This book was written with cooperation and support from some of the most knowledgeable big trout anglers and scientists that study trout on this continent. I personally visited most of the waters and interviewed many of the players in what I described to my wife as "research trips." Field research was supplemented with countless hours in the basement of the Oregon State University Library poring through the primary literature. To obtain the latest information on some of the waters, raw data was begged and borrowed from biologists, limnologists, physicists, aquatic entomologists, and a host of other scientists.

The last forty years have seen an explosion of scientifically validated information (trout growth, feeding rhythms, desirable habitat, etc.) that has as yet had little observable impact on fishing literature. The literature on trout fishing, dating from the 15th century, has relied on the observations and experiences of gifted, often brilliant, fisherman. With the creation of government-supported departments of fisheries in the 20th century, a body of information has been amassed based on the empirical research developed by professional scientists in a wide range of disciplines. In effect, the field is transitioning from a subjective observational approach to a scientific one relying on empirical validation. This book honors that transition and relies primarily on this research to, hopefully, benefit the angler.

The most important lesson I learned during the course of researching this book was that successful big trout angling isn't about the right fly or the perfect cast. The proficient big trout angler spends time researching his destination, listening to others who have figured out pieces of the puzzle, dedicating days on the water to experimentation with old and new techniques and then reevaluating what did or didn't work. This approach may seem academic in nature, but the system works and over the long term can create a more challenging and rewarding experience. It is the difference between catching big trout that just happen to grab the fly versus the ones that you specifically target.

CHAPTER I
GO TO WHERE THERE ARE BIG TROUT

W hen I was a kid, I read an article in one of the major hook and bullet magazines about how to catch big fish. Tip number one was a bit obvious, even for a grade school child, and still stands true today—go to where there are big fish. You may need to spend a few days once you get there, but if you study the water, pick the best periods of opportunity, choose the right equipment and techniques, and focus on big trout, the odds are in your favor to catch one. Line-class record trout are still attainable, and big trout waters for the non-record seeker can be found within a day's travel by auto.

The Waters

There are three types of waters where we find big trout: stillwaters, tailwaters, and migratory trout rivers. Stillwaters are defined as the different types of lakes, reservoirs, and ponds. Tailwaters are rivers whose primary water source is from a reservoir. Migratory trout rivers are those where fish move back and forth between moving water and a larger body of water to feed, find more comfortable water temperatures, or spawn. Migration means that there is a two-way trip. (My definition of migratory trout assumes that a large portion of the population is migrating and not just a select few. Trout also migrate short distances every day in still and moving waters. These waters are not considered migratory trout rivers.)

What is a Trout

When setting out to write this book I first considered only the most common true trouts: the brown trout (*Salmo trutta*), rainbow trout (*Oncorhynchus mykiss*), and cutthroat trout (*Oncorhynchus clarki*). I have also included brook trout (*Salvelinus fontinalis*), or brook *char*. While technically this fish is not a trout, most anglers view them as such. My first "trout" was a tiny, wild brookie, caught in a small stream in the foothills of the White Mountain National Forest. In some areas of Maine and New Hampshire and in the central and eastern Canadian provinces, brook trout are *the* trout. There are places where brook trout do grow big, for reasons similar to the other trout discussed, and many anglers specialize in catching the larger specimens. Thus, they were included in this book. Brook trout live in both streams and lakes, even though their species name, *fontinalis,* actually means, "inhabiting brooks."

Almost all of the big rainbow trout in this book are Alaskan rainbows (*O. m. irideus*) and the redband trout (*O. m. gairdneri*). The redbands are native to the Columbia River Basin east of the Cascade Mountains and in the upper Fraser River Basin. Due to their stunning performance both on the line and in the water, they have since been transplanted into waters all over the world. The redband trout is not a single entity, rather it represents several evolutionary lineages that diverged before the appearance of the modern coastal rainbow trout. Because most of these forms in different drainage basins have come into contact and mixed with each other and with coastal rainbows during and since the last glacial period, transitions in diagnostic characters are commonly found (Behnke). Many of the tailwaters have another rainbow trout, believed to be of coastal origin. From a big trout standpoint it does not appear that there is anything genetically special about these fish, and they only become large when introduced into unique environments with a great deal of food.

Steelhead, an anadromous form of rainbow trout that lives some of its life in the sea and migrates to a freshwater stream to spawn posed another question. This fish has also been transplanted into large water systems such as the Great Lakes. In some of the waters covered there are adfluvial rainbow trout, meaning that they migrate between lakes and rivers and not from the sea. I thought the steelhead issue through deeply and finally decided that I would only focus on the inland trout fisheries. Covering the more common races of trout was a daunting enough task. A number of good books have been written about steelhead by such angling authors as Trey Combs, Deke Meyer, Rick and Jerry Kustich, Jim Teeny, and others. The reader can use the physiology, behavior, and fishing techniques presented here to complement these previously published works.

Steve Hilbert from Lonesome Duck Lodge on Oregon's Williamson River with a big redband rainbow trout that migrated up from Upper Klamath Lake. This fish is probably seven or eight years old.

Some anglers have experience with another variety of rainbow trout (and brook trout) called "triploids." Triploids are not a subspecies; they are fish manipulated by humans. Wild rainbow trout have two sets of genes, one from their mother and one from their father. They are called "diploids." However, just at the point of fertilization, at the last stage of meiosis, the mother has a duplicate set of female chromosomes that are usually lost. By a light pressure, heat, or cold shocking treatment, they can be controlled to maintain both sets. Combined with the father's one set, there are three in total—hence the name triploid. This third set negates their ability to spawn. During the first three years of their lives, the triploids will grow at about the same rate as diploid hatchery trout. But after that point, they can be expected to grow at a greater rate than wild fish up to about five years of age, if the conditions are right. Their growth slows down at this point. This may be because the genetic programming to mature reduces a trout's ability to grow at fast rates. Something in the sterilization technique may also impair normal functioning of the triploid trout. This dysfunction is unrelated to learning (Deeley and Benfey).

The mortality of the triploids is usually low because their success is driven entirely by the environment they live in and not by their own physiological conditions. Triploids can minimize the portion of the population lost due to maturation-related mortality, making them ideal for some stocked ponds. A hatchery in England sells anglers the opportunity to catch 20- to 30-pound triploid rainbow trout and hatcheries on the west coast of North America raise 20- to 25-pound trout for promotional purposes. But if you put triploids in waters that cannot support growth, they will not grow much faster than other hatchery trout. Additionally, although triploids are growing big in some waters, they have not achieved the sizes of some races of rainbow trout.

The cutthroat trout, originally written as "Cut Throat Trout," has the greatest natural distribution of all western trout species. There are four major species of cutthroat trout and ten minor subspecies in North America. Among them, four sometimes grow to the big trout standard of five pounds if the environment permits. They are the coastal cutthroat (*O.c. clarki*), Lahontan cutthroat (*O.c. henshawi*), Yellowstone cutthroat (*O.c. bouvieri*) and the Bonneville cutthroat (*O.c. utah*), specifically the Bear Lake variety. Overall, the cutthroat trout has been on the decline due to hybridization in the wild with rainbow trout, called "cuttbows," and because they are out-competed by non-native brown trout. Fishery managers sometimes intentionally cross-hybrid the rainbows and cutthroats to keep the populations from mating in the wild. The primary reasons why the other cutthroat subspecies have not grown big are that their environments do not have the food sources that allow them to grow large, and their genetic make-up focuses them on an invertebrate diet. (This issue is discussed in more detail in the next section of this chapter.)

Although not native to North America, brown trout may be the most prolific and widely dispersed trout on this continent. Most researchers believe that the United States and Canada were originally stocked with two types of brown trout, the "bachforelle," or "brook trout," from Germany, often clumped together and called "German browns," and the "Loch Leven" from Scotland (Heacox). A later introduction included "seeforelle," or "lake trout," from Germany (Behnke). These "brook trout" and "lake trout" are brown trout and should not be confused with the brook trout (*Salvelinus fontinalis*) or the lake trout/Mackinaw (*Savelinus namaycush*) that is also a char. All of these importations were made in the late 19th century, and they are still the predominant races of brown trout in North America.

The bachforelle were introduced from streams in the Black Forest region of Germany, where they rarely grew longer than 12 inches. The seeforelle came from large alpine lakes where they sometimes grew to over 60 pounds (Garrell). The Loch Leven browns are also a lake-dwelling trout that once grew to 18 pounds in their native environment. Since their introduction, most brown trout subspecies have been intermixed and there may be only small isolated pockets of pure strains in North America. One exception is the recent introduction of seeforellens into some of the Great Lakes.

Despite the natural and human-controlled interbreeding of the Loch Leven and German brown trout, there is a school of thought that the environment has selected out the attributes from both brown trout to help them survive in their new environments. These browns have developed characteristics to survive in their new homes, and fishery biologists have been careful not to introduce new brown trout groups to waters in which they are already established. Like rainbows, brown trout also tend to be stream and river residents in environments where there is a lot of food, and an anadromous or adfluvial migrant when the environments in these smaller waters are less suitable for growth. In some cases, the males will stay near their home waters while the females, which need a greater amount of body reserves to reproduce, will be the more anadromous or adfluvial of the pair. As such, female brown trout will often be the larger ones in the river.

There are also other mixtures of trout, in addition to the cuttbows. One of them is the female brown/male brook trout mix called the "tiger trout." I mention this fish in the few waters that hold them. There are other trout: the Atlantic salmon (*Salmo salar*), which few people recognize as a trout; golden trout (*Oncorhynchus aguabonita*); Apache trout (*Oncorhynchus apache*); Gila trout (*Oncorhynchus gila*); and char such as Arctic char (*Salvelinus*

Most trout become flesh eaters between 12 to 16 inches. When prey fish are not available they will either not grow large or one or two will make the leap to feed on the other trout. A few tailwaters and stillwaters that are highly productive are the exceptions to this rule.

alpinus), Dolly Varden (*Salvelinus malma*), bull trout (*Salvelinus confluentus*), and Mackinaw or lake trout (*Savelinus namaycush*). They were excluded because most are regional fish that few anglers approach on a national level. Additionally, some of these trout and char do not grow large in comparison to the ones focused on in this book. Some of these fish are listed, or close to being listed, as endangered species.

Big Trout Diet

What and when a big trout eats is strictly a function of whether the food is available and when they can consume it efficiently. By efficiently, I mean that they do not spend more energy catching the food than the nourishment gained from the food. To become big, a trout must not only be able to feed on large food items but also must be able to intake more energy from food sources than it needs to sustain itself through a day.[1]

In most cases where there are big trout, they are fish eaters, or what scientists refer to as being piscivorous. Big trout do not start out life feeding on other fish. Juvenile trout, in most big trout environments, are invertebrate feeders. They make the shift to prey fish at somewhere between 12 and 16 inches, depending on the water. Once they make the shift, they rarely go back to feeding on insects even when large quantities are present. A radio telemetry study of large brown trout in the South Branch of the Au Sable River in Michigan found that surface feeding was rarely observed (only 10 times in two years) even when large *Ephemera simulans* and *Hexagenia limbata* were present (Clapp et al.). Those were real bugs with a natural drift. Our chances of catching one of those fish with an artificial dry would be miniscule.

Table 1-1 compares the prey selection for two size groups of brown trout in Lake Michigan. These results are consistent with other studies I have seen. The top row is for brown trout smaller than 11.81 inches (converted from 30 cm) and the bottom one is for those larger than 11.81 inches. These smaller brown trout live on a mixed invertebrate/fish diet that can be found in shallow to medium depths of the lake. Around the time these trout reached 12 inches, they stopped feeding on invertebrates and their diets became primarily composed of fish. In streams (with the exception of some of the tailwaters), trout must also shift from drift feeding to piscivory in order to grow to a large size. In most waters, the maximum size a trout can attain by drift feeding alone is probably less than 16 inches.

Table 1-1: Lake Michigan Brown Trout Diet, Percentage by Weight

Trout Size	Invertebrates	Alewife	All Other Fish
Under 11.8 inches	20.5%	20.2%	59.3%
Over 11.8 inches	0	73.8%	26.2%

Source: Jude, David. 1987. Diet and Selection of Major Prey Species by Lake Michigan Salmonides. 1973–1982. *Transactions of the American Fisheries Society*, Volume 116, September 1987, Number 5.

The brook trout lakes in Labrador may be among the few waters where the trout are wild and native and growing to big trout standards on an invertebrate diet. The stomach contents of this fish shows that it was feeding on water boatmen and diving beetles.

In waters where there are few prey fish, such as in some tailwaters, trout can grow large on invertebrates if there is a tremendous supply of these food items. There are a few reservoirs where this is the case. Henry's Lake and Island Park Reservoir near West Yellowstone are two well-known examples. Sheridan, Dragon, and Stump Lakes in British Columbia and the Blackfeet Reservation lakes in Montana are, too. The Labrador brook trout lakes, such as Osprey Lake, may be one of the few natural exceptions to this rule. A general guide to when the foods of trout are active is shown below in Table 1-2.

Table 1-2: Availability of the Trout's Food Sources

Aquatic Invertebrates	Nymphs/Larva	Adults
Mayflies and caddis	Can be present year round	April through October
Damselflies and dragonflies	Can be present year round	April through September
Chironomidae, Chaoboridae	Can be present year round	Present year round
Zooplankton, scuds, and cressbugs	All year	
Other		
Crayfish	When the water temperature is above 42 degrees Fahrenheit	
Leeches	All year (most active early spring when reproducing)	
Prey fish	All year (except for adfluvial/anadromous spawners)	

Big trout will key in on a food source until their prey has reached the end of its cycle, the trout have changed their feeding habits for environmental reasons (changes in water temperatures, spawning urges, etc.), or the trout have moved on to a larger food source that gives them more energy to maintain growth or recover from the rigors of reproduction. They are not just looking for fish. They are looking for a larger nutritious food. Since smaller fish are often the only other larger food source available, this makes fish look like they are preferred. If dragonfly nymphs, mice, frogs, large diving beetles, etc. are available in equal proportions to the prey fish (fish that trout eat), then they will be in the big trout's diet. Indeed, this is the case on a few big trout waters where faster growing strains of trout were introduced to stillwaters with a great deal of aquatic insects. An example of the concept of keying in on prey items is shown in Table 1-3. It describes the frequency and the percent of the total diet of brown trout in Lake Michigan over the spring, summer, and fall months. These trout primarily keyed in on the alewife, although at times they took other prey fish.

Table 1-3: Seasonal Diet of Lake Michigan Brown Trout Over 30 cm (11.8 inches)

	Spring		Summer		Fall	
	Frequency	% of Total	Frequency	% of Total	Frequency	% of Total
Alewife	62	43.97	69	54.33	63	53.39
Miscellaneous	8	5.67	4	3.15	4	3.39
Rainbow Smelt	18	12.77	14	11.02	7	5.93
Unidentified Cottid (Sculpins)	18	12.77	2	1.57	0	0
Unidentified Fish	35	24.82	38	29.92	44	37.29
Total	141	100	127	100	118	100

Source: Jude, David. 1987. Diet and Selection of Major Prey Species by Lake Michigan Salmonines. 1973–1982. *Transactions of the American Fisheries Society,* Volume 116, September 1987, Number 5.

I do not like to use the word "selective" to describe trout feeding, even though they may only feed on a few food items over the course of a summer. As will be discussed further in the next chapter, the trout does not have the mental capacity to choose the value of one food source over another. There is also not always a choice. In a similar vein, I do not consider "opportunistic" to be a good word either. Big trout do not chase every food item that is available to them. For example, a 15-pound brown trout in Lake Ontario could gain some nourishment from the numerous zooplankton present but it is highly unlikely that they will feed on this food item. Instead, they will key in on food items and, at the same time, take other

You will find the largest cutthroat trout where the trout and the prey fish are native. In waters where one is not native the trout may not know how to hunt the prey fish and they can become competitors.

large morsels that cross their path. Sometimes these items are our carefully presented flies. The trout do not always identify our offering, as we often present flies for which there is no natural to imitate, so the strike may be for consumption, aggression toward an intruder, or perhaps just a knee-jerk reaction.

Genetics

Nature selects winners and losers in the struggle for life based on their suitability to the current conditions and ability to adapt to long-term changes in their environment. These traits are passed down through the generations by the individuals most able to survive and reproduce. Adaptation is a fascinating topic and the reasons why some trout grow larger than others are equally absorbing.

The two primary factors in producing big trout are the environment and genetics. The greatest genetic mutations in animals come from isolation, most commonly a result of the ice ages. From a feeding perspective, individual populations will either learn to specialize or generalize. Sexually mature Lake Iliamna rainbows, for example, feed on prey fish in the lake and then on salmon eggs, and possibly flesh, once they enter the tributaries in the fall. These trout are generalists in that they have the ability to feed on a range of food under different environmental conditions.

A good example of specialization in trout can be seen through the westslope cutthroat trout (existing now in Montana, Idaho, Oregon, Washington, and southern Alberta). This trout did not learn to feed on fish because two other fish in its natural environment, the bull trout and the northern squawfish, were highly piscivorous. The westslope cutthroat trout was left to feed (and specialize) on the invertebrates for which there was no competition (Behnke). Westslope cutthroat trout naturally occur in Lake Pend Oreille in Idaho, and when kokanee (landlocked sockeye salmon) were introduced, the trout did not feed on this fish but became a competitor for the food items that it ate. The introduced Gerrard-strain rainbow trout knew how to feed on the kokanee and as a result grew to enormous sizes.

An understanding of the genetic traits in trout is important for the preservation of the species and the better management of our freshwater systems. This knowledge is also useful for determining which trout are most suitable for a given environment and how large they will grow in it. In most cases, the origination of the trout strain and the type and quantity of the food available to them strongly influences the size of fish produced. The big trout angler can use this information to target waters where larger specimens are present.

Gerrard rainbow trout commonly grow to the size of this buck on a diet of kokanee. This fish weighed in at seventeen pounds before Roy Stokes released it back into Lake Pend Oreille. It was probably eight or nine years old.

The history of the Lahontan cutthroat in Pyramid Lake in Nevada provides a good example of the importance of genetics in the growth of trout. An article in *The Sierra Sportsman* in July of 1932 reported two anglers with a day's catch of 11 trout weighing 238 pounds. The average weight was 22 pounds and the largest was 39 pounds. In contrast, the present-day Lahontan cutthroat trout in Pyramid Lake averages about 4 pounds. An 8-pound cutthroat is a good fish and a 10-pound-plus trout is considered very big and rare. The demise of the original Pyramid Lake Lahontan cutthroat trout began in 1905 when the Army Corps of Engineers built Derby Dam some thirty miles upstream of Pyramid Lake on the Truckee River. By itself, the dam only moderately affected the spawners. However, when combined with the droughts of the 1920s and 1930s that diverted water to other uses, the mouth of the river became silted up and the trout were unable to reach their spawning grounds. The original Lahontan cutthroats native to Pyramid Lake died and were replaced by Summit Lake brood stock.

Historically, Summit Lake in Nevada did not have a prey fish for the cutthroat trout to feed on and the cutthroat's life history strategy was for them to feed on aquatic invertebrates

This average-size Lahontan cutthroat trout from Pyramid Lake is a far cry from the twenty-pound monsters that once were the norm in the lake.

and spawn early in life. They fed almost entirely on small crustaceans and midge larva in the lake and become sexually mature at age two. When introduced into Pyramid Lake, they learned to feed on the tui chubs but have yet to change their life history strategy sufficiently to take full advantage of the new prey (chubs). The restocking of Pyramid Lake with the Summit Lake Lahontans and the inability of the non-native trout to reach the sizes of the original trout in Summit Lake demonstrates the strength of genetics governing life history, growth, and maximum size. The original Lahontan strain that used to inhabit Pyramid Lake is almost extinct, with a remnant population remaining in a small creek on Pilot Peak along the Utah-Nevada border (Behnke).

Trophic Levels

Another aspect to consider for big trout is the "productivity" of the system. Productivity refers to the amount of biomass produced. This biomass is formed at all levels of the food chain and is a reflection of increasing nutrient inputs with increasing trophic level. Scientists generally break the productivity of freshwater systems into three categories: eutrophic, meaning highly nutritious, oligotrophic, meaning low nutrition, and mesotrophic, referring to the middle. Table 1-4 and the illustration on page 18 describe these water types and their corresponding characteristics. These levels of productivity apply to both stillwaters and rivers.

Table 1-4: Productivity and Characteristics of Water Types

Type	Productivity	Perceived Water Color	Characteristics
Oligotrophic	Low	Blue	Steep-sided and deep lakes, rocky shorelines, clear open waters, little shoreline vegetation, phytoplankton, zooplankton, *Chaoboridae* and some bottom-dwelling animals such as crayfish and *Chironomidae*.
Mesotrophic	Medium	Blue/Green	Moderately deep with good shoreline shallows, periphyton, zooplankton, *Chaoboridae*, phytoplankton, limited benthic food sources (mayflies, caddis, scuds, cressbugs, *Chironomidae*, crayfish, leeches, etc.).
Eutrophic	High	Green	Nutrient-rich, turbid waters, shoreline vegetation, shallow waters where light and plants grow across the bottom, periphyton, zooplankton, phytoplankton, *Chaoboridae*, plentiful benthic food sources (mayflies, caddis, scuds, cressbugs, *Chironomidae*, crayfish, leeches, etc.), rich shoals (stillwaters).

Highly productive (eutrophic) lakes and rivers usually have at least two food webs. One is root or bottom based (benthic) and the other is in open waters (pelagic). The foundations for any food web are based on chemicals and minerals in the environment, but for the benthic food web we should start with what we observe; in this case periphyton—a term for a conglomeration of different tiny microorganisms (algae) that live on the underwater surfaces of plants, rocks, woody debris, silt, and other structures in and around shallow waters. Periphyton can also be included in a larger category called biofilm that also includes fungi and decayed matter. Periphyton grows via photosynthesis, the process by which green plants and certain other organisms use the energy of light to convert carbon dioxide and water into the simple sugar glucose. In so doing, photosynthesis provides the basic energy source for virtually all organisms. The more light, warmth, and nutrients, the greater the growth. Scuds, cressbugs, mayfly nymphs, and caddis and midge larvae are consumers of periphyton, as are tadpoles and snails.

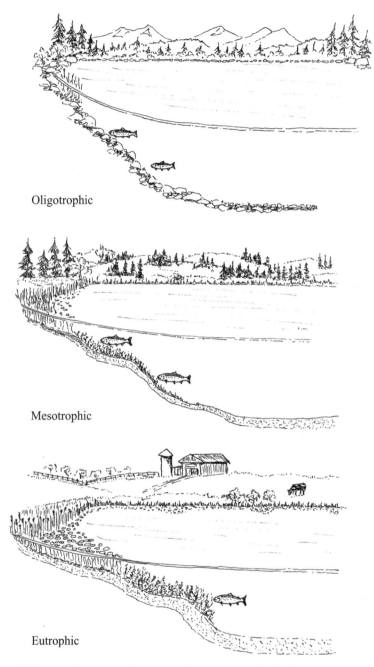

Oligotrophic

Mesotrophic

Eutrophic

When you first approach a body of water, try to think of the system in these categories. An understanding of any water's productivity will lead you to what prey the trout hunt and where they occur in the water column.

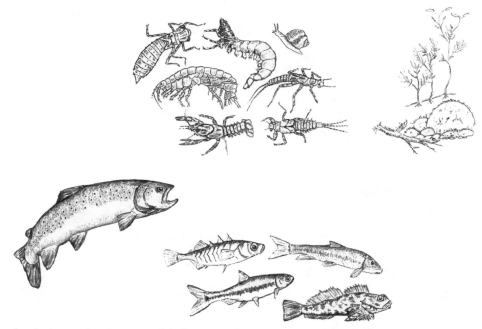

On the bottom/benthic zone of shallow eutrophic waters, trout and their prey usually have an assortment of invertebrate food items.

Another form of algae, called phytoplankton, is found in open waters and commonly consumed by forms of microscopic aquatic crustaceans, generically called zooplankton. By definition, plankton means that it moves passively with the current within the water column. Many fish that big trout prey on are zooplankton feeders, such as sticklebacks, kokanee, chubs, cisco, alewife, and smelt. These zooplankton feeders can be described as being planktivorous. Sometimes insects, such as the *Chaoboridae* pupae (which is more closely related to the mosquito than the *Chironomidae*) and crustaceans such as the *Mysis relicta* (commonly called opossum shrimp) also feed on the zooplankton.

Productive Environments

Bodies of water that have environments conducive to easily produce big trout are those with rich food sources, little competition from other species, and few predators (including man). These are typically large bodies of water where the food sources are not only rich but also stable. Some of these environments are fairly young and wholly or partially created by man. The created environments are usually tailwaters and reservoirs where a major food source for

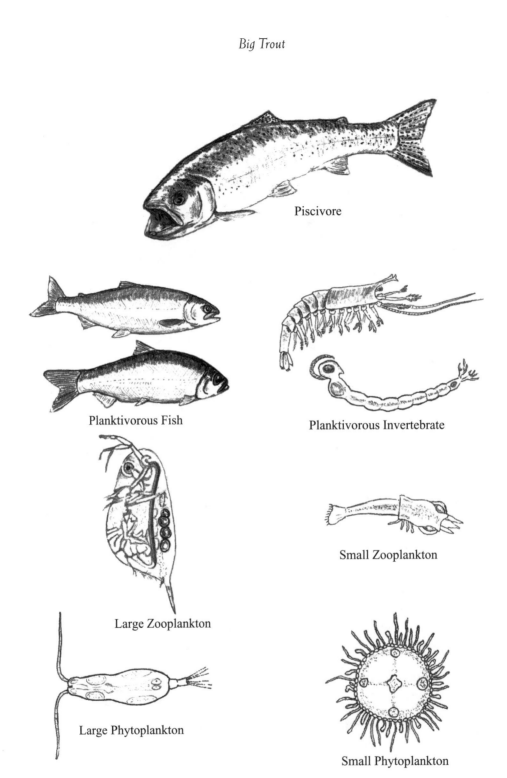

Piscivore

Planktivorous Fish

Planktivorous Invertebrate

Large Zooplankton

Small Zooplankton

Large Phytoplankton

Small Phytoplankton

In open/pelagic waters, big fish eat little fish and little fish eat zooplankton.

the trout and/or the trout themselves have been introduced. In most environments where big trout are native, the primary food source of the adult trout will be another fish. In big trout waters where the trout are primarily invertebrate feeders, these trout are usually fast-growing strains that have been introduced and where invertebrates, in extremely high densities, are the only accessible food source.

Sometimes just a few trout in the population make the shift from feeding on invertebrates to other fish later in life and grow much larger and live longer as a result (Campbell). The prey can be other species or their cohorts. Some scientists believe this to be a kind of "rejuvenation." The advantage of this shift is to exploit a new food source that has less competition than their invertebrate-feeding cohorts while offering more energy for growth. The extended age and increased growth from rejuvenation is considered to be an environmental influence and not a genetic trait of the trout.

Rejuvenation may be one of the contributing factors to how the world-record brown trout from the Little Red River in Arkansas grew to over 40 pounds and probably lived to about 17 years of age. The largest brown trout captured by electro-fishing in the Little Red was only just over 20 pounds. Fishery biologists have seen only a few other brown trout in the river that might run a little larger. Rejuvenation may also be the case for some spring creeks and stillwaters where we find a few large trout that far outgrow their siblings.

The environment is also a major influencing factor for the growth of rainbow trout in Colorado's highly productive Frying Pan River just below Ruedi Reservoir. These non-native trout have the nutrient base to grow quickly and spawn repeatedly, due to easy access to the food needed for recovery from the stresses of spawning. The nutrient base for this tailwater comes from a release of the introduced *Mysis relicta* (opossum shrimp) from the reservoir. Freestone streams may only produce 5 to 10 pounds of trout per square acre, while a typical good trout stream can maintain 50 to 100 pounds, and a productive trout water may have 500 pounds. A stream width of eight feet equals about one surface acre per mile of stream (Behnke). The highly productive Frying Pan River once reached 1,000 pounds per surface acre, although it is probably now at about 600 pounds due to the reduced numbers of opossum shrimp in the lake. There is an example from this extraordinary fishery on a wall in the Taylor Creek Fly Shop—a 30-inch rainbow with a 25¼-inch girth that was estimated to be 24 pounds. Not only does the Frying Pan have a tremendous amount of easy food, but it also has water temperatures that are conducive to year-round feeding.

An abundance of food and ideal water temperatures are also characteristics of the productive Great Lakes (ranging from eutrophic to mesotrophic) brown trout fisheries. The brown trout and their prey, smelt and alewife, were introduced. Brown trout in Lake Ontario will

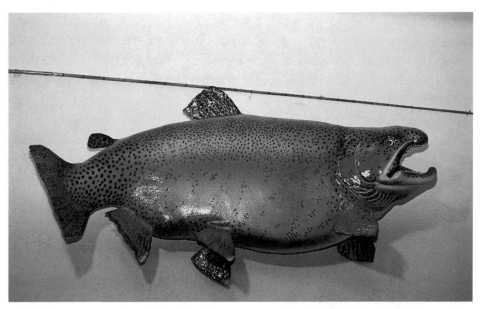

This big rainbow trout, estimated to weigh about twenty-four pounds, was found dead in the Frying Pan River. The fish managed to elude anglers in this heavily fished tailwater. It is highly likely that the fish found a protected feeding lane just where the opossum shrimp entered the river.

grow to over 7 pounds by the autumn of their second year, in part because they have the opportunity to feed almost all year round.

In contrast, Table 1-5 on page 24 describes the growth of redband rainbow trout in Crane Prairie Reservoir, a highly productive fishery in Oregon. The growth of the Crane Prairie rainbow trout is slower than the Ontario brown trout probably due to these trout holding around cooler oxygenated springs during the hot summer months (to avoid the blue-green algae-infested warmer waters) where they have a slower metabolism, and then again in the winter for the three to five months when the reservoir is frozen over. These trout have fewer months to feed. In their early years the trout grow quickly from the abundant supply of invertebrates in the reservoir, but still only to 15 inches by age three. This age and size also coincides with the trout reaching sexual maturation and feeding on the illegally introduced three-spined sticklebacks. Note that the growth rate (length and weight) of the trout declines in the third and fourth years due to energy expenditures associated with producing gamets and spawning.

Rick Kustich displays this fine brown trout that migrated from Lake Ontario into one of the tributaries near Oak Orchard. This is an average fish for these waters, and is probably two to three years old.

Table 1-5: Growth and Age of Crane Prairie Redband Trout

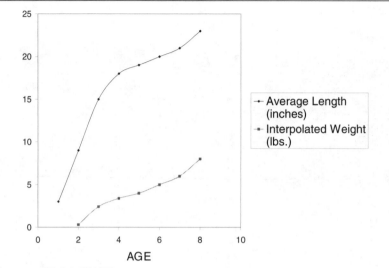

Source: Oregon Department of Fish & Wildlife.

Rainbow trout in Crane Prairie grow quickly on a rich, stable, and diversified diet, but their growth rate slows after they reach sexual maturity.

One could describe the Lake Ontario browns as having extremely fast growth by trout standards and the Crane Prairie Reservoir rainbows as having fast growth. In most environments across North America, for both hatchery and wild rainbows, the trout become sexually mature at two years of age, grow slowly, and do not reach the size of trout in these two waters. There are many reasons. Two common ones are that the trout have not learned to hunt the available prey fish, and in other waters this food source is not present. These trout concentrate on the zooplankton and insects, and when prey fish are present they become competitors. Even if the water has good numbers of small insects and no competitors, it may still not have big trout. The Lower Deschutes is a river that fits into this description. While the river has an abundance of small invertebrate life, redband rainbow trout over 16 inches only compose about one percent of the population over eight inches and average 14 fish per mile (ODF&W). Fish and Wildlife researchers believe that high annual natural mortality combined with slow growth, due to a primarily invertebrate diet, limits the numbers of larger rainbow trout. Growth in the first three years is 7.5 inches and their fourth to sixth years

This large redband trout from Crane Prairie Reservoir in Oregon weighed in excess of ten pounds, which is more than three times the maximum size of nearby Deschutes River rainbows with similar genetics.

only add another 3.5 inches. In contrast, the Crane Prairie Reservoir rainbows were double the size of these trout at three years of age. Crane Prairie Reservoir has an abundance of large food items, most notably sticklebacks, which help trout to live longer and grow larger. What is most interesting about these two waters is that Crane Prairie Reservoir feeds the Lower Deschutes and the genetics of these trout are closely related.

Super Trout

Productive waters are not the only places where we find big trout. Sometimes trout adapt so that they can grow big in unproductive environments. Key to the development of these trout is that they have evolved, over tens of thousands of years, to become sexually mature at an older age. I call these unique varieties super trout. Most, if not all, of these super trout originate from oligotrophic lakes where most of the feeding activity for the adult trout and their prey is in the open water (pelagic zone). Slow growth in the early years as a result of limited food in their environment, and a big leap once they can feed on the pelagic prey fish, just in time to reproduce, is common in these oligotrophic systems. In Lake Iliamna, a large oligotrophic system, the rainbows have slow growth until their maturity at five, six, and seven years of age. If the trout in Lake Iliamna had matured at two to three years of age there would not have been enough medium-sized foods for them to recover from the rigors of reproduction. As it is, less than 40 percent of the spawners survive (Minard).

Table 1-6: Mean Lengths of Rainbow Trout, by Age Group, From Beach Seine Samples Collected During the Spring From the Kvichak River [Kwee-jack], 1989–1991

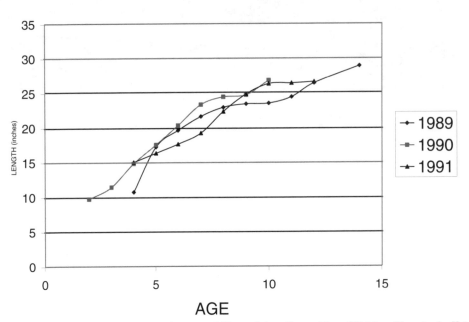

Source: Estimation of Abundance, Seasonal Distribution, and Size and Age Composition of Rainbow Trout in the Kvichak River, Alaska, 1986–1991. Alaska Department of Fish and Wildlife, Fishery Data Series No. 92–51.

Slow growth in their early years, late maturation, and long lives are characteristics of Lake Iliamna trout that migrate into the Kvichak River.

Another oligotrophic lake with super trout is Kootenay Lake in British Columbia, where the Gerrard rainbows do not reach sexual maturation until between five to seven years of age, when they are already ten pounds. One study of Gerrard rainbows in Lake Pend Oreille found that 18 percent of the adult population (over 15.98 inches) reached sexual maturation

The Kvichak River in Alaska is one of the best rivers in the world for big rainbow trout. Guide Scott Williamson is pictured here with an average, late-maturing rainbow from the Kvichak. This fish was probably eleven or twelve years of age.

at five years, 15 percent at six years, and 19 percent at seven years (See Table 1–7). Gerrards in Lake Pend Oreille have been known to live up to eleven years. Anglers can probably better relate this delayed sexual maturation and extra growth to steelhead. A four-year-old (two-salt-year) returning wild steelhead on an Oregon river usually weighs about 9 pounds (ODF&W). If the steelhead stays another year at sea, it would return at about 15 pounds. For the Gerrards, this late sexual maturation, especially those at seven years of age, has resulted in truly large rainbow trout. A number of current IGFA All Tackle Line Class record rainbow trout are of the Gerrard race, including two fish over 31 pounds. Two former world record Gerrards of 37 pounds were caught in Pend Oreille in 1947, and a 42-pound giant was caught in Jewel Lake in 1933.

For the Gerrards of Kootenay Lake, the environment naturally selects the largest fish to spawn successfully. The Gerrards spawn in the Lardeau River, just below the outflow from Trout Lake. The water is particularly swift and the gravel difficult to dig into for their spawning nests, called redds, favoring the largest and strongest females. Similarly, the influence of the warm water from Trout Lake promotes early maturation of the eggs and faster growth of the larval fish. The offspring carry the genetics to grow large and succeed when their time to reproduce occurs.

Table 1-7: Estimated Population Abundance and Average Length and Weight for Gerrard Race Rainbow Trout Over 15.98 inches in Lake Pend Oreille, Idaho

Age	Avg. Length (inches)	Avg. Weight (pounds)	Estimated Abundance	Percent by Age
4.5*	15.98	4.41	4452	30.47
5	19.48	6.24	3335	22.83
6	23.34	6.69	2498	17.10
7	26.61	8.17	1871	12.80
8	28.93	14.51	1401	9.59
9	32.12	19.40	1050	7.18
Total			14607	100

Source: Vidergar, D.T. 2000. Population Estimates, Food Habits and Estimates of Consumption of Selected Predatory Fishes in Lake Pend Oreille, Idaho. 2000. Unpublished Master's Thesis from the University of Idaho.
*adjusted based on predatory size

Rainbows are not the only super trout that come from unproductive (oligotrophic) systems. There are races of brook, cutthroat, and brown trout that also mature later in life and reach larger sizes as a result. Some of the most famous brook trout are the Coasters of the Nipigon River, Ontario, the Assinica strain from the northern regions of Quebec, and those from the Eagle River (Osprey Lake) and Minipi region of Labrador. The Nipigon brook trout mature at age three, when males are about 16 inches and females 18 inches and averaging about 3.3 pounds. Some Nipigon River brook trout live up to eight years of age and reach quite large sizes, such as the world record fish at 14 pounds, 8 ounces (The Brook Trout Subcommittee). Assinica brook trout have been known to reach 11½ pounds (Karas). Similarly, some Labrador brook trout live to be about nine years old (Flick and Webster) and reach over 10 pounds. These fish are quite large and old in contrast to the average stream-dwelling brook trout in the lower 48 states that matures as a yearling and will rarely reach weights of more than 2 to 3 pounds.

Sometimes a larger predator can influence the life history strategy of the trout. The lakes in Labrador (such as Osprey, Big Minipi, and Anne Marie) that have the largest brook trout also have pike and few brook trout under 4 pounds, while nearby lakes without pike have many brook trout below 4 pounds and few above 5 pounds. The smallest brook trout that I caught in Osprey Lake was about 3½ pounds, while the average was over 5 pounds. The

Arkansas fisheries biologist Darrell Bowman with a 35-pound brown trout from the White River that was estimated to be over 15 years of age. At the time this book was written this trout, and a few others in the same size class, were known to be swimming in the White River. One of them could very well be an IGFA All Tackle World Record. (Photo courtesy of the Arkansas Game and Fish Commission.)

smaller brook trout live in the adjoining rivers and creeks until they are big enough to avoid the pike in the lake. The pike/brook trout balance is much like that of wolves and caribou. The wolves cull out the weaker animals so that the strongest can survive and reproduce. Researchers who studied brook trout in the Assinca/Broadback system in Northern Quebec came to a similar conclusion. If planning a trip to the fishing camps in the region, ask them about the availability and health of the pike population (Flick).

Older age of sexual maturation is closely related to the age of trout, with early spawners living fewer years. The maximum life span of most native western trout in most environments is six to seven years (Behnke), with few trout reaching this age. Kvichak River rainbows that migrate out of Lake Iliamna have been estimated to live up to fourteen years of age and reach lengths of over 30 inches (Minard). While this old age is the exception, a good portion of this population lives to eight or nine years of age. In extremely productive waters, such as Upper Klamath Lake and Crane Prairie, trout mature at three to four years and only live up to eight years. Nevertheless, in most waters these are generally considered old trout.

Some subspecies of cutthroat trout also have a long life characteristic. Bear Lake-strain cutthroats, from another unproductive lake, have been shown to live to eleven years of age (Nielson and Lentsch). Repeat spawning in Bear Lake cutthroat trout is also rare (less than 4 percent) so that the energy that would have gone into reproduction can go into growth. As age is one of the keys to producing these super trout, please release them so that they can grow larger, reproduce, and be available for other anglers to enjoy.

What happens when you plant a late-maturing/long-lived strain into a highly productive water? The results vary. Forest Lake, just northeast of Williams Lake, British Columbia, is a successful example of a well-managed fishery that has had success with this strategy. Provincial fisheries biologists planted late-maturing Quesnel Lake-strain rainbows into this shallow, highly productive, and insect-based 240-acre stillwater. The result is that there are good numbers of four-year-old rainbows that range from 7 to 12 pounds and a few larger ones that go over 20 pounds. The two keys to the success of this program are that most anglers release their trout so that they can grow to be old enough to get big, and the provincial fish and wildlife biologists balance the number of trout with the available food supply. According to Brad Kerr, an aquatics consultant, the most productive natural habitats have mechanisms to regulate the number of trout surviving to reach trophy size. Otherwise, there would simply be lakes with dense populations of average trout.

While Forest Lake is an outstanding example of fishery management and angler cooperation, highly-productive Strawberry Reservoir in Utah is just the opposite. Original plantings

This six-pound brook trout from Osprey Lake in Labrador is slightly larger than the average for the lake and many times the size of those found in the lower 48 states.

This chunky Quesnel Lake stock rainbow trout from British Columbia's Forest Lake, being released by Dennis Schmidt, demonstrates the success of fishery management and angler cooperation.

of late-maturing (five to six years of age) Bear Lake cutthroats produced trout in excess of 26 pounds. This stillwater became popular, and the trout were so easily caught by anglers, that they were harvested before they had the chance to mature (reduced to three or four years in their new environment) and grow large. The result is that the fish rarely grow beyond the mid-teens in inches. Fishery biologists understand the potential of the resource but are hampered by the local angling population, who prefer Strawberry Reservoir to be managed as a meat fishery.

Not all plantings of late-maturing trout in productive environments result in larger fish, even if the conditions exist for them to grow big. The New York State Department of Environmental Conservation (NYDEC) planted late-maturing seeforellen brown trout, originally from acidic, unproductive alpine lakes in Germany, into Lake Ontario. (Acidity in water is measured by its potential of hydrogen pH, on a scale of 1 to 14, the lower numbers being more acidic. At 7.0, the water is neutral. The ideal range for trout is from 6.5 to 8.7.) They found that growth performance was not unlike the domestic hatchery strains that had been planted. Their conclusion for both the seeforellens and the domestic brown trout was that early maturation is a function of rapid growth.

If the food source is there, they will grow and reproduce in relation to it. Fishery biologists in Michigan also planted seeforellens into Lake Michigan, with eggs from New York, and had similar results. However, older fish did return on some rivers, such as the Menominee River. Age seven was the upper limit, as compared to the domestic three-year-old limit of their domestic strains. In general, the size of the older fish was not much different than the younger domestic stocks. Nevertheless, some extremely large seeforellens have appeared. Two fish in one year, 35.11 pounds and 35.12 pounds, broke the Wisconsin state record. Both were believed to be older brown trout that fed efficiently after they matured. This would suggest that their genetics (in combination with their environment) gave them the opportunity to grow to trophy sizes, although on average they will not be this large.

Record Trout

Many big trout that could be records, whether they be Fly Fishing, Line Class, or All Tackle, are never recorded in state record books, the International Game Fish Association (IGFA), the Official World and U.S.A. State Fresh Water Angling Records published by the National Freshwater Fishing Hall of Fame, or by other organizations. Record-book contributors also have their own preferences as to where they want their trophies to be listed so the largest world record trout in one book might be different than another. Some records are based on weight while others measure length. Which are the correct methods and the larger of the two fish? I do not think that it matters. I consider the record books to be a valuable resource to tell me where the big fish are being taken. If a few of the line-class records for one species are taken in the same river, lake, or region in recent years you can bet that there are more big trout in those places. You can find all of the fish and wildlife state records on the Internet, or you can join the IGFA or the National Fresh Water Fishing Hall of Fame to receive their book. A glance at Table 1-8 and Table 1-9 below will key you into some of the places where there are big trout.

Table 1-8: World Record Freshwater Trout Caught in North America

Species	Line Class/ All Tackle	Pounds	Ounces	Where	Date
Rainbows	6 lb. test	31	12	Santa Cruz Lake, NM	March 13, 1999
(not steelhead)	20 lb. test	31	5	Lake Pend Oreille, Idaho	November 18, 1983
	16 lb. test	31	10	Lake Pend Oreille, Idaho	October 1992
Brown Trout	4 lb. test	40	4	Little Red River, Arkansas	May 9, 1992
		34	6	Lake Ontario, Mississauga, Ontario Canada	September 9, 1994
		34	6	Bar Lake, Arcadia, Michigan	May 16, 1984
Brook Trout	All Tackle	14	8	Nipigon River, Ontario, Canada	July 1916
	16. lb test	10	12	Osprey Lake, Labrador	June 24, 1996
	4 lb. test	9	0	Lake Nipigon, Ontario, Canada	July 1, 1996
Cutthroat Trout	All Tackle	41	0	Pyramid Lake, Nevada	December 1925
	8 lb. test	18	0	Omak Lake, Washington	July 1, 1993
	6 lb. test	14	4	Pyramid Lake, Nevada	February 28, 1988

Source: IGFA 2000 World Record Game Fishes.

Table 1-9: World Record Freshwater Trout Caught on a Fly Rod in North America

Species	Line Class	Pounds	Ounces	Where	Date
*Rainbows (not steelhead)					
Brown Trout	12 lb. test	35	2	Rio Grande, Tierra del Fuego, Argentina	March 1998
	16 lb. test	29	12	"	January 19, 1992
	8 lb. test	29	0	"	March 9, 1996
Brook Trout	8 lb. test	10	7	Assinica Broadback River, Quebec	September 1982
	4 lb. test	10	0	Minipi Lake, Labrador	June 29, 1987
	12 lb. test	9	7	Minipi River, Labrador	August 8, 1988
Cutthroat Trout	16 lb. test	13	1	Pyramid Lake, Nevada	March 14, 1994
	8 lb. test	14	1	"	April 4, 1982
	12 lb. test	10	0	"	February 9, 1990

Source: IGFA 2000 World Record Game Fishes.
*There are only large steelhead listed in IGFA Fly Rod World Records.

While these are truly large trout, traditional fly fishers do not often frequent some of these waters. In Lake Pend Oreille, for example, which is a large body of water (surface area 94,640 acres), only a few fly fishers hunt big trout. Oddly enough, gear anglers on Pend Oreille troll streamers on the surface. According to Keith Snyder, a guide on the lake, "When you run spoons you definitely knock your size class down—flies catch the biggest fish." Lake Pend Oreille holds world records that can be taken on a fly with non-traditional techniques. I fish Pend Oreille and Kootenay Lake with fly gear and have had no less success than the conventional anglers. Most of the IGFA Fly Rod line-class world records for rainbow trout are steelhead in the high teens and mid-twenty-pound range. These records are definitely breakable. The fly fisher just has to change his tactics, focus his efforts, and consider his timing.

I have developed a top ten list of big-trout waters in North America. I thoroughly researched the genetics of these trout and the environments that they live in. These waters seasonally hold good numbers of big trout that I can qualify from my personal fishing experience. Most of them contain wild fish and none of them are stocked ponds. There is no particular order to these waters. There are other waters that I visited, but did not have the chance to fish for enough time or under optimal water flows, that could be on this list. The Little Red River and White River in Arkansas are two that could very well have been in the top ten. There are 75 other big trout waters listed in Chapter 6. Some that I did not have the chance to visit, such as Bear Lake in Utah and the Naknek River in Alaska, likely would have qualified for this list.

Top Ten Big Trout Waters in North America (in no particular order)

- Crane Prairie Reservoir, Oregon (rainbow trout)
- Lake Pend Oreille, Idaho (rainbow trout)
- Quesnel Lake, British Columbia (rainbow trout)
- Kvichak River, Arkansas (rainbow trout)
- Upper Klamath Lake, Oregon (rainbow trout)
- Oak Orchard and nearby Lake Ontario tributaries, New York (brown trout)
- Pyramid Lake, Nevada (cutthroat trout)
- Osprey Lake, Labrador (brook trout)
- Frying Pan River, Colorado (rainbow trout)
- Kootenay Lake, British Columbia (rainbow trout)
- Williamson River, Oregon (rainbow trout)
- Connetquot River, New York (rainbow and brown trout)

The Next World Record Trout

While researching this book I often thought to myself about what it would take to catch the next world record trout. One approach would be to look for an existing trophy trout lake that is at the low end in a cycle—has a reduced population of trout but is expected to come back—whether naturally or with the help of man. For example, the increase in fertilizer to stimulate the phytoplankton in Kootenay Lake, that in turn will increase the number of kokanee, might be a factor to generate a world record fish. Another approach might be to analyze the current trophy trout fisheries to determine which ones have fish in the size class that you are looking for. The White River in Arkansas, for instance, holds brown trout that could surpass the current All-Tackle records. I would start by interviewing the fish and wildlife biologists about their electro-fishing surveys to see if such a fish exists in the targeted water. I would then try to learn everything that is possible to know about that trout. Its physiology, genetics, behavior, food sources, etc. I would fill a book with information about that trout. I would then devise a plan to stalk that trout during the times of day and periods of the year when it is most susceptible.

Another strategy to catch a world-record trout would be to research new plantings of late-maturing trout in highly productive waters with little competition from other species and low fishing pressure, monitor the growth of the fish through the fishery biologists who are managing the water, and then arrive at the time the fish reach the age class required for the record size. Many of the state and world records have come from early plantings of such fish.

State records are probably more easily achieved for most anglers, largely because you have a better chance of frequenting waters that are a few hours' drive from your house than the international class-record destinations—such as Labrador for big brook trout or the White River in Arkansas for browns. To catch a state record fish, I would focus on waters where the largest fish are frequently caught. These can be found in the record books. I would research the patterns of when and where they are caught and then focus on those times and places. In my home state of Oregon, I would target a state record brown trout in Paulina Lake on the first day the ice is off the lake and the trout are hungry and unpressured. I provide many examples of windows of opportunity to catch big trout across North America in this book. Each state has waters with such opportunities.

Who is the Hero?

Many record fish are released out of choice by anglers who are concerned about preserving the genetics of the strain. They are content with a picture on their desk and a story to tell their peers. Some anglers do not know the procedures for entering such fish and by the time they figure it out the evidence is destroyed. Other anglers do not want their fishery to be publicized by the exposure from such a story. This is not to say that entering a record fish is wrong. Indeed, favorable press often brings attention and resources to a fishery. The angler must make the decision for him or herself whether or not to enter the fish. If you do decide to keep the fish, inquire with the local fish and game department if there are any body parts that they are interested in studying. Scientists who study the genetics and life history strategy of trout seek extremely large fish. The researchers often handle these fish in a live state during electro-fishing surveys, but they rarely have the chance to examine their anatomy after they are deceased.

Ordinary, but skillful, anglers who happened to be at the right place at the right time, and took the time to fill out the forms, caught most of the record trout on the books. There was no magic or hidden secret involved. Since the right time more often has to do with the genetics of the trout and history of the water, the true hero of the world record fish is the trout (and sometimes the managers of the fishery) and not the angler. Consider that the IGFA All Tackle World Record brown trout from the Little Red River in Arkansas probably lived to the extraordinary age of seventeen years while most browns across this continent do not live beyond four or five years. There is clearly little that the angler did to make this possible. The life history of this trout would probably make a better movie than the story of the angler who caught it, with no disrespect intended to the late Howard "Rip" Collins.

CHAPTER 2
GET INTO THE
MIND AND BODY
OF YOUR PREY

You have to get back to the basics of the salmonid itself—his physiology and his environment.
Charlie White

There has been a great deal of research in both the angling and scientific worlds on the behavior of trout and other freshwater fish. The scientific research is usually aimed at building a foundation for the better management of natural resources or basic research about the physiology, genetics, and behavior of fish. While these studies are not conducted under fishing conditions, their findings often relate to issues of interest to anglers. Sometimes anglers with scientific minds conduct their own studies to better understand the interactions between fish and fisherman. These studies are especially important because they are usually designed to solve specific angling questions.

The Mind of the Trout

Trout do not have complex thought patterns, and trout in one river are no more intelligent than those in another. Research may someday find that one race's brain is larger than another, but we are still talking about dumb and dumber. Trout raised in a hatchery environment may instinctively react to a human approaching as a sign of food, and your beadhead caddis pattern hitting the water may look like a protein pellet. The wild trout may inversely consider any large object above it to be an avian predator, but the hatchery-raised trout may react in the same way after being dived upon a few times. The trout's behavior, regardless of whether it is wild, a pure-strain hatchery fish, or a triploid, is really a matter of conditioning, although there may be some behavioral differences between the species. How trout hold in the water column and diet preference also vary by species and these characteristics are often misinterpreted as intelligence. They are actually the result of trout adapting to their environments. In rivers, brown trout tend to hold closer to the bottom and farther under shade than other trout (Butler and Hawthorne) and, as a result, tend to be less susceptible to anglers.

The illustration below compares the size and midline view of a human's brain (A) to that of trout (C). (A blown-up view of the trout's brain is shown in B.) The cerebral hemisphere is shaded in darker gray and the brainstem is in lighter gray. Note that trout lack a complex brain, especially enlarged cerebral hemispheres (dark gray) composed of neocortex. This neocortex is the gray matter that gives us cognitive thought. The brainstem is responsible for basic functions of life, such as breathing and blood pressure. According to Dr. James Rose from the University of Wyoming, who did a great deal of research on the trout's brain, this fish cannot think and doesn't have to think in order to feed. Feeding is a visually guided behavior that is processed mainly by the brainstem, especially by a structure called the optic

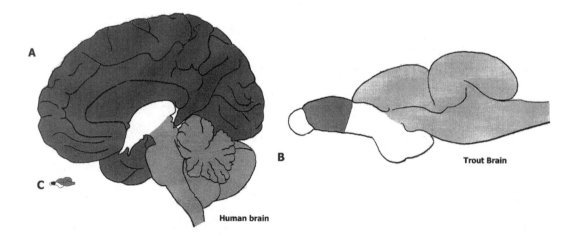

B

Trout Brain

A

C

Human brain

tectum. An understanding of big trout behavior should be based on the fish's brain capacity, and our approach to catching them should consider their behavior and how they react to stimuli in their environments.

While trout do not have the capacity to think, there is a great deal of evidence that this fish has the ability to remember. In laboratory conditions, trout have been shown to retain a memory for three months (Adron et al.). An angling survey on the heavily fished Lake Pend Oreille showed that the frequency of the same rainbow trout being hooked had a medium number of days of 186 and ranged from 8 to 551 days (Videgar). Studies on the pike, another predatory game fish, have shown that after being hooked once with a spinner, they avoided this lure for the remainder of the test period (approximately one month). Meanwhile, the same pike would continue to feed on live roach that were offered on a hook and line (Beukema). As a side note, none of the fish in the study were believed to have learned how to throw a hook to avoid being captured. This presents a strong argument for angling on opening day, periods when few fishermen are on the water, and at rivers and lakes that are not heavily fished.

Trout react instinctively to food and predators as opposed to strategizing about how to deal with them efficiently. They react differently to some colors and movement can excite them. They key in on prey foods that look and behave similarly and studies have shown that they do not quickly adjust their behavior to new opportunities, even if the newly introduced food items are more energy efficient (Ringler). When big trout focus their behavior so intently on feeding, their guard against predators often goes down. Fishery biologists on the Little Red and White Rivers in Arkansas do most of their electro-fishing at night and have higher catch rates (greater than 2 : 1) during this period than the daylight hours. The biologists reason that this is because they can get much closer to bigger trout when they are feeding and less alert to predators. Most anglers have been in a super hatch when the trout seemed to swim around them to reach the drifting insects while the same trout would dart for safety at much farther distances at another time. Alaskan anglers drift in their boats for rainbow trout that are keying in on sockeye eggs. Sometimes the trout shuffle a few feet away while at other times they hold under the boat as it passes over them. My hypothesis is that during heavy feeds or times when they are hunting prey fish the trout are concentrating on something besides the angler. There is a great deal of research with other freshwater fish to support this conclusion (Milinski). As a result, trout can be much easier to catch during major feeds.

Size of Prey

An important question for any body of water is what size fly should be presented. Fishery biologists have observed that the rainbows in Quesnel Lake, British Columbia prefer to feed on prey fish that are one-third their own length (Fisheries Branch, B.C. Ministry of Environment). Just as important as the length is the outer diameter of the prey fish and the size of the trout's own mouth and throat. A trout that tries to consume a food item that doesn't fit down the hatch isn't going to live for long. (This dimension also includes the fins.) Prey fish like three-spined sticklebacks are bigger than they look once the spines go up, and the trout learns this (Moodie). Does this mean that we should fish such large flies to big trout in other waters? It all depends on what size prey is available and if the trout feed on that prey item. Big rainbow trout in Crane Prairie Reservoir in Oregon feed almost exclusively on three-spined sticklebacks that have a maximum length of about four inches. While a 10-pound trout can probably suck down a fly much larger (girth + fins) than a big three-spined stickleback, I wouldn't present a longer or deeper fly. This relates to presenting a fly that is similar to what the trout are used to. As an aside, the size of prey fish is not a determining factor in the reactive distance of the predator.

The degree of ambient light behind the prey is more important than the size in this respect, so a 4-inch fly can be seen just as readily as a 3-inch one.

Working big flies will help to ward off smaller fish on waters where the trout hunt larger prey fish, although I have seen 20-inch trout take an 8-inch streamer, so this is not a hard and fast rule. Many of my big fish flies, such as the Stinging Fly series (Bucktail, Bunny, Sculpin, and Hair), are tied on fairly large hooks by freshwater standards and have sweeping tails that make them appear even larger. There are a few exceptions to the "big fish, big fly" rule. These include fishing the opossum shrimp drifts on tailwaters, or stillwaters where there are intense concentrations of insects and scuds, such as in the Blackfeet Reservation lakes. Fishing *Chironomidae* to trout resting along the bottom of shallow, productive lakes, or drifting Glo-bugs to migratory browns in the Great Lake tributaries and to Alaskan rainbows feeding behind spawning salmon are other exceptions.

The Attack

The trout is a fast swimmer but not a swift ambush feeder in comparison to some other freshwater game fish. The tiger musky, for example, can move 37 inches per second from a dead start when attacking a fathead minnow, while a rainbow trout of a similar length moves

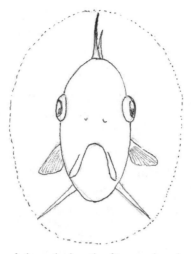

The trout is not only concerned about the length of its prey but also the outer diameter, including the fins and spines.

about 20 inches per second (Webb). The start-up speed for the rainbow equates to just over a mile per hour, about as fast as our walking pace. Once the trout gets going it can swim at over 10 mph (Black). The speed of trout also depends on their size, typically expressed in relation to body length (a 24-inch trout swims three times faster than an 8-inch trout) (Behnke). Somewhere between zero and 10 mph is the right speed to retrieve line or troll. The amount of energy the trout puts into the individual hunt or to chase your fly will be based on how hungry it is, the water temperature, physiological issues, and how fast and in what direction you are hauling your fly to or away from it.

The trout often has to chase a prey fish that has detected its predator and goes on the run. The blind spots for the fleeing prey items will be from below and behind and the trout will probably pursue their prey from these angles. The strike will be hard, as the trout grabs the prey fish and tries to crush this food item with its jaws. On a large prey fish, the food item will most likely be taken in the back half of the body, as this is the direction of attack. Dr. Eric Moodie, who has done a great deal of research on the feeding interactions between rainbow and cutthroat trout and sticklebacks, also suggests that the farther back the trout grabs the fly (imitation prey fish), the less likely it is to be hurt by a spine.

Trout feed differently on small food items that drift to them than on larger prey items that they have to catch in open water. Foods taken off the bottom and/or those that have drifted into their path are picked up, tasted, and swallowed. Often, these smaller food items easily fit into the trout's mouth. Prey fish are first searched for, then encountered, chased, grabbed, stunned, manipulated, tasted, and then swallowed. Less "spiney" fish, such as sculpins, also require less manipulation before swallowing, as their spines are minimal. However, some have ugly little spines on their heads that the trout are painfully aware of. Soft-rayed and spined prey fish are crushed so as to fold down the spines or rays and then manipulated around to go down head first.

Trout and other freshwater game fish rarely consume these prey fish tail first as the spines can rip out the insides of the trout while being swallowed (L'Abee-Lund et al.). Large trout can swallow small minnows, and even small sticklebacks, tail first when the prey diameter is less than one half the gape of the predator (Reimchen). Smaller prey can also equate to less protein for the same amount of energy expended and will not be the first choice for big trout. Many anglers misinterpret the head down swallowing direction, thinking the trout attacks the head of the prey fish. This is a maneuver that the salmonid could not easily accomplish. Can you imagine running ahead of a fleeing deer and then grabbing it by the head? Most of the trout's strikes on prey fish are at the tail section, just as most predators pounce on a fleeing animal when trying to catch it.[2]

Some anglers suggest that when the trout grabs the tail of the prey fish it has a "short strike." I, too, believed this for a long period of time, but after careful observation and research, I am convinced that most of these missed hook-ups were not a mistake on the part of the trout but a result of the angler's fly design or action. The angler didn't exert enough force into his hook-set, the hook is not being placed within the trout's mouth for a good set, or the trout believed that it crushed the prey item, and after starting to be turned around in the fish's mouth the angler pulled the fly out. In the latter two cases, the angler should *stop the retrieve* or let the fly hang back once the hook-set has been missed to keep the fly within sight of the trout and let the predator have another chance at it. Dr. Moodie observed that trout feeding on sticklebacks often attacked and lost their target but would come back for a second time if they could see the food item (e.g. the stickleback was not too far away because it was badly hurt).

The length of the hook in relation to the fly can also determine whether or not there will be a solid hook-up. Traditional streamer flies, such as the Mickey Finn and Gray Ghost, have short tails and use a long-shanked hook that extends almost to the end of the fly. Modern streamer flies have been developed with flowing tails and body parts to look more lifelike—in my opinion, at the expense of reliable and solid hook-ups. Take a look at the streamers in your fly box to see which ones have a body that extends far beyond the hook. You might find a few that are two to three times the length of your hook. Do you remember all of the fish

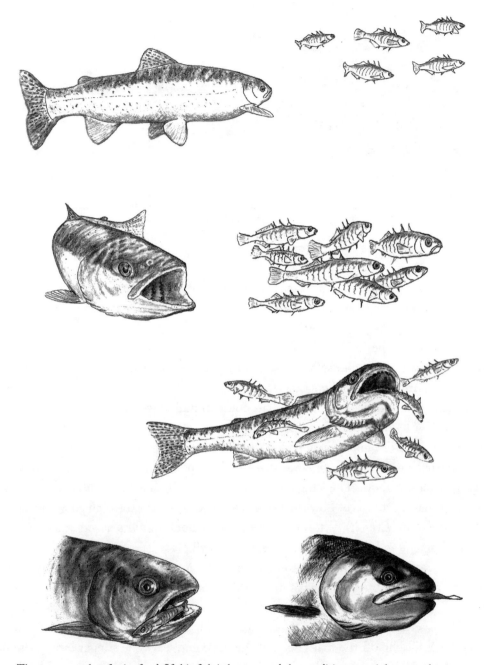

The trout searches for its food. If this fish is hungry and the conditions are right to catch a prey fish, the trout will attack it from behind and stun it at the tail. The trout then turns the prey fish around in its mouth so that this finned food item goes down head first. This maneuver prevents the spines or rays from flaring out and getting caught in the trout's throat during ingestion.

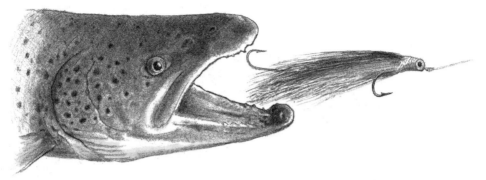

The trout will instinctively grab at the tail of the streamer to avoid the prick of the presumed fins of this prey fish imitation. Some anglers misinterpret this as a "short strike."

that hit them without a hook-set? Don't worry about the hook hanging exposed behind the body of the fly. Fish fixate and strike on the hook if they cannot see the point, especially with hooks that actually wiggle (White).

The position of the hook is important for other prey imitations, as well. I had a big Alaskan rainbow attack a mouse pattern skittering across the surface during ten retrieves before making a firm hook set. This experience taught me two lessons: trout will come back if not threatened and the hook set-up on that mouse imitation was less than ideal.

Streamers with one hook that holds body materials often do not have the flowing motion of the larger ones. The angler may be unintentionally leveraging these long-shanked hooks out of the trout's mouth. A better approach that incorporates the old and new is the stinger hook set-up shown above. The stinger hook is attached with a piece of flexible nylon monofilament so that regardless of how the hook is set, the hook will travel in a path towards the mouth of the trout. Even if the trout tries to drop the hook from its mouth, the flexibility of the monofilament and the wide gape off-set hook will place it in the right zone. It will also make it more difficult for the hook to be leveraged out of the trout's mouth. Big trout anglers that use this set-up report that almost 100 percent of their hook-ups are on the stinger hook.

Not all fisheries allow a two-hook set-up. If your targeted water does not permit two hooks on one fly, clip off the main hook at the bend and leave the stinger intact. Use octopus-style hooks for the stinger, but be sure to straighten out the point. These hooks have been shown to provide much greater hook-ups than standard flat hooks (White). Treble

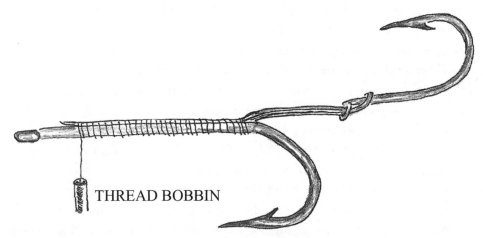

THREAD BOBBIN

Tie a two-hook system to catch trout that are stunning the prey fish at the tail. You can easily double your catch. If local regulations prohibit a two-hook system, clip the main hook off at the bend and leave the stinger intact.

hooks have even greater hooking potential, but I do not use them. It is a matter of preference (and law) on many waters.

How Big Trout Find Their Prey

Whether the big trout is in a river or stillwater, the process of hunting food starts with a desire to feed. If the trout is hungry, and the water temperature, oxygen, and light levels are conducive to feeding, the fish will position itself to take food in the drift or swim to locate prey. Trout are primarily visual predators and this sense can be influenced by turbid water, rain, currents, wind, and the degree of illumination. When their sight is impaired, they must use other senses to survive. One of them is acoustic reception, or what we call hearing.

Hearing

Trout do not have external ears like mammals. They have internal ears within their skulls, and this organ is jointly used for balance and distinguishing sounds that food, or friend or foe may make. The sounds are amplified by the trout's swim bladder.[3]

The ear does not respond to the thrashing sounds of prey fish very well and perhaps can detect other sounds at a greater distance. But, assuming that their sensitivity is not great, the distance over which they will detect sound is not very far, either. The distance would depend on many factors including sensitivity of the ear to the amount of background noise, such as wave action or water running over rocks, that would mask detection (Popper). Considering that rivers typically have more background noise than lakes, you stand a better chance of getting close to a trout in moving water, from a sound standpoint, than in calm water. Moving waters also have a ruffled surface that obscures fish's vision above water.

Another hearing organ is the trout's lateral line. This line extends from the head to the tail of the trout and picks up low frequency vibrations, or pressure waves, reflecting from structure, other fish, and sometimes us. These pressure waves have lower vibrations than sound waves. A workable understanding of the lateral line and inner ear starts with physics. To begin with, the speed of sound travels about four times as fast in clear water as it does in air. We have to be careful with this figure, though, as the waters that we fish in are not perfectly clear. They are often soaked with algae, floating debris, and have air bubbles and other obstructions that dampen sound and the distance it can travel. Nevertheless, the speed stays the same. Sound waves travel much like the ripples when you drop a pebble in a pond. A ripple spreads over the surface of the water in an ever-enlarging circle. As the circle gets larger, the energy, or pressure wave, spreads out and becomes less intense. By the time the pressure wave reaches the other shoreline, the ripple is barely perceptible. This ripple is a pulse, meaning that one beat of energy is being released. Such a pulse would probably notify a trout that something is amiss, but a constant series of pulses would be required for the trout to locate the source. A school of swimming prey fish might create a significant enough series of pulses, at that point termed a "frequency," that could travel for some distance for the trout to pick up with its lateral line. A single prey fish, hiding or intermittently swimming along, probably doesn't create the disturbance required for such detection at any great distance.

Although trout can detect certain movements at fairly close distances, when developing a strategy to take big trout the hearing senses (or taste or smell, for that matter) are not efficient enough to play a major role. Consider walking through the forest at night: You hear deer around you and can roughly guess where they are, but your chances of grabbing one with your hands is highly unlikely. The trout's ability to catch prey fish in rivers or stillwaters with their non-visual senses is no different.[4] An interesting aside: The lateral line system may provide warning of imminent capture, allowing a quick movement away from the predator just at the moment of the strike (Blaxter et al.).

Even if trout are able to catch small prey (such as minnows) that do not have spines or large rays when they are confined in small quarters, this is not likely to happen with any degree of efficiency in a natural setting. Some angling writers have suggested that the trout can discern the type of prey from long distances with their hearing system. If this were truly the case, they would not be attracted to flies or lures that do not sound like live prey fish.

Prey fish can also use their hearing senses to avoid the trout. I could probably hear and grab a deer in my living room when the lights are turned off, but this is not a likely feat on a dark night in an open field. In a natural environment, prey fish tend to be more cautious when they come into contact with predatory game fish, or they simply try to avoid them altogether (Huntingford et al.). Even under good lighting conditions, trout are not always successful at grabbing prey fish, and a test of cutthroat trout feeding on sticklebacks showed that about a third escaped from the trout's mouth (Reimchen).

Some prey fish (sticklebacks, chubs, shiners, minnows) specialize in using their lateral lines to detect insects feeding on the surface in stillwaters (Bleckman) and on zooplankton in darkness (Montgomery), although the feeding rate of these prey fish is not as fast as when they can see their prey (Batty et al.). This may give the prey fish an advantage by allowing them to feed when the big trout cannot see them. However, the feeding period of the prey fish will be over an extended duration as their lateral lines are not as efficient as their visual sense during the illuminated hours of the day.[5]

The regularity of some sounds may be an important issue. Wading anglers, fly lines slapping on the surface, and noisy watercraft are not a common occurrence in most waters and may spook the fish if the pressure waves reach the fish. However, Charlie White, from British Columbia, found that he could stomp on a boat and bang a wrench against metal fixtures and only alarm the chinook salmon momentarily before they came back to follow his lure. He did find that changing engine speeds negatively affected the fish. White also observed that boats with rough idling engines catch fewer fish than those that are smoothly tuned.[6] So with respect to the angler, hearing in trout is probably most useful for the fish in avoiding us rather than as a means of luring them.

At first glance, it would seem that the farther your fly is from your craft (the more line out), the better off you will be. But more line also equates to more stretch and chances for a missed hook-up. What is the optimal distance? It depends; I have had trout snatch my fly a few feet from my pontoon boat in soupy green lakes. Trial and error, with close observation of the water clarity and lighting conditions, is probably the best answer.

Some anglers will be asking how they have been able to catch trout under dark conditions if hearing plays such a small role. I can offer two explanations: The first, which will be discussed in more depth later, is that trout can see under fairly low illumination equivalent to starlight. The second is that trout can find and catch a large, noisy, and slow-moving fly or

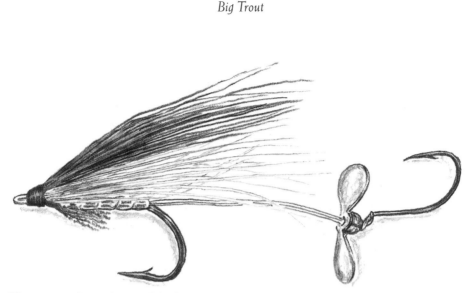

The streamer fin on the tail of the Stinging Bucktail sends out pressure waves to draw big trout to the fly and incite them to strike. This is an ideal fly for both day and nighttime angling.

lure (with continuous pulses) that is presented to them under conditions where they cannot see. But how do we create enough noise to attract the trout without spooking them? A similar problem exists in soupy green lakes or in those where the trout are spread out over vast distances. A Woolly Bugger probably generates more pressure waves than a Mickey Finn, but they still do not travel far. Test this for yourself by pulling both types of flies on the surface next to your boat and see how far the ripples (pressure waves) travel. I have addressed this problem with my "streamer fin" pattern, as shown in the illustration below. The streamer fin is constructed from a durable and lightweight metalized thin sheet of plastic and can be cast or trolled. Just behind the streamer fin is a glass bead on which the fin travels. An alternative to the streamer fin is to use a metal spoon with a folded clevise. The streamer fin is a better option, as the blade is lightweight and spins with very little movement, such as the tailing action of a hovering prey fish. In contrast, the metal blades of a spoon are heavier and need to be jerked to rotate, thus limiting your range of retrieval options.

Field of View
The trout and the angler are both primarily visual predators. As such, visual factors should determine our approach, lure selection, and presentation. (Dr. William Hanneman's book, *What Trout Actually See,* provides a thorough examination of this subject.) The first perspective is the trout's field of view. This helps us to predict the angle that the trout is most

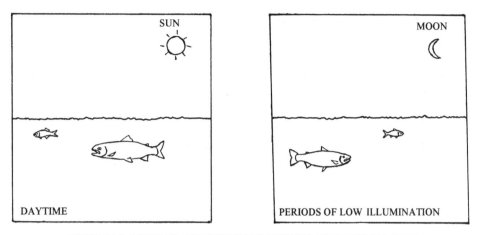

OPTIMAL VISUAL DETECTION ANGLE FOR BIG TROUT

When fishing during the day, consider keeping your fly lower in the water column, casting into the sun, or trolling away from it. During the evening hours present your fly closer to the surface and retrieve or troll in the direction away from the illumination the moon provides.

likely to take to our fly. Trout can see an area of 300 degrees in front of them and to their sides. Their blind spots are a small area directly in front of their nose and a wider one extending from one flank to the other. This might make a prey fish moving in their direction or across their path preferable, as they can start to chase the prey on the approach as opposed to trying to catch up to a fish that has already moved past them. It is unlikely, though, that prey fish will swim into the waiting mouth of a trout. Most prey items that come into sight of the trout will probably be from an angle or the side, which the trout will see with its monocular vision (one eye), or from above and in front of them, which utilizes their binocular vision (two eyes). This monocular vision has little depth perception and does not help the trout to catch moving or zigzagging prey items. If the trout decides to chase the prey item farther, the fish must use its binocular vision. That means it has to swim towards the prey fish.

Where you present your fly should depend on the available illumination. In open water (pelagic) systems where trout primarily feed on other fish under generally low light conditions, visual acuity is less important than detecting the contrast between prey and its background (Vogel and Beauchamp). Note in the illustration above that the trout can better see the prey item when it is across and above the trout and in the opposite direction of the sun. Trout do not have eyelids and use depth, cover, changes in the structure of their eyes, and their angle to the sun to avoid the sun's harsh rays. In a series of experiments in a hatchery environment and on open water, Charlie White found that the fish only attacked surface prey with the sun at their backs. Inversely, during periods of low illumination, the effectiveness of the trout will depend on its ability to strike at backlit prey from below. Thus, during the nighttime, the angle should be above the trout and in the direction of the light source (moon).

Distance at which the Prey Can Be Visually Detected By the Trout

Trout are nearsighted and cannot see objects at long distances. Table 2-1 describes the distances that trout can see during daylight under varying water conditions. As light intensity decreases, whether it is related to the turbidity of the water or illumination from the sun or moon, depth perception also decreases.

Table 2-1: Horizontal and Vertical Reaction Distance to Prey for Trout in Moving and Stillwaters During Daylight Conditions[7]

Type of Water	Crystal Clear (Blue) Water (1)	Turbid (Green) Water (2)	Murky (Brown) Water (3)
Stillwater (4)	10 to 15 feet or less	Less than 5 feet	Less than 3 feet
Moving Waters (5)	5-plus feet	6 inches to 1½ feet	Less than 6 inches

While trolling from a boat you can increase your chances of coming into visual contact with trout by spreading your rods out to cover more area. The illustration on page 53 describes two scenarios for rod placement in the boat. In the first, the fisherman has two rods facing directly out of the back of the boat; in the second, they are at an angle away from the craft. Because the first anglers have their rods close together, their reach is overlapped and they are fishing their flies to the same fish. These anglers have a maximum spread of about 36 feet, while the second anglers cover around 56 feet.

Visibility

Refraction, or how light waves are bent as they pass from the air to the water, is the final field-of-view issue for the angler to contend with in a river. The trout may seem to be directly diagonal to the angler, but the fish will be closer and deeper than it appears. This issue is important for river anglers, as they often have the opportunity to target big trout by sight. I had difficulty with this for many years, thinking that my fly was being swept away from trout by the current. The reality was that I was not placing the fly in the correct position. A right-angle nymphing system can help the angler to overcome this problem.

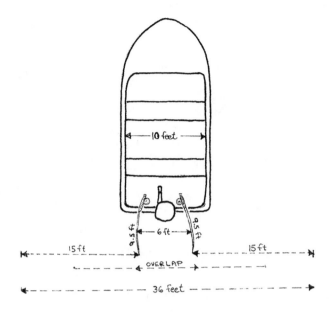

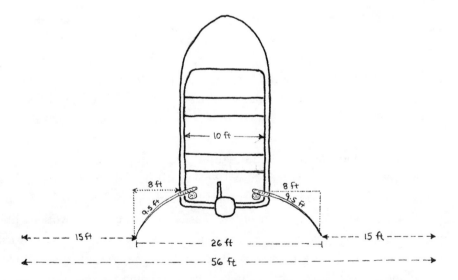

Try to spread your rods out to cover more area when trolling. The more trout that can see your flies, the greater your chances for a hook-up.

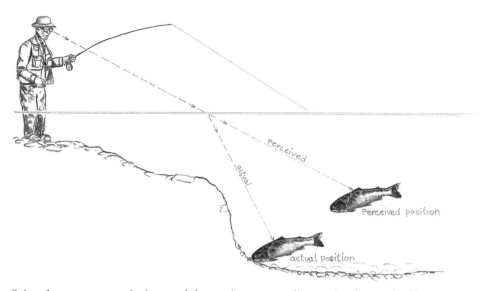

Subsurface trout are much closer and deeper than we actually perceive them to be. You may think that you are accurately casting your fly to a trout, but you may actually be laying your line over the fish.

Color and Light

Another vision issue of interest to the big trout angler concerns color and light. The angler needs to understand light from two perspectives. The first is related to how and under what conditions trout see colors, and the second is how light helps to determine the daily rhythms of the trout and their prey. (This second topic is the primary focus of the next chapter.) Within the color issue there are three aspects: the first is the process of how trout see color; the second is the physics of colors; and the third is how combinations of colors affect trout.

Most anglers consider color but do not use a systemized approach to choosing color for the trout's environment or color combinations that will best entice the trout. Many anglers fish one color, perhaps a favorite pattern, until the fishing conditions have become conducive for the trout to take that color. Others recognize the importance of color and continually change flies, or the color of flies, until they find one that works. This is the classic Atlantic salmon angler who has a box of multicolored flies, with at least one color, or contrasting ones, in a pattern sure to attract a fish. Many migratory trout anglers follow this same route with boxes of Glo-bug patterns in various color combinations. The big-trout angler also recognizes the importance of color and analyzes the trout's environment to determine the best color, or combination of colors, to present to the trout.

How Trout See Color

There is a great deal of academic and industrial research related to how fish see colors. Studies have shown that some trout have keen color discrimination (Ginetz and Larkin). As a baseline, we have to understand that the trout have learned to adapt to a huge range of illumination through the evolution of two distinct receptor systems in the retinas of their eyes—rods and cones.[8]

The rods function at low light levels and do not see color or contrast well. The advantage of the rods is that they are super light-sensitive and allow trout to see the shapes of objects under low illumination. These shapes, or silhouettes, will be in shades of black and white. Cones function during the heavily illuminated hours of the day and allow the trout to see sharp contrasts and colors.[9]

The next time you wake up early in the morning when the sun is just coming up and your shades are down, take a look around your bedroom and see if you can identify the colors in the paintings on your walls or even the color of your carpet or rug. I have a series of prints on my walls that are sparsely colored on white paper with a green mat. At the above degree of illumination, the green border looks black, the white paper a light gray, and everything else is a dark gray. Trout see objects under low illumination much like this. Low light flies for big trout need to be designed with this idea in mind.

The Physics of Color

The trout use their cone vision to see colors during the illuminated hours of the day. However, we have to understand that the trout can only see the colors of its prey if the wavelength of that color is transmitted to the depth of the trout and its prey. The amount and distance that surface light transmits below the surface of the water varies by the color of the object that reflects it, the clarity of the water, and the intensity of light above the surface that penetrates below. The color spectrum for the adult trout goes from the short wavelengths (high energy) to the longest wavelength (low energy). This order is blue, green, violet, yellow, orange, and then red. The order that light dissipates below the surface (the downward scale) starts with red, then orange, yellow, violet, green, and finally blue. The shorter (high energy) wavelengths penetrate the deepest in clear water (tropical oceans) because they are the least absorbed by water.[10]

If we apply this portion of the light issue to big trout in the large and clear oligotrophic lakes—such as Kootenay, Pend Oreille, and Quesnel—and the tailwaters, blues and greens should penetrate the deepest as these waters have a small amount of organic matter. In the mesotrophic and eurotrophic lakes, green should penetrate the deepest. In migratory rivers where the brown trout are moving up to spawn during higher and murky water flows, the waters are shallow and the visibility of the trout is probably a more important issue. In all three water types, fluorescent colors will penetrate the farthest and be more visible. One would think that since these colors penetrate the deepest, that fly patterns should be tied with these colors; but if the fly color and the background are the same, they will blend together and be difficult for the trout to see.

Color Penetration

If the angler wants to develop fly patterns with contrasting colors, he must first determine how each color will look under varying water conditions. Table 2-2 shows how trout see colors under lighted conditions in three types of water conditions: crystal clear (blue) water, turbid (green) water, and murky (brown) water.[11]

Table 2-2: Subsurface Penetration of Colors Under Clear Sky Daylight Conditions

Color	Crystal Clear (Blue) Water		Turbid (Green) Water		Murky (Brown) Water	
	Max. Depth Color Penetrates Before Shift	Color Shift	Max. Depth Color Penetrates Before Shift	Color Shift	Max. Depth Color Penetrates Before Shift	Color Shift
Green	50'+	None	<30'	Dull Green	<10'	Gray/Brown
Red	20'+	Black	20'+	Black	<8'	Red/Brown
Yellow	40'+	White	<20'	Pale Green	<8'	Light Brown
Blue	75'+	None	<20'	Blue-Green	<10'	Black/Gray
Purple	35'+	Black	<15'	Black	<10'	Black
Orange	25'+	Black	<10'	Black	<8'	Dark Brown
White	80'+	None	<20'	Pale Green	<6'	Light Brown
Black	100'+	Black	<20'	Black	8'+	Black
Olive	30'+	Brown	<15'	Brown	<8'	Brown
Gray	80'+	Light Gray	<20'	Pale Gray	<8'	Dark Gray
Fluorescent Chartreuse	150'+	Highly Visible Chartreuse	15'+	Highly Visible Chartreuse	<10'	Highly Visible Chartreuse
Fluorescent Orange	150'+	Highly Visible Orange	15'+	Highly Visible Orange	<10'	Highly Visible Orange
Fluorescent Red	150'+	Highly Visible Red	15'+	Highly Visible Red	<10'	Highly Visible Red
Fluorescent Green	150'+	Highly Visible Green	15'+	Highly Visible Green	<10'	Highly Visible Green

(Estimates provided by Paul Johnson.)

There is a theory of offset colors that suggests certain pairs of colors, whether they are next to each other or against contrasting backgrounds, will be more or less conspicuous. A white fly against a bright sky may not be as conspicuous as a black one. This is why the bellies of surface feeding fish are usually white. This color, or lack of it, serves to camouflage them in their environment. Inversely, a black fly seen against a dark bottom would also not be as conspicuous as a white one. This is why most insects are combinations of brown and black. A fly that looks black against a bluish-water background will be visible, and a white one will stand out when there is a green background.

Sometimes prey fish change colors to be more or less conspicuous, such as when breeding males want to attract females or when they camouflage themselves to avoid predators. To better understand how contrasting colors relate to fish, let's take a look at how trout prey on three-spined sticklebacks. One study with rainbow trout found that they were more likely to attack male sticklebacks with red throats than those without this feature, even though there were an equal number of males and females and only 14 percent of the population of male sticklebacks had red throats. When the researchers painted red onto the sticklebacks that did not have a natural red throat, attacks increased (Semler). The breeding female may also be more nutritious, further suggesting that the color pattern is eliciting the strike from the trout.

To understand the trout's behavior, one has to see what three-spined sticklebacks look like. Out of the water, the females and non-breeding male sticklebacks are black on top with silvery sides. The breeding male stickleback has three colors on its body—black (back), blue (flanks), and red (throat)—with a green eye. This breeding pattern is characteristic of the male for about four months or so, starting in the spring, and will show well under brightly lit and cloudy days as discussed under the theory of contrasting colors. The breeding stickleback has this red throat to attract females (McLennan and McPhail), and one of the reasons why the rainbows prefer to feed on the breeding male stickleback is that the trout sees the contrasting color.

Red is a highly conspicuous color against a green background, as evidenced in our own use of red in stop signs. One study with cutthroat and Dolly Varden found that the reaction distance to prey in both species was greatest for red, followed in descending order by green, yellow, and blue (Henderson and Northcote). Another interesting observation made by the Nobel Prize-winning behaviorist Niko Tinbergen was that sticklebacks in his fish tank went into a defensive posture whenever a red truck drove by the window of his lab. Frightened minnows similarly flare their gills when confronted by a predator. Thus, the color red can spark the interest of fish. This color can also make the difference between a trout that casually observes your fly and one that decides to strike.

While monitoring the reaction of rainbow trout to color while ice fishing, Charlie White made similar observations. When he introduced a red lure with bait on the hooks he found that the trout would repeatedly strike at the red lure and not the dangling bait. In my own experiments I have trolled flies with and without red in them, and at equal lengths behind my craft, and observed that the ones with red were almost always the first taken by trout.

When you go into a fishing camp that is stocked only with a dozen or more flies, take a look at the common color combinations. You will often find that each fly has some red or orange. Guides will probably tell you that these colors emulate the colors of salmon, trout, or other fish eggs, the flanks of a male brook trout (orange), or rainbows (red). My suggestion is that the trout's attraction to the flies is instinctive and not a function of their food.

How we, and other animals, see color changes throughout the day in response to shifts in light over the photoperiod. Consider when you are on the river during a bright afternoon and see a lot of greens along the shoreline, while at dusk on the same day they would have more amber tones. At dusk in the natural world, red and orange are the first colors to go, followed by yellow, green, and blue. At dawn, the colors blue and green are the first to appear, then yellow, orange, and red. Red and orange flies fished at dusk are likely to look black to

The trout tries to separate a prey fish from the school. He will target the one that stands out from the group. The triggering factor may be color, movement, size, or shape.

the trout, while green and blue ones will be more visible, although they are likely to blend into the blue/green water background. The same is true at dawn.[12]

Certain contrasting colors can also serve to protect the prey fish while they are in schools. The effect is much like a zebra herd in the wild. When they are together, there is almost a dizzying effect, and a lion has to sort one out of the group to actually catch it. The zebra that he chooses will be the one that doesn't follow the rhythm of the herd—the one that acts or looks different. Once the individual zebra is separated from the group, it will be more visible. A group or school of prey fish can be viewed in much the same way. When one is singled out of the group, the prey becomes much more visible to the big trout. When these prey fish have a color change that creates contrast, they will also be more conspicuous and susceptible to visual predators such as trout.

A common attribute of the old, colored wet flies and streamers is that they had flossed or dubbed bodies that were ribbed with silver or gold, creating contrast when viewed from the side and the bottom. Streamers often included a feather, called a hair wing, that traversed the length of the fly (tied from under the head) and created additional contrast from the side and bottom when the fly was rocking in the ripples. I am not necessarily suggesting that the angler use these patterns, but they demonstrate that the use of contrasting colors has worked for generations of anglers. Black flies are extremely popular these days because when trout look up they are seeing a silhouette against the lit surface. To create contrast for the trout's view from the bottom of prey fish, tie a thin white base with darker layers going up. Traditional flies such as the Muddler Minnow created this effect with the dubbing and tinsel tied tightly around the shank of the hook and a black deer hair or bucktail wing extending back. The modern angler can take advantage of contrasting colors at the vise by integrating this concept with newer materials.

The fish's brain interprets white when all of the colors in the spectrum are reflected and none are absorbed. The concept of white is extremely important in fly design. White contrasts against black in blue and green environments and penetrates fairly deep in these waters. In a blue environment, it will look white, in a green environment pale green, and in brown environments it will look light brown. So why don't we tie all of our flies in black and white? One answer is that most flies are designed for the fisherman and not the fish. Shades of these two with a few colors mixed in would sell more flies to fishermen and possibly attract more trout, as well.

The shift in fly fishing from traditional multicolored wet flies to more natural tones has not always replicated the prey items or made them visible to the trout. Match-the-hatch concepts

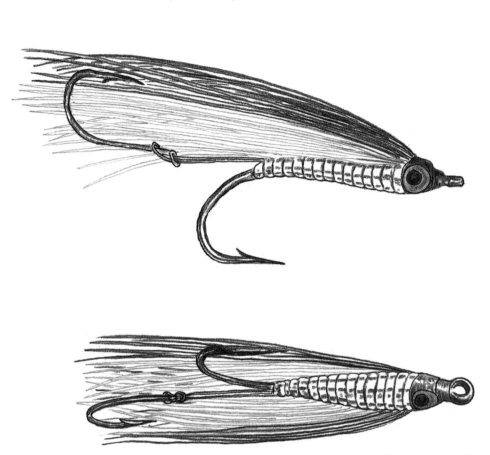

Creating contrast, from both vertical and horizontal angles, is crucial to creating effective big trout flies.

are often reasonable for slow-moving, clear waters where the food drifts to the trout. I also subscribe to this approach for tailwaters where large amounts of one food item drift to the fish. On migratory trout rivers, when the fish are gorging on salmon eggs and flesh, it also makes sense to match the color of their food item, especially since the eggs are red or orange. However, on migratory trout rivers where the fish are moving up to spawn, the trout are not always feeding actively, so matching a natural isn't an issue. In stillwaters, the food items, especially forage fish, do not swim into the waiting mouth of a trout. The trout must be able to find and catch them. Trout are primarily visual predators so they must be able to see their prey to catch it. This can be particularly difficult in murky waters or under complete darkness.

Applying Colors to the Trout's Environment

This leads us to consider colors, contrasting combinations, and the environment in the design of our trout flies. Fly design and color selection must be analyzed differently for waters where the trout move to find their prey (stillwaters), and where the trout's food drifts to them or they chase it at close distances (tailwaters and migratory trout rivers). For stillwaters, the design and color selection should also be analyzed differently for flies that trout view above them, those to the side, and under varying degrees of illumination. The primary consideration is that the trout must be able to see the fly. The best approach is to tie flies for the different water and light conditions. I call my oligotrophic lake and river flies blue water patterns, my shallow eutrophic stillwater and river casting and trolling flies green water patterns, and my murky water river flies brown water patterns. As a side note, feathers and fur do not dye well, and there is a great deal of inconsistency among different manufacturers, even within the same dyeing operation. Colors that appear bright to us at the bench may not have any color under water and will look either white or be a pale tone of the intended color. You will have your best success at holding colors by using synthetics.

I have variations of each type that are designed for low light levels. During daylight conditions and the first part of the evening and end of the morning transitional period, in clear (blue) oligotrophic waters, as was shown in Table 2-2, the trout will see any color that you present to them. Thus, brightly colored flies are not necessary and may only frighten the trout. When targeting open water feeding trout on these large oligotrophic lakes during the daytime, start with a light belly and end with a dark top. Between these two, use combinations of blue, silver, and gray. Consider darker patterns that run shallow and provide a strong silhouette deep into dusk and at night. In eutrophic lakes and rivers (green water), all of the colors will be visible during the daytime at the distance that the trout can see them. Eutrophic waters are generally shallow, and it is rare to present a fly deeper than 15 feet. Again, start with natural tones such as brown/green and brown/amber, but add metallic or iridescent materials such as Diamond Braid, Krystal Flash, and Zonker bodies to increase visibility. At dusk, go to brighter flies and at night go to darker ones. Incorporate some red into all of your patterns during all daylight conditions. I usually place this color at the throat. Under normal daylight illumination, when trout are keying in on prey fish feeding on bottom-feeding insects and crustaceans against a white bottom (such as marl or sand), present fly patterns that contrast with these. When approaching deep-feeding fish, consider flies with more white in them to contrast with the darker bottom. In the murky, brown waters typical of some migratory trout rivers and tailwaters, visibility is often low, and highly visible colors that contrast against each other or their environment are critical. Consider chartreuse and other fluorescent colors—especially in orange and red.

Fly Movement

The last issue related to vision is how the trout detects, and is stimulated by, movement of the prey item. Once the big trout sees the prey item, the fish has to be enticed to take it. As stated earlier, in natural environments, big trout prey on small fish that are set apart from the others. Sometimes this difference is movement. The male breeding three-spined stickleback entices the female into the nest, carrying out his courtship dance in a series of zigzag motions. Perhaps this movement also attracts the trout.

While trolling, I have found that most takes occur when I change the craft's direction. Something in the movement tells the trout that this prey fish is a taker. Is this movement also how a prey fish escapes from the predator? Dr. Moodie describes the escape pattern of the stickleback as a jump (very fast swim) for about one meter after they see the predator is too close. As soon as they are about one meter away, they stop and freeze as long as the predator is not still chasing them. A start-stop-start or fast-slow-fast-slow movement is the best way to copy the movement of this prey fish, especially when trying to entice a predator that has spotted the fly.

While stripping in line on a stillwater, it is difficult to change the horizontal direction of the fly, but the angler can change the vertical direction and the speed of the retrieve. This may be one of the reasons why flies with lead heads such as the Clouser Minnow have been successful—they move up and down when stripped and paused. This fly also has a horizontal pattern that will be highly conspicuous to the trout when moving vertically. Trout and prey fish maintain neutral buoyancy by adjusting the amount of gas in the swim bladder, so most movement is horizontally planar. The injured or dying fish is the one that includes vertical movement when moving erratically. Some of the more popular retrieves are long pulls with a pause, slow hand twists, and short quick strips. Most retrieves with a pause will allow the fly to dip downward. Buoyant streamers with fast-sinking fly line will have the same effect.

Taste and Smell

After the trout has seen the prey item, the next step for the trout is to capture it. I say capture because this step may not be followed by ingestion. When trout come close to a food item, they can taste and smell their prey and have the choice of accepting or rejecting it without actually taking it into their mouths. The decision to ingest the prey depends on whether the food item tastes or smells good to the trout and, to some degree, on the size and texture of the food.[13]

The first time I fished (not fly fished) for steelhead, my guide set me up with a fly reel, running line, and a long noodle rod. My bait was a sack of blue-colored salmon eggs called "blue goo." The guide motioned to cast to a spot at the top of a run and remarked that the first cast usually gets a hook-up. He further said that the chances would diminish on each drift until another sack of eggs was tied on. I inquired, "Why not change egg sacks after a few casts?" To which he replied that I wasn't paying him enough. I didn't have the chance to fully test his hypothesis as a steelhead did take the blue goo on the first drift through the run. I did lose a few sacks that day on the first and second casts and the guide switched me to his hand-tied flies as a cost-saving measure. I haven't fished an egg sack since.

If scents can attract trout, as in the blue goo, then it would also seem logical that some scents could deter trout. If a salmon can smell his way to the waters where he was born hundreds of miles away, surely a trout can sense chemicals that are in the feathers and fur and those that we accidentally put on them. In a river situation, Pacific salmon have been seen to veer away from upstream bears and humans, presumably with the aid of their chemical receptors, as they could not see these animals from the perceived distance. A friend related a story to me about a fellow who spilled a bottle of suntan lotion into his fly box. He couldn't catch another fish on the flies and ended up throwing the box and all of its contents away. These observations and experiences raised questions that I followed up on with the researchers at Pure Fishing.[14]

John Prochnow, a chemist with Pure Fishing, graciously offered me some of his research findings on fish reactions to scents. To summarize his findings, there are four scents the common angler uses that will reduce his chance of catching fish. The first is sunscreen, a product that I have since handled with more care. According to Prochnow, there are chemicals in sunscreens that fish perceive as a real negative. No one is suggesting that anglers forgo sunscreens; however, we caution anglers to wash their hands well after they have applied the lotions.

Another detrimental product line is insect repellant. There is a chemical found in many insect repellants, known as DEET, that can really turn fish off in a big way. Prochnow jokes that if you want to catch more fish than your buddy, just spray his lures with insect repellants. Anglers should also take care how they pack and store insect repellants. An accidentally-jarred dispenser can make your clothing, gear, and flies smell like mothballs.

Fragrances can also be problematic. "Many of the various fragrances that are put into soaps, for instance, are synthetic. And most synthetic compounds are viewed negatively by fish," according to Prochnow, who worked in the fragrance industry before joining Pure Fishing in 1986. Nicotine, from cigarettes or chewing tobacco, also rated high on the list of fish-deterring scents. If you think that smoke doesn't stay with you for long, smell a late night bar hopper's jacket the next morning, or even a week later. Secondhand smoke may not only have serious consequences to you and your fishing buddy, but to your fishing success, as well.

A few other items can limit your fishing success, including many preservatives, alcohol towellettes, and waterless washes, as they have many surfactants that can turn fish off. "The bottom line is just to keep your hands clean and as odor-free as possible, and in tough fishing situations it will definitely increase your odds," the chemist says. He also notes that it is important for anglers to understand that people and fish live in two different worlds. So what may be positive for humans may well be a negative for fish. "For fish, things need to be water soluble in order for them to relate to it as food. For humans, things need to be air volatile. What we smell, and what fish smell, are totally different things," Prochnow said.

So how long will an odor stay on your fly? The answer is probably related to a combination of two factors: the velocity of your retrieve or troll, and how much odor is pulled off the porous nature of your fly. For example, a silicon-coated fly will probably not hold as much odor as an eggsack or a more porous one made from feathers and fur. Prochnow's tests were in a fish tank with calm water. A great deal of the odor probably stayed on or around test samples as they were dunked in the water.

Another salient question is how severe a deterrent these negatives are. If the trout is aggressive and on the bite, you are really dealing with how long they will hang onto it. (If you are fishing flies with more metal than fur, it will not be long.) But when fish are negatively inclined to bite (resting), as will be discussed further in the next two chapters, or when you are making short casts and the odor does not have the chance to dissolve into the surrounding water, you have to pay attention to details and make sure you are not presenting any negatives to the fish. Just keep this in mind when you travel a thousand miles, spend a month's wages, and miss a family reunion to have a shot at a trophy fish. You do everything else that can possibly be done to catch that trout, yet your fly is carrying a chemical with a big neon sign on it that says "Keep Away."

Prochnow also addressed the effect of spraying WD-40 and other oils on gear before going fishing. Prochnow believes that WD-40 is a masking agent, covering up both the negative and positive odors. His reasoning is that oils, or large molecules, cannot be detected by a fish's olfactory system (taste buds). The taste buds are the locks and the molecules are the keys.

Spraying your flies with WD-40 just before use can mask scents that may otherwise deter the fish from striking.

These types of chemicals do not allow the fish to send a message to the brain because the key doesn't fit into the lock. Some of the dyes that are used to color our feathers and fur have a strong odor. This may be affecting how long the trout holds the fly before rejection. Covering this smell with WD-40 may be effective. Dale Williams of Screaming Reel Fly and Tackle on Kootenay Lake rubs cod liver oil on his hands before setting out for the day. Dave Whitlock rubs his flies with the bottom of a rock or a piece of aquatic vegetation to help mask scents that may seem detrimental to the trout. Charlie White uses bilge water from his motor.

Summary

The trout's ability to feed is a physiological issue and the taking of one natural food item over another is a matter of instinct. Where to take this information will be discussed further, but close attention to the situation and giving some thought to what is going on in the mind of the trout will go a long way. I cannot definitively say, nor can anyone else, that any one stimulus is more important than another, as no significant research has been done on trout in this regard. There have been a number of studies that examined the basic instincts of other fish, which can help us to explain the instinctual reactions that we see in trout. One found that fish preferred red and pale colors over dark colors, fast over slow movement, straight and rectangular over globular shape, and larger over smaller size. When red was replaced with a pale color, the order of preference became movement, shape, and then size (Ibrahim and Huntingford). Since big trout usually need to see in order to hunt, it makes sense that colors will similarly be the main attractors during daytime illuminated conditions. When colors are not apparent, such as during the evenings when the trout primarily utilizes its rod vision, then movement can incite the trout. Perhaps a combination of both these triggers will yield the most success.

CHAPTER 3
DETERMINE THE TROUT'S RHYTHM

Trout feed because they are active, and are not active because they are feeding.
E.C. Black

There is a continuous cat and mouse game played every day in our stillwaters and rivers. The prey are sometimes caught, which sustains the predators and the higher forms that in turn feed on them. But the prey isn't captured at will, as this food source would become depleted and, in time, the food pyramid would collapse. Nature has created ecological balances that keep the predators fed and the prey plentiful. Some of these balances are physiological and others are environmental. We often join in this game as a predator of trout.

The major difference between wild predators of trout and most anglers is that we choose our hunting periods out of convenience and they hunt when they will have the best chance at success. Avian predators, such as osprey, hunt the same waters every day and need to catch fish in order to survive. Their stakes in the game are much higher, but the time they spend around their prey keeps them in tune with the activity cycles of the trout so that they can most efficiently catch them.

The advanced angler has a lifetime of angling experiences on which to draw. Most of us usually remember only the most fruitful days or a change we made that seemed to make the difference between a pleasant day on the water and a memorable one with a trophy trout. The root of these successful days may be based on many factors: water temperature, light intensity, feeding interest, availability of prey, biological urges of the trout, etc. It is difficult for us to observe these variables on a given day and, thus, the trout sometimes appear moody. You may be on your favorite river or lake when there is no apparent hatch, the fish are concentrated, and the bite on, and only minutes later all of the fish seem to vanish. Where did the trout go? What were they doing when they were there? We would know if we hunted trout every day like the osprey.

There are recurring environmental patterns, or rhythms, that can only be observed by analyzing data gained over a period of time. As my friend and former feather merchant Henry Hoffman related to me, when you take an extended fishing trip, over weeks, and watch the changes in the environment around you, patterns emerge. Some of these patterns occur on a daily basis. Most, if not all, of these daily rhythms are driven by an internal clock. The internal clock is entrained mainly by the day/night or light/dark cycles of the day.[15]

During my travels while researching this book, I met an angler who kept detailed records over a long period of time. Twenty-four years ago, Kamloops, British Columbia angler Ron Newman was coached to start keeping records about his fishing experiences. A registered professional forester with the province of British Columbia by profession and a statistician by nature, Newman obliged and took the advice one step further. He included other anglers' strikes and catches. He kept records on the weather, water clarity and temperature, wind, time of day, retrieve, location of fish in relation to the depth of the lake, fly pattern, size of fish, moon phase, stomach samples, water surface temperatures, and so forth. During these years, 755 days of fishing experiences were logged (approximately 33 days per year) that covered many samples of fishing and daily variables.[16] There have been many scientific studies of trout behavior and an angler's success with fishing for trout, usually lasting for only a few months or years. Newman's tabulated results are extraordinary because they cover such a long period of time and allow us to look at trout feeding and other behavioral patterns from a statistical perspective. These trends help us to separate factors that have a strong influence from those that only have a minor effect.

The Photoperiod

For many years, fishermen have attempted to predict where and when they would have their best chance at success. This quest is the angler's Holy Grail. Instead of eternal life, this chal-

Ron Newman of Kamloops, British Columbia, has been keeping detailed records on his trout catches for over 24 years. His findings are priceless.

ice offers the ability to time your fishing efforts to when the big ones are on the bite. For the professional bass fisherman, there are significant dollars riding on the guess, but for most of us it is a measure of time spent trying to catch big fish. The most common approaches to predicting fishing success are based on solunar tables, "Sol" for the sun and "Lunar" for the moon, as originated by John Alden Knight and described in his book *Moon Up, Moon Down*, first published in 1942. These tables are available through bait and tackle shops, newspapers, and magazines. Knight's hypothesis was based on the gravitational pull of the earth and moon or lunar tides. The major times of the day, or when the fish are most active, are when the gravitational pull is directly overhead (high tide) while the minor periods are when the moon is directly to the side of the earth (low tide). Knight's hypothesis was that the best periods of the moon to fish were during the new moon and worst during the full moon. He reasoned that since the earth, moon, and sun are practically in line during the full and the dark of the moon, they will have the greatest effect. Knight also suggested that "solunar pull" is at its maximum when the sun and moon pull together—during the dark of the moon; and at its minimum when they pull against each other during the full of the moon.

Freshwater fish behavior can be predicted, to some degree, although not for the reasons that Knight proposed. Gravity is a static force that the trout uses to maintain equilibrium, but there is no evidence that tidal pulls have a significant effect on freshwater systems, and even in the largest lakes the effect is small, perhaps just a few millimeters (Wetzel). As suggested earlier, daily rhythms are cyclical. This behavior is based on gene expression in the brain and the light/dark cycle that synchronizes them. Knight gave no indication that he was aware of daily rhythms when he wrote his book, and his tables do not accurately reflect them. The daily rhythms of trout are conditioned to the photoperiod, or the daily cycle of light and darkness. The photoperiod entrains the trout's internal clock, thus maintaining its temporal relationship to the illumination in its environment. In this way the trout knows where it should be and what physiological state is required. There is extensive evidence that the trout's pineal gland (a part of the brain) is responsible for the production of a chemical called melatonin. Melatonin production in trout is rhythmic, with high activity at night and low activity during the day, in tune with the photoperiod. The melatonin release factor has been demonstrated for brook, rainbow, brown, and cutthroat trout (Ali). This rhythmic activity affords the trout the ability to predict the time of day and alter its physiology to anticipate a food source in advance so that it can be prepared and in the right location to deal with it most efficiently. Locating, chasing, catching, and digesting food is metabolically demanding. If the trout was always prepared, or constantly fed opportunistically, then its daily energy would be utilized inefficiently, and the fish would not be able to work at its full operating capacity. The fish would not be able to feed successfully and big trout would not be produced.

Humans also have an internal clock. Scientists have shown that certain proteins occur in the brain that enable animals, including humans, to synchronize their internal clock by responding to light signals conveyed through the optic nerve to a different part of the brain from the center for vision (University of North Carolina at Chapel Hill). Every day we experience profound changes in our mental and physical condition as body and brain alternate between states of high activity during waking day and recuperation, rest, and repair during nighttime sleep. These cycles are not a passive response to the world around us; they are pre-adapted, driven by an internal clock. They are not only tied to our visual systems but are also entrenched at the cellular level. Animals have different chemical processes during active and resting periods of the day (Young).

Consider the timing of your daily activities: You eat, rest, and digest during the same periods of the day. The light doesn't force you to make these decisions; it reminds you what time of day it is so that your activities can be tied to when you can accomplish them most efficiently. The hours that restaurants are open are tied into our internal rhythms. The steak house that opens at 2:00 P.M. and closes at 5:00 P.M. will not be in business for long as the availability of food does not coincide with our physiological requirements for food, as timed by our internal clock. The same is true with trout, and if you can time your presentation to when they will most likely be feeding, you will have a better chance of catching a big one.

We can relate the trout's daily rhythm to our hunting efficiencies, as well. Imagine an elk-hunting trip in the mountains that requires you to stay awake and active for two to three days, twenty-four hours a day. It would be fair to say that your chances of taking one would be slim as compared to a hunt when you were only awake and active when you had your best chances of seeing an elk up close. For humans, this would be during the hours of the day that are illuminated by the sun. Problems occur when we work outside of our natural boundaries, or when our internal clock tells us to slow down. If we present a fly to trout when these fish are not at their peak of efficiency, they may be less likely to take it.

Seasonal changes and behavior are also tied to the internal clock. As the seasons progress, changes in the photoperiod (day length/night length) are detected by the internal clock, which in turn drives a variety of changes in the fish, reproductive status being a major effect. The prey species will also undergo seasonal changes along with environmental factors such as day length, light intensity, light quality, temperature, and so on, many of which will be driven by the photoperiod via the internal clock. These seasonal changes may affect factors such as diet and location of the trout and their prey. Environmental factors, such as water temperatures and oxygen levels, also affect where trout position themselves (King).

Light is a foundation for life, both on land and in water, and strongly influences the daily rhythms of many fish and aquatic invertebrates. My own research also shows that the most important factor influencing trout behavior is light, which can be predicted, to a large degree, and tied to the three types of natural illumination: direct sunlight, sunlight reflected off of the moon (called moonlight), and starlight (light from other suns). Changes in illumination from these sources can be timed to the rising and setting of the sun and moon and the phases of the moon, called the Synodic period. The Synodic period has 29.5 days starting with the new moon on day one. (In scientific circles, counting the days of the moon's position starts with the new moon on day zero.) The first quarter will occur on days 6, 7, or 8, depending on cycle. The full moon occurs on days 14 to 16 and the third quarter on days 21 to 23, depending on cycle. When checking the time between similar moon phases, calendars and almanacs will sometimes give 29 days and other times 30 days because of the half-day in the cycle. Clouds can also affect the degree of illumination that penetrates below the water's surface, as can the turbidity of the water and depth.

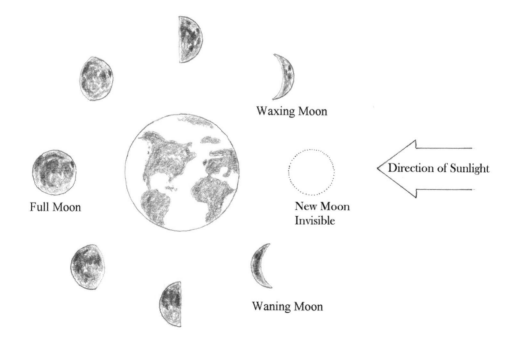

Waxing Moon

Direction of Sunlight

Full Moon

New Moon
Invisible

Waning Moon

Daily Migrations

Phytoplankton (microscopic algae), one of the bases of aquatic life, grows via photosynthesis. The more direct sunlight, warmth, and nutrients, the greater the growth. During late spring and into the summer, the days are longer and more photosynthesis occurs than over darker seasons. Other factors can also affect phytoplankton, such as seasonal turnover in lakes, which is discussed in the next chapter. Regardless of the season, phytoplankton grows and reproduces in a daily rhythm, related to direct sunlight. Various forms of zooplankton (microscopic aquatic crustaceans) feed on phytoplankton. In many environments, zooplankton spend their daytime hours in the cool, dark depths of lakes or, in the case of shallow waters, on the sediment where they maintain a low metabolic rate and expend little energy. At dusk, or when the illumination diminishes, they migrate up to the surface to feed (Hutchinson). Limnologists refer to this activity as a diel vertical migration.

Many prey fish (small fish that trout feed on), such as kokanee, cisco, smelt, shiners, chubs, shad, minnows, sticklebacks, and alewife are primarily zooplankton feeders. These small fish are also sight feeders and can most efficiently feed on this food source when there is some degree of illumination.

There is a wealth of research to support a similar and concurring hypothesis that fish secrete chemical cues, commonly called kairomones, that trigger a response from their prey (Lambert and Sommer). In the news we often hear about another chemical cue,

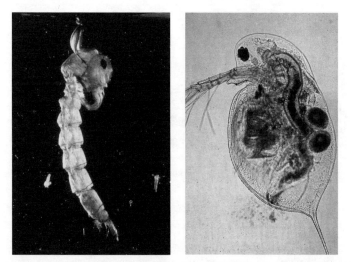

Chaoboridae larvae (left) and zooplankton are photosensitive and avoid illuminated zones when fish are present. (Photos courtesy of Dr. Norman Anderson and Dr. Winfried Lambert.)

pheromones, which are chemical signals that animals within the same species send to one another. In trout, pheromones are utilized to communicate alarm or danger, crowding, pair formation, and spawning.

With respect to the interactions between zooplankton and prey fish, the zooplankton migrates away from areas where the prey fish's kairomones are present. Aquatic invertebrates can learn to associate illumination with the kairomones from fish predators and then adjust their activities to the photoperiod. Zooplankton and *Chaoboridae* will hold in the water column just below where the light penetrates and the prey fish cannot see them. The *Chaoboridae* larvae rest on the bottom during the day and then rise up in the water column at night (by adjusting their buoyancy) where they feed on zooplankton. *Chaoboridae*, insects that feed on zooplankton, are often called phantom midges because their body is almost transparent, except for two crescent-shaped hydrostatic organs that regulate their buoyancy. As is characteristic of zooplankton, the *Chaoboridae* and opossum shrimp control their vertical movement by swimming up and down, but are at the mercy of water currents for movement in a horizontal direction.

One study that examined *Chaoboridae* found that individuals exposed to fish were considerably more sensitive to light than those that were not and showed a panic response when their environment was suddenly illuminated (Dawidowicz et al.). Another study of *Chao-*

Response of Pelagic Prey Fish to Light in Bear Lake, Utah

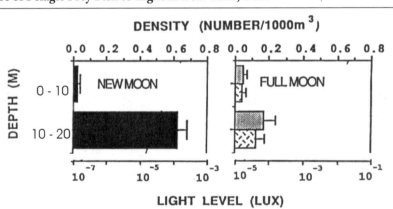

Bonneville ciscoes in Bear Lake migrate vertically to reach their prey (zooplankton) and avoid the big Bonneville cutthroat trout (Bear Lake stock). This chart shows that the Bonneville ciscoes shy away from the illuminated areas during the evenings, where the trout can more easily capture them. (Chart courtesy of Dr. Chris Luecke and Dr. Wayne A. Wurtsbaugh from the Department of Fisheries and Wildlife, Ecology Center, Utah State University.)

boridae, in Lenore Lake in Washington, reported that the appearance of migration in larvae, where previously only non-migratory larvae had been found, coincided with the introduction of cutthroat trout into this stillwater (Luecke). Note that few insects, other than the *Chaoboridae,* occur in the water column away from shallow areas. They do not have neutral buoyancy like zooplankton and need a place to sit. When farther up in the water column, these other insects are only passing through to emerge.

When the zooplankton and *Chaoboridae* migrate up towards the surface, the prey fish will move up to feed on these small animals when they can also take advantage of the protection low illumination provides. The effect of the different degrees of illumination can be observed in the following chart, which shows the feeding depths of Bonneville ciscoes relative to light intensity. Bonneville ciscoes are a food source for the big cutthroat trout in Bear Lake in Utah. Note that during the new moon phase (lower light) the fish were found to be holding higher in the water column than the (more illuminated) full moon evening (Luecke and Wurtsbaugh). The data suggests that the Bonneville ciscoes migrate vertically under different light intensities to avoid the trout; the food (zooplankton) for these prey fish also migrates under different light intensities. As this hydro acoustic survey was taken on a boat, one could assume that the lower numbers of fish holding in 0 to 10 feet is a result of the presence of the watercraft above them. They would otherwise be on top.

Studies of the movements of other prey fish such as smelt, perch, and shiners have found that, in both shallow, nutrient-rich (eutrophic) lakes and medium, productive (mesotrophic) ones, these fish migrated from their refuges at dusk (smelt from the hypolimnion and perch and shiners from inshore) to offshore areas where they fed on zooplankton in depths that ranged from the surface to about thirty feet. These prey fish migrated back to their refuges at dawn when they could find their way with the morning light (Gliwicz and Jachner). During the daytime, open water (pelagic) fish form tighter schools and drop down to dark depths, while near bottom feeding (benthic) ones immerse themselves in the shoreline weedbeds where they have protection from predators.

Schooling is an anti-predator behavior and few prey fish school at night. Fish need to see each other in order to school, and when the degree of illumination goes below their visual threshold, the schools break up (Radakov). Clear, full-moon evenings can also introduce a great deal of light and make feeding less efficient for the prey fish because the illumination can suppress the normal feeding rhythms of many aquatic invertebrates and push these fish farther down in the water column or into heavy shoreline vegetation. During brightly lit nights, the trout may not be able to feed efficiently on the prey fish because these smaller fish will not be accessible in deeper sections of the water column or in dense shoreline cover. This

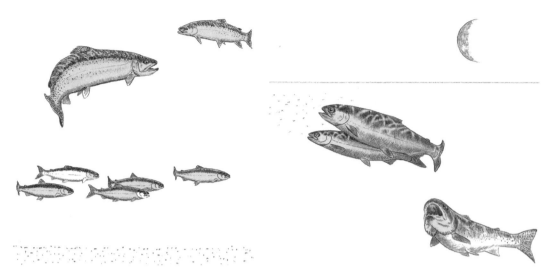

In nutrient-poor oligotrophic lakes, the trout and their prey will rest in the deeper sections of the water column where the water temperatures are low and where there is enough oxygen. In lakes with a thermostratification during the warmer months, their resting position will often be around the thermocline. During periods with lower illumination the food chain will rise up to the surface, and when there is transitional illumination, the trout will go on the hunt.

In shallow, nutrient-rich, eutrophic lakes, the trout and their prey will rest close to the bottom or over springs during the illuminated periods of the day. The trout will have the advantage over the prey fish under transitional illumination conditions, such as during dusk and dawn, and go on the feed.

daily migration allows these prey fish to feed during the low light period to avoid piscivorous birds and larger predatory fish, such as the trout, while still being able to feed on the zooplankton. The big trout's internal clock helps them to tune into this behavior and, at dusk and dawn, they will migrate towards the surface so that they can efficiently hunt the prey fish. The conditions for a trout to grow big require that the fish feed in rhythms when all of its ducks are in a row: optimal degrees of light, water temperatures and oxygen levels, and prey available and easily captured. Full-moon evenings can reduce their chances for success, something anglers should keep in mind.

Aquatic insects like caddis and mayflies, and Crustacea such as scuds and cressbugs have behavioral patterns similar to zooplankton. Under strongly illuminated conditions, these animals will often hide under rocks or in dense vegetation. During periods of low illumination, the insects will move from one plant or rock to another to scrape (feed on) periphyton (algae on the surfaces of plants and rocks). Most anglers have picked up a rock or two and seen a *Baetis* nymph clinging to the bottom. If you picked up the same rock at night and quickly flashed a light on it, you would see them scurrying on top. An important point to understand is that these low light periods are when the invertebrates are drifting to other places to feed or are dislodged by the current while feeding. This is not a transformation/reproductive function. Scientists call this activity behavioral drift. Similar behavior takes place in stillwater environments. Instead of drifting from one food source to another, these invertebrates crawl or swim. There are many other types of drift. Those of importance to the angler are continuous drift—where constant low densities of drift occur by accidental displacement—and catastrophic drift, which can result in high-density drift movements as a result of major physical disturbances such as heavy releases of water from a dam.

While anglers have generally been focused on when insects experience metamorphism, more commonly called hatching, or the emergence, as this is what we can see, the more significant activity for trout is when the insects feed. The reproductive terrestrial phase is short in comparison to the growth and feeding aquatic part of the life cycle. Most species of caddis have a one-year cycle, with the larval stage being nine to ten months, the egg and pupal stages requiring two to three weeks each, and the adult from a few days to three to four weeks. There are wide variations among species of caddis with some having a two-year life cycle (that means the larvae will live for more than a year) and others have two to three generations per year (Wallace and Anderson). Most studies of trout stomach contents reflect these short terrestrial stages. They show that where insects are the most available food source, the nymph and larval stages of the insects, and not the adults, are the most common.

Depressant Effect of Moonlight on the Activity of Aquatic Insects

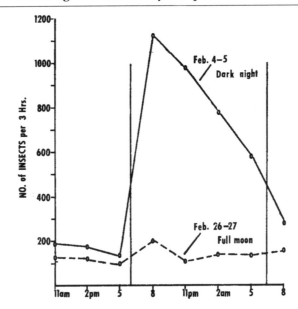

Aquatic insects have greater drift during dark evenings than illuminated ones, such as during the full moon period. Scientists believe that these insects are more active during darker periods to avoid predation by fish. (Graph courtesy of Dr. Norman Anderson, Entomology Department, Oregon State University.)

One hypothesis why the insects maintain a behavioral drift during the low light periods is because they will have the least chance of discovery by predators such as trout. The reasoning is similar to the one proposed for zooplankton and *Chaoboridae*. An interesting study demonstrated the validity of this hypothesis by transplanting insects from a trout-less stream, where they did not have a strong nocturnal rhythm, to one where trout were present. The insects were observed to have changed their periods of activity to take advantage of the lower light levels (Cowan and Peckarsky). They became strongly nocturnal in response to the trout's kairomones.

Drift is not constant each evening and is affected by the natural illumination. A study by Dr. Norman Anderson, an aquatic entomologist with Oregon State University, found that there was a distinct difference between the drift during a new moon (when the insect's predators could not see them) and during a full moon (when they could). The former, more heavily illuminated evening, had a continuous drift while the alternative dark moon had a strong behavioral drift. Insects do not always hide during illuminated evenings. Researchers have found that the emergence of the mayfly *Povilla adusta* only occurred within five days of the full moon, with the greatest number of swarms on the second night (Hartland-Rowe). It was hypothesized that the nighttime illumination synchronizes the emergences of some swarming insects and helps them to find mates. Although small aquatic invertebrates may time their feeding activities to the photoperiod and presence of the prey fish, these smaller animals do not all hatch from the egg on the same day, so the behavior of individuals in the groups is learned by experience and is not consistent. Those that did not learn as fast and ventured outside of the safe limits can become food for the fish.

Behavioral drift is closely tied to the activity of trout, as shown in the following chart describing the hourly movements of brown trout in streams in Wyoming. This data was obtained from radiotelemetry studies. The closed and open circles represent "average" times of sunset and sunrise. Note that the movements of the brown trout increase sharply as the sun rises and sets. Underwater observations on eutrophic rivers such as the Henry's Fork of the

Hourly Movements of Adult Brown Trout in a Mountain Stream

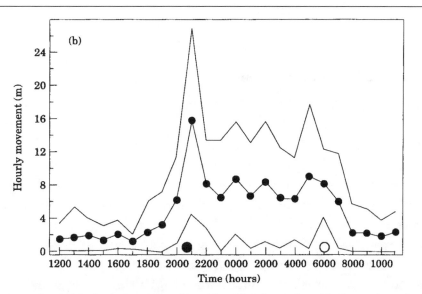

Trout are most active during the dusk and dawn (transitional light) periods and in the evenings when their prey is present and they can catch it. Trout can still be caught throughout the day by focusing on where they rest during inactive periods. Drifting nymph and larval imitations through resting zones on a river is a common technique to catch them. Hanging a *Chironomidae* pattern in a deep and cool section of a shallow lake is another. *Source:* Young, M.K. 1999. Summer diel-activity and movement of adult brown trout in high-elevation streams in Wyoming, U.S.A. *Journal of Fish Biology.* 54: 181–189.

Snake (Riehle and Griffith) and Silver Creek in Idaho (Contor and Griffith) have similarly found that the rainbow trout were closely synchronized with when they could visually see their prey and the behavioral drift of the invertebrates. Where trout feed on invertebrates or the prey fish that feed on this food item, I suggest that the angler focus his or her efforts on the behavioral drift (and similar movements in stillwaters), especially the fringes of the behavioral drift when the invertebrates are most abundant, and not during what the angler calls the insect hatch.

Low illumination feeding is not strictly tied to aquatic insects and small crustaceans. Larger crustaceans, such as crayfish, have also been shown to feed during periods of transitional or lower illumination to avoid visual predators, and small crayfish that are more vulnerable to predators react more dramatically to sudden illumination than larger ones. The larger crayfish tend to hold in the deeper pools during the daytime where and when the predator fish are present while the smaller ones feed and rest in the riffles and runs (Englund and Krupa). The different foraging cycles among these life stages and position in the water column could be interpreted as a size-mediated response directly related to predatory vulnerability. A good portion of the food (cressbugs and scuds) of bottom-feeding sculpins also have strong low illumination rhythms. This situation stimulates other predators to these crustaceans, and prey to the trout, to feed during this condition.

Role of the Pineal Gland in Predation

Earlier I suggested that the pineal gland secretes melatonin to help the trout keep its physiology in sync with the photoperiod. One effect of the melatonin release is to shift the eyes of the trout from cone vision (day) to rod vision (evening) and vice versa. Unlike humans, trout can't quickly adjust the amount of light entering the eye by changing the diameters of their rather large pupils. As a result, trout can't quickly accommodate to extreme changes in light levels. You can relate to this light change to some degree by walking from the outside during a dark evening into a house and then switching the lights on. For a moment you will be blinded. Trout experience the same blindness, just over a longer period of time.

One study conducted by Dr. Griffith and his associates from Idaho State University at Pocatello demonstrated that rainbow trout in the Henry's Fork of the Snake, a eutrophic water, actively feeding at starlight would cease this activity when illumination equal to a full moon was presented. Similarly, I have noticed daytime fishing activity suddenly stop when a series of clouds passed overhead. Full adjustment for rainbow trout from bright light to dark takes about 30 minutes to an hour. With dim to less dim transitions, it may only take a few minutes (Douglas).

In a laboratory environment, the retinomotor activity of brown and rainbow trout is two peaked with transient migrations toward light adaptation restricted to dawn and dusk (Douglas and Djamgoz). In trout, the melatonin-induced conversion to the evening light levels (cone to rod vision) begins before it gets dark. For the brook trout, this shift takes place at 20 lux (Zachmann et al.). On most days, 20 lux occurs about the same time as dusk.

The inverse shift from rod to cone vision takes place at dawn. The internal clock drives this activity and predators such as trout that make this adjustment faster, via more intense melatonin activity, can have the jump on their prey. The trout is not a particularly swift ambush feeder and needs some advantage to catch prey fish. During these transitional hours, the predators can see their prey before they can be seen. During more illuminated hours of the day, the trend is reversed (Howick and O'Brien). Where the big trout primarily prey on other fish under generally low light conditions, visual acuity (needed for feeding on small food items such as zooplankton) is less important than detecting the contrast between prey and its background. The opposite is true for small prey fish that feed on tiny organisms. Contrast will be affected by available light, turbidity, and the backscattering of light between the predator and prey (Vogel).

Numerous studies have found that when rainbow trout were in an environment with a degree of illumination below where they needed to see the prey fish they didn't exhibit any foraging behavior even in the presence of food. Other studies have found that trout can feed on small insects and crustaceans even under starlight (Riehle and Griffith). The type of food present is the key to when trout can hunt, and we have to consider these food items when choosing our hunting periods, as well.

This melatonin release is a major reason why fishing for big trout at daybreak and dusk is prime, and even better when there is a long transitional light period (as will be discussed later in this chapter). During low light conditions, zooplankton move up to the surface to feed on phytoplankton and hold fairly close to the surface, sometimes in the top few inches. Scuds and cressbugs that feed on decayed matter on the bottom and in weedbeds become more active, as well. In this narrow window, the smaller prey fish will key in on zooplankton.

When small schooling prey fish, such as alewives and cisco, feed on zooplankton, they disperse or have looser schools and grab individual zooplankton breaking from the swarm. Looser swarms will be more advantageous to the feeding prey fish, as the higher densities have a "confusion effect" on the fish (Milinski). Similarly, when visual feeding predators such as trout prey on schooled fish, they normally try to weed a few fish out of the bunch. They choose those fish that move or look differently. In many cases these may be ones that are injured and more easily captured. At other times, the trigger can be color (Ohguchi).

The low illumination feeding of zooplankton, *Chaoboridae,* and the opossum shrimp that feed prey fish mimics the big trout's strategy of loosening up the schools and makes this an opportune condition for them to feed efficiently. Moreover, in the case of zooplankton and *Chaoboridae,* all of the food items will be concentrated in a narrow window while at the same time the trout can utilize their transitional light feeding advantage. The zooplankton is especially enticing to prey fish, as they can gain all the nourishment they need for a day or more while feeding in a brief period of time and without expending much energy. One study of sticklebacks found that this fish could receive its maximum daily intake in only two hours of feeding on zooplankton at 59 degrees Fahrenheit while it would take over ten hours to achieve the same from insects consumed near the bottom (Ibrahim and Huntington). There is an increased risk of predation on the prey fish during their feed because they more often fail to detect predators when they are feeding on high-density food sources than low ones (Milinski). I believe that this is also the case for big trout, making this a great opportunity for anglers.

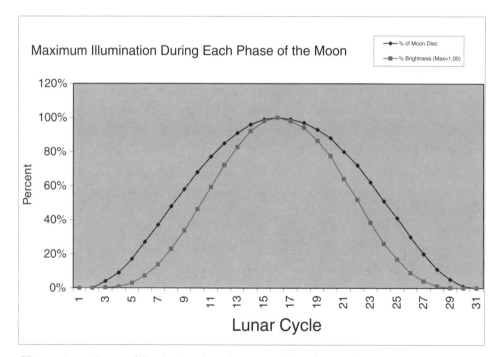

The maximum degree of illumination from the moon is dependent on the percentage of the disk illuminated and its angle to the earth, and changes over each day of the lunar cycle. The top line shows the amount of light reflected from the moon's disk and the bottom adjusts it for the angle to the earth's surface.

Changes in Light Over the Lunar Cycle

Nighttime illumination does not have the same intensity in every place, on each day, and varies based on the phase of the moon, cloud cover, and terrain. The chart below shows the maximum intensity of illumination on the water's surface for each day over the lunar cycle. It assumes a clear day and level terrain. The degree of illumination from the moon on the surface is based both on the percentage of the disk illuminated and the angle of the moon to the earth. When the moon is low on the horizon, such as in the early and final days of the lunar cycle, very little light penetrates below the surface of the water. These figures are calculated with the full moon being at 100 percent. The full moon provides a luminance of about .267 lux. Starlight during the new moon provides about .0002 lux. Although the quarter moons appear to have half the illumination of the full moon, these phases are at 90-degree angles to the earth and only provide us 8 percent of the illumination of the full moon.

I suggest that the activity level of the trout and their prey is not only a function of the maximum degree of light but also the length of time that the illumination occurs. One reason is that longer transitional light, or an extended dusk or dawn, provides the trout with a longer period to hunt efficiently. Another is that the relocations of the prey fish and zooplankton are not instantaneous. They sometimes move long distances, both vertically and horizontally (for prey fish), and the longer periods of reduced illumination can facilitate this.

The chart below relates to July and August in southern Canada and the northern regions of the lower 48 states. Note that during the first few days of the lunar cycle there are few "night hours illuminated" and many "night dark hours." This would be an optimal period for the zooplankton to migrate up and feed on the phytoplankton on or near the surface and for insects to feed on periphyton in and around the surfaces of plants and rocks. The opposite extreme is between the 14th to 16th day of the lunar cycle during the full moon period. Note that during the new moon in August, the "night hours dark" period is longer. This trend would continue until its peak at the end of December, at which time it would then work backwards in the opposite direction.

As a side note, just because a trout can't see well during a new moon (low illumination) doesn't mean that fish will not take your fly or lure. All trout may take a streamer if the fly is big enough and close enough for the trout to sense and moving slow enough for them to catch it even under challenging illumination. Ron Newman and I have found that during evenings with reduced illumination, we have had the most success with large attractor/streamer patterns that were slapped on the water, allowed to settle, and then retrieved slowly so that the trout could find them with their non-visual senses. But these are not periods when trout are on the hunt, and I believe these fish were caught almost incidentally. You are better off targeting trout when they are on the feed.

One would expect the upward slopes of the "night hours dark," after they intersect with the "night hours illuminated," to have good evening fishing, as they have increasing transitional light and they are relatively dark evening periods when the zooplankton and insects can be active. However, there is more to the story. At new moon, moonrise occurs at about the same time as sunrise and moonset occurs at about the same time as sunset. In the first half of the lunar cycle from new to full moon, the moon rises later each day and sets later each night. At full moon, moonrise occurs at sunset and moonset occurs at sunrise. During the second half of the lunar cycle from full to new moon, the moon rises later each night and sets later each day. When the sun sets and it starts to get dark before the moon rises, there isn't a smooth evening transition in illumination from light to dark. On day 21, until the end of the cycle, the sun may set at around 8:00 P.M. It becomes dark, without enough light for the trout to feed effectively, and then the moon rises later in the evening. The feeding advantage experienced by the trout during the evenings of the first half of the lunar cycle is shifted

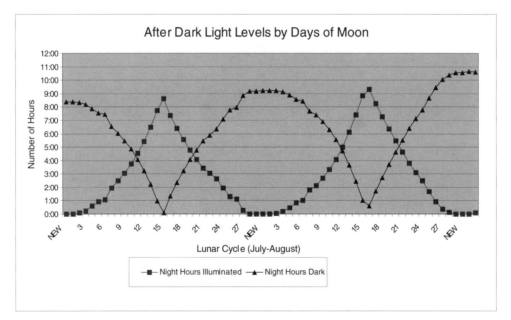

Source: Data from *The Old Farmer's Almanac,* Canadian Edition for July–August 2000.

During each day of the lunar cycle, the number of hours of light during the day and evening changes. Trout and their prey are highly sensitive to these changes. The periods with longer transitional light will provide an extended hunt for the trout.

to the mornings in the second half. Since the moon rises late in the evening, there is a long and smooth transition in illumination for the trout to feed before and around dawn.

Table 3-1: Transitional Illumination (July–August 2002)

Date	Moon Phase	Sunset	Moonrise	Sunrise	Moonset
July 10	New Moon (Day 0)	8:33 P.M.	6:00 A.M.	5:56 A.M.	9:18 P.M.
July 18–19	Days 8–9	8:29 P.M.	3:20 P.M.	6:02 A.M.	1:58 A.M.
July 24–25	Full Moon (Days 14–15)	8:25 P.M.	9:10 P.M.	6:06 A.M.	7:13 A.M.
August 1	Day 22	8:18 P.M.	12:22 P.M.	6:13 A.M.	2:02 P.M.

Source: Dates and times from *The Old Farmer's Almanac 2002*, United States Edition.

The time of day that the moon rises partly determines how much light is in the trout's environment and its feeding success rate. Note that the transitional light periods are longer during the evenings of the first quarter (days 8–9) and morning of the last quarter (day 22). These extended transitional light periods are excellent times to target big fish.

The effects of these changes in illumination can be seen in the "Angling Success for Rainbow Trout" chart below, which shows Ron Newman's catch statistics for the first eighteen years of his record keeping. The Y-axis is for pounds/hour and the X-axis is the lunar cycle with the new moon on day zero. The lowest point in the evening fishing success is during the highly illuminated full moon period at days 14 to 16. This may also be a physiochemical response: Studies have shown that the pineal gland releases intermediate amounts of melatonin under dim light conditions in a light/dim/light sequence (Gern et al.).

Since the retinomotor shift is largely governed by the amount of melatonin released, the trout would not be active for a long duration. Where there is no transitional light advantage the trout's physiology may adjust itself to this environment so that it does not waste energy on an advantage that doesn't exist. The absence of a rhythm under conditions of constant high light or light/dim (really constant light) is a basic characteristic of all biological rhythms in plants and animals. They are frequently not expressed under conditions of constant high intensity light or constant low temperature. In these situations arrhythmia is frequently observed.

Newman's day and nighttime fishing success lines also intersect approximately where the "night hours illuminated" and "night hours dark" do on the preceding chart. The fourth

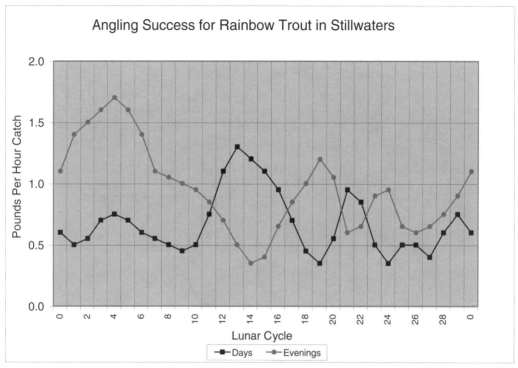

Source: Ron Newman's catch records from 1976 to 1993 on lakes in the Kamloops region of British Columbia.

The trout's daily rhythms are closely tied to changes in illumination over the lunar cycle. Anglers can use this information to target key times of the day and month to catch the biggest fish.

quarter evening angling success is low, as predicted due to less transitional light. Newman did not fish through the night or very early in the morning and does not have these periods in his data set, although I have been able to put together the pieces from other research to show the long morning transitional illumination feeding during the last third of the lunar cycle. My personal observation also supports this hypothesis.

Newman's data for stillwaters also shows that the average evening fishing (lower overall light), after 7:00 P.M., is always better than average daytime fishing (strong light), except around the full moon period, days 11 to 16, when the evening illumination is most intense and extends throughout the entire night. On average, the best evening fishing occurs through the first quarter of the moon, in particular, days 4 through 9 (low to medium evening light with long transitional periods). He also found that the proportion of larger rainbow trout caught is significantly greater on days 2 through 8 of the moon than virtually all the other days of the moon. While Newman's data shows strong correlations between the feeding activity of the trout on the days of the moon, they were not observed as being more or less active during the minor and major periods during the course of each day, as suggested earlier by John Alden Knight. This is because Knight's hypothesis was primarily based on gravitational pull and not light.

Timing the Hunt for Big Trout

While none of us can positively predict the future, we can use our experiences and scientific data about trout behavior to give us an informed guess about what will happen. If we were to rate predicted fishing success for trout during the lunar cycle it would look something like the table below. On my website (*www.bigtroutbook.com*) there is additional information on these patterns and my Annual Game Fish Feeding Rhythm Tables that give the best windows by the time of each day over the calendar year. The feeding periods on my tables were determined by calculating the amount of light striking the water (brightness and angles of moon and sun to earth), factoring in the trout's visual thresholds, feeding cycles, and the activity of their prey. They have been adjusted for two azimuths in Canada and the United States. They are an easy to read source of information to start studying the most productive times of day to fish and to help you plan the best days for your angling trips. Although created before the printing of this book, these tables were not included, as they need to be updated each year.

Table 3-2: Daily Feeding Rhythms and Predicted Fishing Success for Big Trout Over the Lunar Cycle

Moon Phase/Days	Morning Transition	Daytime Period	Evening Transition	Nighttime Period
New Moon/Day 0	Short	Low	Short	Low/Poor
Waxing Crescent/Day 1	Short	Low	Short	Low/Poor
Waxing Crescent/Days 2–3	Short	Low	Lengthy	Low/Poor
Waxing Crescent/Days 4–6	Short	Low	Lengthy	Low/Poor
Waxing Half/Day 7	Short	Low	Lengthy	Low/Poor
Waxing Gibbous/Days 8–10	Short	Low	Lengthy	Low/Poor
Waxing Gibbous/Days 11–13	Short	Low	Short	Low/Poor
Full Moon/Days 14–15	Sporadic	Sporadic	Sporadic	Sporadic
Waning Gibbous/Days 16–17	Sporadic	Sporadic	Sporadic	Sporadic
Waning Gibbous/Days 18–20	Lengthy	Low	Short	Low/Poor
Waning Gibbous/Day 21	Lengthy	Low	Short	Low/Poor
Waning Half/Day 22	Lengthy	Low	Short	Low/Poor
Waning Crescent/Days 23–25	Lengthy	Low	Short	Low/Poor
Waning Crescent/Days 26–29	Short	Low	Short	Low/Poor

- **Lengthy Feed** Morning and evening transitional periods when the illumination changes over a longer period of time—the zooplankton concentrate in the upper stratum of the water column and the aquatic invertebrates in rivers have a heavy behavioral drift. When this feed occurs during the morning transitional periods it starts early, after moonrise, and ends as the zooplankton slowly drop down or the invertebrate drift diminishes. Target active trout with streamers in feeding zones (shallow areas).

- **Short Feed** Morning and evening transitional periods when there is a relatively abrupt change in the illumination or periods. Target active trout with streamers in feeding zones (shallow areas).

- **Sporadic Feed** Periods between short and low feeds when the trout looks for food even though conditions are not optimal. Expect infrequent bites. Target active trout with streamers in feeding zones (shallow areas).

- **Low Feed** Periods when the trout cannot feed efficiently due to intense illumination or when they are satiated after a lengthy feed. The prey fish are often tightly schooled, in dense vegetation or low in the water column. Invertebrates will have a lower density continuous drift. If a hatch is coming off this may stimulate the prey that the big trout feed on and excite them. Target inactive trout in streams by nymphing in resting zones (deep and cool oxygenated areas). In stillwaters, run a leech pattern or hang a *Chironomidae* pupae pattern just off of the bottom.

- **Poor Feed** Periods when the natural illumination is below the visual threshold of the trout and they cannot feed efficiently on prey fish. Slowly work big and noisy streamers near the surface or go home to sleep.

The light-feeding factor will not only be influential on stillwaters but on tailwaters and migratory trout rivers and with smaller trout feeding on invertebrates in streams. There is a twist on some tailwaters, though. In the Colorado tailwaters, the flow of water from dams mostly regulates the distribution of food. However, since zooplankton rises during dark evenings, it is not likely that these aquatic animals will be caught in the flow of water from the bottom of the dam at that time. Opossum shrimp feed on the zooplankton at night, but they are also photosensitive and migrate to the reservoir bottom at daylight where they can be pulled into the dam outflow.

Trout in a stream environment have been shown to become more aggressive as the water velocity suddenly increased, carrying more food to them and putting them in the drift. They also became less wary. This may be the case for the tailwater trout feeding on the opossum shrimp drifts. Thus, brightly lit periods during the days and evenings may be more beneficial to the Colorado tailwater angler to get a trout to take his fly, assuming that the opossum shrimp are in the vicinity of the reservoir dam.

The reader must be wondering how he or she can catch trout at all hours of the day in some streams and stillwaters. Dr. Robert Bachman's study on brown trout invertebrate feeding in Spruce Creek, an oligotrophic water in Pennsylvania, gives us some clues. Mark Sosin chronicled Bachman's research in a 1982 issue of *Sports Afield.* He reported that, "Throughout the day, however, we observed that the fish never stopped feeding. As far as we were concerned, any time was as good as another." He also noted that the trout held almost motionless in what he calls "seats in a restaurant." I would suggest that these trout positioned themselves during the daylight hours in places where it takes little energy to catch their food items and they were by and large in resting mode. The daytime feeding activity during the summer in such nutrient-poor creeks is also sometimes tied to terrestrial drift. However, these trout are less cautious and more vulnerable to anglers when feeding on large numbers of aquatic invertebrates during their behavioral drift. The peak of the invertebrate drift is during dark evenings, which the researchers were unable to visually observe, and the trout can best feed on these items during the transitional fringes, around dusk and dawn. Since Spruce Creek is also oligotrophic and heavily stocked, the evening behavioral drifts are probably not intense enough for the trout to become satiated in a short period of time.

Spruce Creek is typical of many trout waters in North America, especially streams on the east coast and in high mountains. The reader should be careful not to consider the feeding of small trout in these streams as an example of how big trout behave. Size and range of movement in trout are related to the type of food that they feed on. In most stillwaters, with the exception of downwind shorelines, the food sources do not drift to the trout. In most rivers where big trout are present, these fish have made a shift to larger food sources (such as prey fish and crayfish) that are not available to them at all hours of the day. These big trout feed on the move and typically have to chase their food. A great deal of energy can be expended for food items captured, whether they be large or small, and a big trout needs to find substantial meals.

The difference between the availability and density of foods between eutrophic rivers and stillwaters, large oligotrophic lakes and stillwaters, and small oligotrophic streams and lakes is also what often differentiates small trout waters from big ones. The largest trout are often found in waters where there are large food items that these fish know how to feed on and that are accessible to them in short pulses. Big trout feed in rhythms and trout that feed in rhythms grow big (where the food is present). There is considerable evidence to show that trout feeding in phase with their normal feeding rhythms utilize their food more efficiently for growth than do trout feeding out of phase with the natural rhythms (Gelineau et al.). If you can determine when a big trout feeds, your chances of catching this fish are much better. This hypothesis is the crux of this chapter. In contrast, small trout are often present in waters where they must feed on small food items over a longer period of time.

Rhythms in Trout Migrating to Spawn

While this book does not focus on steelhead, some observations and scientific research regarding their daily rhythms may be useful. The main behavioral difference, with respect to the angler, between resident river rainbow trout and steelhead is that the mature steelhead rainbow trout does not usually feed in the riverine environment—although this is not an absolute. For example, the steelhead that follow the brown trout up into the Lake Ontario tributaries aggressively feed on the eggs of the fall spawners. In most cases, however, the steelhead typically uses its stored reserves to carry it through the migration and spawning period (Barrett and McKeown). So does a steelhead have a daily rhythm like the trout previously discussed? A study that was conducted on juvenile winter steelhead in Oregon's Alsea River trout hatchery might shed some light on this issue. The researchers found that these steelhead trout had melatonin releases from the pineal gland (Smith and Weber) that are similar to river and lake resident forms of rainbow trout. This finding should not be surprising, as this rhythmic activity is critical for the wild juveniles to survive and grow in the river environment before they head out to sea. So what was the melatonin release rhythm of the steelhead after it returned from the salt? The researchers did not test this age class of fish, but one of them suggested to me that it is unlikely that their rhythms are different from the juveniles.

Other research has shown that starving trout have weak rhythms (Spieler) so another factor might be if the steelhead has been eating lately. A fresh winter steelhead on the coastal rivers isn't likely to be starving, while one that has reached the Clearwater River in Idaho might not have had a meal in awhile. If daily rhythms apply to steelhead that are not starving, then anglers can time their presentations to the steelhead when this fish is either resting or active. This timing could be the difference between when a steelhead is on the bite or has lockjaw. I have observed fresh coastal steelhead go on the move at dawn and dusk, taking my fly more readily than during daytime hours. I often see steelheaders on the water at first light, but rarely at dusk—a prime period.

Veteran steelhead angler Jim Teeny demonstrated in his video *Catching More Steelhead—Breaking Tradition* that when he threw rocks in the vicinity of lethargic steelhead during the afternoon, they would get riled up and were more likely to take the fly. I am not advocating that anglers "stone the pool," of course, but the practice demonstrates that an active steelhead is more likely to take the fly than one that is not. The gauntlets on some heavily fished Great Lakes' fisheries may have the same effect. This may especially be the case where there is a great deal of flying lead. In lieu of stoning the pool, the angler can time his presentation to when the steelhead are most active as a result of their own physiology—long term/genetic response to when the best feeding periods and opportunities occur. The steelhead's rhythms will most likely be tied strictly to the photoperiod, and they will be active during the morning and evening transitional light periods (and not adjusted for whether or not their food was available or if they had a successful hunt). Although we do not have scientific evidence on the rhythmic activity of mature steelhead trout, all of the peripheral evidence supports this conclusion.

With respect to inland migratory brown trout rivers such as Oak Orchard or the Racine, whether the trout are moving to spawn or feed they will often become more active during the transitional light periods (around dawn and dusk) because their daily rhythms have been programmed in this direction. Trout feed because they are active instead of being active because they are feeding (Swift). Therefore, it is possible that the peaks of activity from when brown trout fed in a stillwater before the spawning run can carry over into the river environment when they may not be feeding. During these periods of activity a non-feeding trout may become aggressive and be susceptible to the fly. At dusk on a Lake Ontario tributary near Oak Orchard I watched a group of brown trout that had been lazily holding all day behind a protected bridge pillar become active and disperse at dusk. As the brown trout started moving around, nearby anglers hooked up almost simultaneously. I have observed this behavior on a number of other migratory trout rivers, as well, although this was a particularly interesting situation as I could see the fish and anglers from a bird's eye view on the bridge.

Barometric Pressure, Clouds, and Wind

I live in the Pacific Northwest, a region that receives storms continuously from October until June. Most of my fishing takes place during this stormy period, sometimes called the "Oregon Eclipse," when the rivers are flowing and the reservoirs are at full pool. I always watch the activity of the trout and prey fish through my fish finder on lakes and the results of the anglers around me in both moving and stillwaters. You can plan the days and times for your trips based on the illumination from the sun and moon, but understanding the weather can give you additional opportunities for big trout.

I often hear anglers on the water attributing their lack of fishing success to a changing barometer. One idea is that the barometric pressure causes a change in the water pressure, which in turn affects the trout. This is a topic that we can look into further from a scientific perspective. Barometric pressure is a measure of the weight of air in the atmosphere measured with an instrument called a barometer. There are two types of barometers. One is the "aneroid." This type has a metallic surface, a pointer, and a graduated scale, and is the kind found in most homes. The other is "mercurial," which has mercury in a graduated glass tube. Pressure is measurable at 14.7 lb./sq. in. = one atmosphere (atm) at sea level and out of the water at the surface, and increases by one atm for every 33 feet of depth (33 feet = 2 atm).

The trout is a remarkable animal and through a blood capillary exchange can adjust its internal pressure in the air bladder so that it equals the external pressure. The rainbow trout has been shown to hold at depths below 200 feet (Behnke). But more importantly, the differences between the greatest barometric pressure on earth (above water) from the highest to the lowest elevations, and through the greatest swings with weather, are less than a three-foot movement up or down in the water column. Many of us have played trout that dove more than three feet. I have hooked surface-feeding trout that tore 50 feet of line almost straight down. If actual pressure were a critical factor, then why would they have attempted to escape in that direction?

An understanding of the barometer can be most useful for the angler in timing the weather with changes in illumination. The actual pressure is not as important as the change in pressure. Changes in pressure indicate shifts in vertical motion in the air between the earth and the atmosphere. As a rule, falling pressure means deteriorating weather (for humans) and rising pressure means fair or improving weather. The changing barometer doesn't tell us what weather is happening on the ground at that moment, but it gives us an indication of what weather we will have.

Throughout this chapter, I have placed a great deal of emphasis on the intensity and timing of natural illumination. Weather patterns closely tie into these issues. An outflow of air in the upper atmosphere is one of the most common mechanisms for drawing the atmosphere upward and setting off the vertical motions that lead to rain; this situation would be indicative of falling pressure. Inversely, when the atmosphere is forced to sink towards the earth's surface, the weight of the air will be greater, and the pressure will rise. The skies might be stormy, but as the barometer begins to rise, the skies will clear. High pressure can thus be associated with bright sunny days or conditions that make non-hatching aquatic invertebrates and prey fish wary. One could expect zooplankton to migrate down below where the prey fish can see them, the prey fish to become tightly schooled or hide in the weeds, and the aquatic insects to hunker under the rocks and deep in the vegetation. Since these are not optimal hunting conditions for the trout, their instinctual reaction may be to rest and digest, if they are not involved in those activities already.

Cloud cover can have mixed effects on both daytime and evening fishing. Cloud cover can deteriorate dusk and dawn fishing, as there is not much of a shift in illumination. The skies go from dark to dull in the morning and dull to dark in the evening. The illumination from a full moon can be completely suppressed by a major storm, and heavy cloud cover can eliminate the benefit of starlight. Inversely, continuous cloud cover may improve daytime fishing, as the trout may not have to look up into the sun at your offering or start the melatonin-induced shift in vision. This is usually only the case when the clouds are thick and not when patches are mixed with sunlight.

Another explanation is that winds preceding changes in barometric pressure break up the placidity of the surface, create a chop, and dilute the subsurface light. This theory may help to explain why Ron Newman and other anglers who have kept accurate records and analyzed them in a statistical manner have found strong correlations between wind intensity and catch, and no correlation with current barometric conditions and catch. For rainbow trout, Newman found a high correlation between the chop of the water and fish strikes. He rated the water's surface as calm, light breeze, strong breeze, windy, and very windy. He observed that the worst fishing was when there was a calm surface and fishing gradually became better during the light breeze and into the strong breeze. Fishing steadily declined during windy and very windy conditions. Fishing was best when there was a slight ripple on the surface. An extensive study of angling success for brown trout in a highly productive (eutrophic) reservoir in the United Kingdom reported the same findings as Newman's (Taylor).

High winds may affect the angler more than the fish by the resulting loss of control. The craft is rocking up and down, there may be anchoring/drift problems, the anchor may be causing more noise than usual, casting is less efficient, and concentration more difficult to keep. If the angler is trolling, he probably isn't following the path that he would like to and he has to constantly readjust his engine to the gale.

The situations discussed above refer to insects that are drifting to feed (behavioral drift) and not during their metamorphosis/reproductive stages. My observations have been that insects delay their metamorphosis/reproductive functions when there is a stormy period. The angler that is fishing near the surface or looking for trout keying in on hatching insects generally has slow fishing during these periods. The insects are still active lower in the water column during the darker hours of the day in stillwaters (Hartland-Rowe) and on the bottom in rivers, so a change in tactics to a different time (dark period) and place (bottom) is really all that is needed to catch the fish.

Many anglers suggest that the reasons are barometric pressure and/or changes in the water temperature. I do not believe that pressure is the cause for the reasons previously mentioned. I have also noticed that surface temperatures on lakes vary slightly, if at all, during a week of storms, and I believe that the temperatures at the lower depths where the insects live are even less variable. Thus, I discount temperature, as well. Scientists have shown that some insects synchronize their reproductive behavior to the lunar cycle and others to seasonal day length and the photoperiod. If a storm covers the illumination of the moon, then the insects would probably not be able to synchronize their movements to this natural clock, and we would not expect any major hatches during this period. After the storm has passed and the insects' photoreceptor cells have adjusted to the new photoperiod, we would expect the hatches to resume, perhaps even a huge hatch that makes up for the days lost. I have seen this occur on many rivers and lakes.

Digestion

If big trout feed a great deal at one time, does this reduce our chances of catching them during other periods? The answer is yes, if they can feed until they are satiated. Satiation refers to being satisfied, an amount that could change every day for each trout. In humans, a croissant is found to be only half as satisfying as white bread while a boiled potato is more than three times as satisfying. Some days you are satisfied with one potato and on another day it may be two. Satiation is not something the trout are consciously aware of. Regulatory processes in all organisms, including humans, occur without conscious awareness. The fact is, we overrate the degree to which consciousness regulates our functioning, including our behavior.[17]

Fish are probably controlled by similar factors and these operate without awareness to initiate behaviors, like taking a position in a feeding lane, that increase contact with foods and that also interact with external stimulus factors. For example, emergence of a particular invertebrate, like a caddis, can enhance surface feeding in trout that feed on them. Awareness of regulatory behaviors is often not essential, and in fact is often irrelevant. Trout don't have the mental capacity to feed selectively or choose one feeding period over another (Rose). The internal clock, however, does drive feeding behavior at some times over others, or at least a preference for feeding at some times and not others. The timing of the trout's feeding is also based, in part, on the time taken to evacuate the stomach and digest food, which depends upon the temperature and to a lesser extent on the type of food.[18]

I have watched trout through my fish finder in the depths of stillwaters that were suspended without moving. Had they already taken their meal? Do we mistake selectivity in trout with those that have already reached a point of satiation? Charlie White observed that 90 percent of all fish turned away from his lures, and he noted a lethargic period in which the fish just looked lazily at his lures. I would suggest that these trout were satiated or inactive.

But when and how much food can a trout consume until it is satiated? Biologists on Quesnel Lake examined the stomach of a 20-pound plus rainbow that had taken a large plug. They found eight fresh kokanee that measured an average length of almost 8 inches. The amount of food that a trout can consume is directly related to its size. On productive waters where the trout feed on insects and small fish, and in unproductive waters where the trout primarily feed on other fish, the big trout feed until they are satiated and then don't feed again for a period of time. If they do feed at other times it is infrequently on items that are easily obtainable nearby.

There are many studies on the digestion rates of trout. As shown in the following table, the rate of digestion is primarily influenced by the water temperature and then by the density of the food item. In colder zones, digestion will be slower than in warmer ones. (The temperature affecting the rate of digestion is the temperature of the water where the trout digests.) In many waters where trout hold over springs during the warmer summer months, the differential between the surface feeding zone temperature and the deeper water where they rest can sometimes be thirty degrees Fahrenheit. This table also suggests that trout will feed less often in winter than during the warmer months. It is important to know how cold the temperature is in your targeted water.

Table 3-3: Time for 50% and 100% Gastric Evacuation of Protein Pellets and Worms by Rainbow Trout at Various Water Temperatures

	Hours to Evacuate Protein Pellets		Hours to Evacuate Worms	
Temperatures	50%	100%	50%	100%
41 F	24.7	72.4	17.9	58.5
50 F	15.1	44.2	11.3	38.3
59 F	9.2	26.9	7.1	25.1
68 F	5.6	16.4	4.5	16.4

Source: Windell, J.T., Kitchell, J.F., Norris, D.O. & Foltz, J.W. (1976). Temperature and rate of gastric evacuation by rainbow trout, *Salmo gairdneri. Transactions of the American Fisheries Society.* 105: 712–7.

The trout's digestion rate is partly controlled by the water temperature where it is digesting its food. Trout will digest their food more slowly in colder waters than warmer ones. In the wild, a stomach full of insects will take less time to digest than protein pellets and flesh since they are less dense and contain more water.

If big trout feed in cycles governed by their physiology and the photoperiod, then how are they caught during the day? The primary answer is that they do not just feed during the transitional light periods. If they can feed until they are satiated they will focus on these periods, just as we saw from Ron Newman's data set. Big trout that did not become satiated during the morning or evening transition periods may feed into the next period, just not as effectively during each feed. This inefficiency results in more resting periods after each hunt and careful selection of food items. Trout may also continue to feed while they are resting, but infrequently and on small food items that are present in their resting zone and easily caught. In shallow lakes, emerging *Chironomidae* pupae would be ideal as they are coming off the bottom in fairly large numbers and the trout do not need to expend much energy to catch them. Trout must also hold some reserve energy to escape from predators that threaten them while resting.

Summary

This chapter has presented ideas to anglers that conflict with the Knight's solunar (gravitational pull) tables and other commonly held beliefs. While the solunar tables have the weight of tradition, they are not grounded or supported by empirical science. Current scientific research provides an alternative, well-supported explanation of the feeding of trout, with convenient, practical applications. Knight may have reached too far by suggesting that all of the birds, fish, and big game he pursued were active at the same times of day. In *Moon Up, Moon Down*, Knight provides no data to support his hypothesis, nor have I seen any articles written by Knight that provided any supporting data.

Many anglers have noticed patterns in freshwaters and attempted to explain them. One well-known bass angler suggests that the periods of increased activity are related to ionic particles from space. Numerous magazines use tide tables but describe them in different ways. Hunger, digestion rates, availability of prey, enough light to feed, the transitional light feeding advantage, and the internal clock—and not gravitational pull—stimulate trout feeding.

There is a strong relationship between the timing of changes in illumination, and the most important reason to pay attention to this factor is that it is the only one that we can predict. Anglers, myself included, have caught big trout for years without the aid of this information. But neglecting to check our angling experiences against these data points doesn't mean that they have no effect. And if they do have an effect, will they give us the edge? On rivers, anglers probably do not notice the light issue because the heavier evening drift of insects are a subsurface phenomena and especially difficult to see during periods of low illumination. Perhaps, as a group, we have not previously seen these relationships because we have not looked deeply enough for them.

CHAPTER 4
LOCATE WHERE BIG TROUT HOLD IN THE WATER COLUMN

When you go elk hunting, you don't just start shooting into the bush.
Jim Teeny

Earlier chapters have established the periods of the lunar cycle and times of day that big trout are most actively feeding. It has also been hypothesized that resting trout can also be caught, and there are techniques to approach them when they are in this state that will be discussed in more detail. However, your chances to catch big trout are much better when fish are active and on the hunt. So let's first explore the places where big trout are located and tie this into the periods that they feed and rest and digest.

Feeding and Resting Zones

Trout, regardless of their size, are not found throughout any body of water, whether it is a tailwater, migratory trout river, or stillwater. In all waters, trout move within each day and throughout the seasons. Their routes and destinations are predictable. They will travel as far as it takes to feed, find suitable environmental conditions, or spawn. But if the trout does not have the ability to think then how does this fish know where to go? Research indicates that their movements are instinctual and that a genetic imprint in their biological clock tells them where to be at a certain time (much like juvenile steelhead know when to migrate to sea and return as adults.) In large fish tanks, researchers have found that trout spend their daytime activity close to the bottom and are more active during the evenings and near the surface (Sanchez-Vazquez). Food was not always present in either of these zones so it could not have been a stimulating factor. I have seen similar behavior through my fish finder. The study and my observations show that trout hold in two distinct zones over a 24-hour period. The first is where they are active and are feeding, herein called feeding zones. The other is where they find safety while they rest and digest their food, resting zones. The notions of feeding and resting zones can help us to better predict where trout will be at any given time of the day and link these zones into their daily rhythms.

Hunting quick and agile prey fish can be a strenuous activity and the trout need to rest from this exercise. Salmonids often feed in warmer and shallower waters where the food production is greatest, and after being satiated, they migrate to cooler water at a temperature more favorable for maximum food conversion (Brett). Sometimes a trout will take risks to obtain food, or a maximum supply of food at one feeding. The food may be in waters that are too warm for them to stay in for long, or in the shallows where larger predators can harm them. For example, trout will swim to the downwind side of a lake in the warm months to feed on snails in water that has a temperature high enough to kill the trout if it stayed in the zone for too long. After feeding, they will become almost dormant, especially if their resting zones have cool water temperatures that enable them to lower their metabolism and digest their food over a longer period of time. This was shown in the previous chapter when we looked at radio telemetry data for adult brown trout in Wyoming streams. The data indicated that trout move greater distances during the transitional light and evening periods (active periods) than they do during the daytime (inactive periods). We do catch big trout during the daytime, and there are techniques, such as dead-drifting a nymph, to catch them during this period. Bead head nymphs have become popular in recent years because they have the weight to drop down into the trout's resting zone. However, since trout are more active and on the move during the periods of lower illumination, techniques like this are not likely to work as well. Casting streamers or other flies that cover more space will be effective. The concept of using the right fly and approach for each specific activity period of the trout is important to remember.

Structure

Feeding and resting zones are behavioral in nature and correspond to the trout's physiological needs. Two more areas can be identified that are more structural (based on geological and environmental factors). The first of these is what I call hard structure. The most dramatic hard structures are the shorelines, banks, and the bottom, as they create physical limits within which the trout must live. These hard structures (there are others described in Table 4–1) are relatively permanent fixtures in the environment.

The second type is soft structure. Soft structure can be currents in river and lakes, temperature stratifications, waves or chop on the surface, etc. I consider the surface of the water to be a soft structure as this feature often moves based on volume of flow, the wind, and currents with water level fluctuations. Some soft structures can change significantly or even disappear entirely from one hour to the next.

Table 4-1: Significant Structures for Big Trout Waters

Water Category	Hard Structure	Soft Structure
Stillwaters	Points, shoals, channels/edges, inlets/outlets, islands, standing timber, shorelines, brushlines, flats, rocky areas, drop-offs, underwater humps, deltas	Lake temperature zones, currents, chop and waves from the wind, shade, sunlight, weedlines, algae blooms, water surface, oxygen depleted areas, flows from inlets and outlets
Tailwaters	Islands, flats, pools, shelves, drop-offs, depressions, eddies, gravel bars, channel edges, flats, rocky areas, drop-offs, banks, submerged logs, brush, boulders, log jams, waterfalls, bridges	Floating debris, foam lines, shade, sunlight, mats of vegetation, water surface, man-altered flow rate (water storage and hydroelectric power need changes)
Migratory Trout Rivers	Islands, root wads, pools, boulders, flats, depressions, banks, gravel bars, flats, channel edges, logs, brush, waterfalls, bridges	Floating debris, muddy water, water surface

Stillwaters

The concept of structure is critical for reading all waters, especially stillwaters, as it creates boundaries and areas of opportunity for the trout and their prey. Casual observers look at a large lake and only see the hard structures along the banks. However, under the surface there may be submerged islands, shoals, weed beds and/or a stratification of temperatures and currents from rivers that enter and exit the lake. Within the soft structure we can break a stillwater down into four more zones. Close to the shoreline, where light penetrates to the bottom is called the littoral zone. Open water, outside of the littoral zone where light penetrates is called the pelagic zone. The region below the pelagic zone where light does not penetrate, is called the profundal zone. The bottom area in the littoral zone is called the benthic zone. These classifications are important to understand as they will each have different types of plant, invertebrate, and fish life.

Oxygen and water temperatures are probably the most important types of soft structures in both still and moving waters, and they will usually designate where the trout resting zones will be. Often these factors will also be instrumental in determining the trout's feeding zones. Trout need oxygen to breathe. Plants in and around their aquatic environment gener-

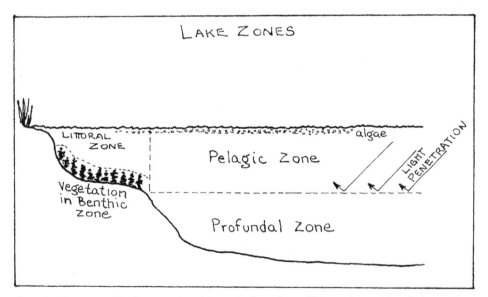

Consider the types of food sources in a lake and where they will be positioned in relation to these soft structures.

Sun River Fly Shop proprietor Bob Gaviglio with a big Crane Prairie Reservoir fish caught while fishing over springs during the heat of the summer.

ate the trout's oxygen and utilize carbon dioxide during photosynthesis. During high water temperatures and high light periods, plants produce oxygen, while microbial (bacteria) decomposition removes much of it. When light levels are low there is less plant activity and lower amounts of oxygen are produced, but carbon dioxide is still given off. Cooler water is capable of holding more oxygen than extremely warm water, so during cooler nights there can still be more oxygen in the water even though less is being generated (Waters). This is also a reason why trout will choose resting zones in cooler water. There must be a balance, though, and the trout will seek out resting zones in the middle ground where oxygen is adequate and water temperatures are low.

Seasonal Variations

The seasons can have a strong influence on the location of suitable oxygen and water temperatures. During the hot summer months in many lakes, trout will rest in cooler areas such as over springs, where the shoals in a lake break off to deeper water, where a cool creek enters a larger body of water, or at the lakeside base of dams. Many of the prime periods to take big

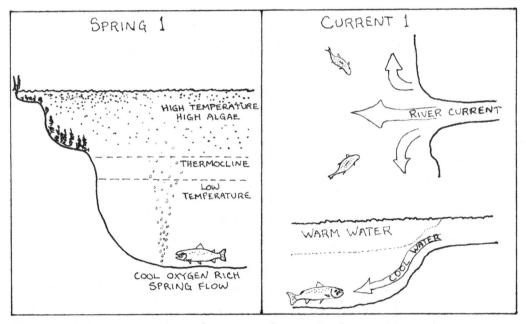

Cool oxygenated water can percolate up from springs on the bottom. Trout will often rest over them during the warm summer months.

Streams that flow into lakes tend to attract trout during the warmer water periods. These can be feeding and resting zones for trout.

trout are a result of these environmental issues. For instance, a key time to take big rainbow trout in Oregon's Crane Prairie Reservoir and Upper Klamath Lake is during the daytime on the hottest summer days when the fish gather/rest over springs or at the mouths of creeks.

I fished one morning with Bob Gaviglio, an experienced guide and proprietor of the Sun River Fly Shop, and two big rainbows weighing nine and thirteen pounds were caught. A few more in that range were lost. Gaviglio knew the right spot on a 4,000-acre impoundment and had planned a day when the fish would be concentrated because surface water temperature would be high. In this case, the location of the trout was both a feeding zone and a resting zone. The prey fish, three-spined sticklebacks, were forced by the high water temperatures and dense blue-green algae near the surface to hold within close proximity of the big trout in deeper water.

During the summer months, in many deep lakes, there is a stratification of oxygen and water temperatures that can determine where the feeding and resting zones will be. During this period, there are often three layers in such lakes: the hypolimnion (deep, oxygen-depleted, cold-water layer), the epilimnion (surface, warm-water layer), and the thermocline (layer which prevents mixing of the lighter, warmer epilimnion with cooler, denser hypolimnion). During the warm summer months, the trout will rest in and around ideal temperatures or in the thermocline. They may also feed in this area if the prey fish or zooplankton are in the same zone. If not, big trout will feed during low and transitional illumination near the surface in open water on schooling fish that in turn feed on zooplankton. These conditions are not constant and change throughout the year.

In shallow, eutrophic lakes, big trout will feed around hard structure such as on shoals and shallow vegetated areas where the algae and small invertebrates are most prolific. They will rest in deeper waters or over springheads where the water is cool and hospitable. In both deep lakes and shallow eutrophic ones, they will stay in these resting zones to achieve two objectives: digest food and regain energy.

Lake 1 in the diagram shows the contours of this stillwater, which may give us an indication of where the trout will be resting during the non-feeding periods. Lake 1 is a small, eutrophic lake that has resting zones at the deepest regions (20 and 24 feet). These deep waters are the coolest and safest places in this small stillwater for trout to rest where they will have a lower metabolism and can digest. However, if such a lake is very eutrophic, by the end of the summer most of the oxygen in the deeper water will be depleted by microbial action to the point where the trout are no longer found that deep. They will have to move into shallower water with more oxygen.

Temperature Stratification Through the Seasons

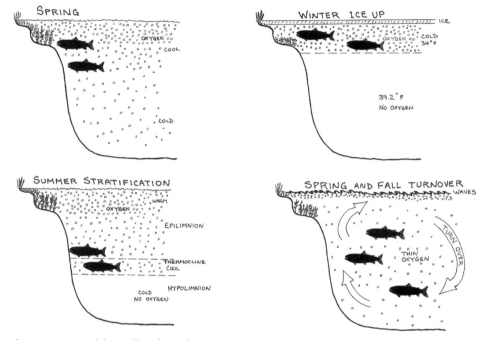

Over the seasons some lakes will undergo dramatic changes in the stratification of water temperatures and the distribution of oxygen. These temperature zones will partly determine where the trout will hold.

Sometimes small stillwaters such as this do not have prey fish and the trout are invertebrate feeders. The benthic invertebrates will be most prolific in two to eight feet where there is heavy vegetation on which periphyton can attach and on which insects can feed. The trout will cruise these shorelines to feed on the insects and crustaceans.

As summer turns into fall, air and water temperatures begin to cool. When the wind comes up and surface water temperature reaches about 39 degrees Fahrenheit, the stillwater will turn over. There can be a great deal of oxygenated waters for the trout to feed in while storing up fat reserves for the winter or for reproduction. Therefore, after this turnover occurs is an ideal time to take big trout. This turnover period can also produce a burst of phytoplankton that may spark zooplankton reproduction. Ultimately, predators farther up the food web will also be more active. The resting zones will not be determined by temperature, as one area will not be significantly different from another. The trout may rest at depths where avian predators cannot target them. Their feeding zones will be determined by the location of the prey.

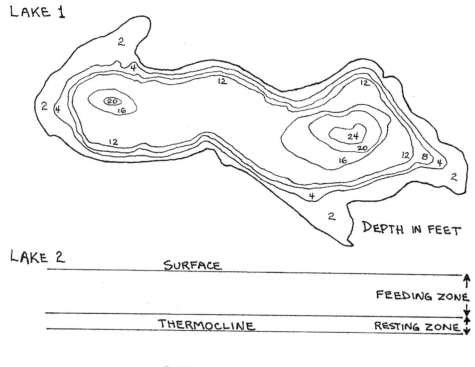

The trout in small stillwaters such as Lake 1 tend to rest in the cooler and deeper waters during the daytime and cruise the shallows for food during the evening. The open waters of large and deep stillwaters such as Lake 2 are more likely to be structured by oxygen and water temperatures. Trout will rest in and around the thermocline and hunt their prey in the warmer waters that are closer to the surface.

In winter, there will be another change in the stillwater; the plant life along the lake's shorelines begins to decompose. It is not the plant life or decomposition that determines the depth of the mixing; it is only a function of heat and wind that influences this process. The feeding and resting zones may be anywhere in the stillwater, but note that feeding will be at a minimum due to low water temperatures and the limited production and supply of food.

The habitable zone for trout may also change throughout the winter if oxygen depletion occurs in the lake bottom areas as decomposition progresses. The trout's physiology adapts to these changes so that they can survive into the spring in the absence of food. This can be a good period to fish the downwind shorelines. The trout will also feed around warmer waters where the productivity of life is greater. Such feeding zones can be around rocky shorelines that radiate the sun's warmth in ice-free areas, over springs, northwest areas of a lake that may be protected by trees from the northern exposure, and the north side of a lake, which receives more sunlight at low angle in the winter in the northern hemisphere.

The next event is at ice-out when there will be a short period before the spring winds start mixing up the lake. This feeding zone is usually on the downwind side of the lake, or the northeastern side where the water gets the most sun. The most important aspect is that ice-out is where the first pulse of production occurs. Big trout move into the downwind shallows during this period, feeding on prey fish that target zooplankton and *Chaoboridae* and possibly mating leeches. These warm waters will be conducive to feeding, and they are an important feeding zone where the angler should concentrate his efforts. The fish are also just getting active after a long winter and, since they are hungry, can be caught by anglers. In many large and deep reservoirs, ice-out is when most of the big fish are taken.

The turnover period may extend into spring, when the lake starts mixing up again. This period is easily identified by its murky waters and may last for a week or two. The plant life will bloom with the increasing sunlight and nutrients, and the oxygen layer will expand. The formation of the epilimnion layer will begin anew. At this time, as food becomes increasingly more available, the trout in eutrophic stillwaters will begin to feed aggressively in the littoral zone and pelagic zones and those in oligotrophic lakes will feed in the pelagic zone.

Currents and Wind

Currents and wind play an important role in the distribution of food in many stillwaters. A key area to look for trout is where they heave water upwards when they come into contact with hard structures such as points and shoals. Take, for example, the currents flowing from the north to the south in the diagram below. (This situation could also occur with strong winds.) When the current reaches the point, part of the flow may be diverted out into the lake while the remainder will be pushed over the submerged point, where swirls can sometimes be evident on the surface. The water at the depth of the current will not be the only thing being lifted. Food that was caught up in the current can be directed towards the surface, as well. Anglers can expect the major feeds to occur where the current breaks over the shoals and where it is diverted off into the lake.

Wind can also distribute the food on stillwaters. Wind and ripples on the water can diffuse more oxygen into the water and this may cause trout to be more active, too. Wind does not blow evenly across any body of water; contours and points in the land, trees, and other barriers break or give greater access to wind. These hard structures can create areas where there is variable chop on the water. The transition zone between waves of different intensi-

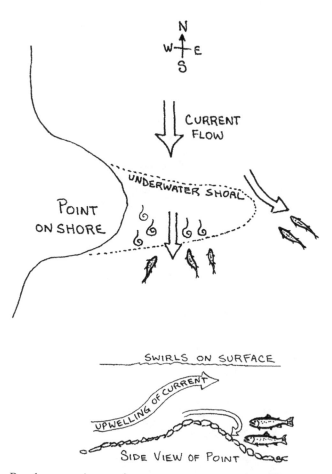

Pay close attention to where currents pass over points. These can be prime areas for feeding big trout.

ties is where the trout can find broken-up light and where the food sources of their prey fishes are displaced. This provides an area where prey fish can be easily hunted by trout. This would especially be the case where trout feed in open water on prey fish following zooplankton and *Chaoborus*.

In a lake where the wind is blowing from north to south and a point comes out from either the western or eastern shoreline that breaks the wind, a wind line can extend from the end of the point downwind. The distance will depend on how tall and dense the trees are, and it will be much like a seam that runs down a river. Anglers who fish big oligotrophic and

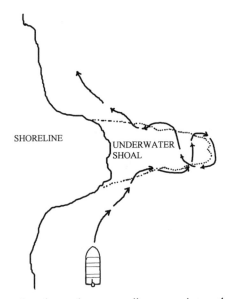

A good trolling strategy is to make a loop when you troll past a point so that your offering has a longer presentation in the target zone. Another approach is to position your craft and cast into the zone.

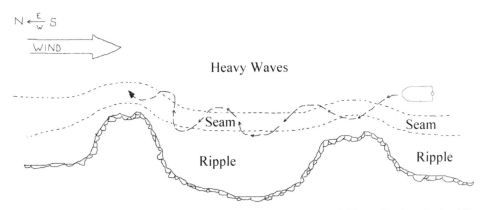

On windy days focus on the transition zones where heavy waves subside to flowing ripples. The foam line between the two will often be a key zone for feeding trout.

mesotrophic lakes look through their fish finders for prey fish, and big trout that feed on them, in this region of the lake, and concentrate their trolling on the choppy, but less rough, water inside of this seam.

Animals, whether they be deer, birds, or trout, tend to hunt or hide on the edges. The angler should present his fly by trolling across the wind in a zigzag pattern to present his offering to more trout. When trolling in open water, rock the fly back and forth between the waves to increase the trout's ability to see it. A second direction to the cross-current troll/retrieve is downwind, where the fly or lure is heading in the direction of the trout and there is good visibility (although not visibility as good as with the crosswind retrieve/troll). The least preferred direction is upwind, as the fly will skitter across the top of the waves with little visibility to the trout. The fly will also be moving away from them.

Wind can also influence the distribution of the zooplankton. The illustration below describes lakes at dusk where the wind is blowing from the west to the east. Note that zooplankton become concentrated on the downwind side of the lake. One study demonstrated a 20-fold difference in the density of zooplankton between two ends of a lake due to the wind (George and Edwards). Wave action can also have a similar effect. At dusk on Lake Ontario, schools of adult alewives swim inshore along the bottom in approximately eight to ten feet of water. Suddenly, a school will move into shallower water, even to a depth of one foot, and

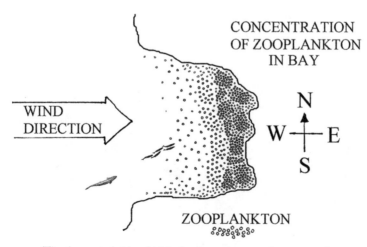

The downwind side of a lake has been shown to have as much as twenty times as much zooplankton as the upwind end of the lake. Prey fish feed on zooplankton and will key in on these zones if the temperatures are suitable.

feed upon the zooplankton at the surface. This zone, often marked by foam lines, would be a prime place to look for big browns at this time.

If the water temperature and quality (oxygen level) are good, it is preferable to fish the downwind shore of the lake. If temperature and water quality are poor for trout, such as during a mid-summer algae bloom, it can be preferable to fish at the upwind end of the lake. At these times, the downwind shore can be a green soup of concentrated algae, a lethal environment for trout due to high bacterial loads or low oxygen concentration. Cooler water can be

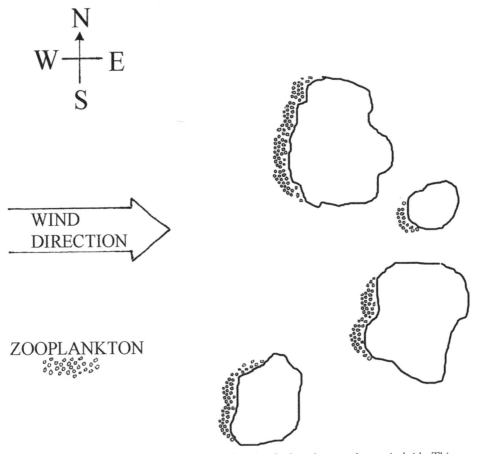

Islands often trap zooplankton and attract prey fish that feed on them on the upwind side. This can also be the case for submerged islands and gravel bars. The shoals around islands often provide easy access to deeper waters for daytime resting.

upwelling at the upwind end of the lake. This raises its oxygen concentration and provides productive nutrient-rich water for food production. Anglers should look for the rapid temperature change/gradient in the water column.

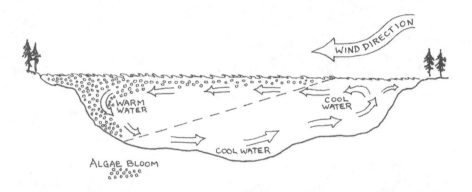

One of the observations I have made over the years, which is supported by Ron Newman's data, is that big trout are not caught when small ones are present and active, and vice versa. This may be because small trout often do not rest and feed where big trout do.[19] Would a deer bed down or feed near a cougar?

I also observe this through my fish finder, and it is especially apparent in stillwaters where the larger trout are feeding on prey fish such as kokanee, tui chubs, alewife, or shiners, while the smaller trout are feeding on insects and zooplankton. What we are really seeing is that small trout will feed in the productive feeding zones while the big trout are resting. When the big trout move into the feeding zones, the smaller trout move elsewhere. Indeed, when an area with a great deal of food seems barren of fish, it may be the case that there are just a few larger trout in the area. Therefore, I am extremely cautious in dismissing potentially productive areas when I do not see fish on my fish finder.

The big trout angler needs to research the types of prey fish available and determine which ones the trout may actually be feeding on during different times of the year. (A list for the general behavioral patterns of a number of prey fish is provided in the next chapter.) On stillwaters where trout feed on zooplankton-feeding school fish such as kokanee, shad, or cisco, the soft structure/open water will be their feeding zone and soft and hard structures will be their resting zone. Feeding zone areas depend on the type of food that big trout feed on and the food's position in the water column. If the trout feed on shoreline bottom-

Bob Jones caught this fine brown trout in Wickiup Reservoir in central Oregon. A northeastern wind was blowing the zooplankton towards a dam on the impoundment that created a concentrated feed for the chubs and the big trout that feed on this prey fish.

dwelling (benthic) fish, insects, or crustaceans, their feeding zones will be in this area and their resting zones will be the deepest, coolest, and most oxygenated areas of the stillwater.

Case Studies

The preceding examples of the behavior of trout and their prey in stillwaters were based on research from many different waters. Stillwaters can be broken down into various categories. The following are five examples of how these conditions apply to the trout over a one-year cycle on specific waters.

Shallow, Man-Made, Nutrient-Rich (Eutrophic) Trout Ponds

These relatively shallow, man-made ponds are typically no larger than 200 acres, formed by damming up a small creek. Perhaps a few years ago the rancher dropped a few trout in for their kids and now the fish are whoppers. Their kids, now adults, don't have the time to fish for them anymore, and a clever fly shop owner is leasing out the pond for his clients. Sometimes the rancher figures out what he has and forms his own booking service, paying a commission to fly shop owners and guides who throw business his way.

Although all farm ponds do not produce big trout, a few ranchers have gotten lucky by having high quality, trout-producing environments. There are many prominent private big trout stillwaters of this type across the West that are sometimes called "hog pens" and open to pay to play fishing. There are few that have big trout that naturally grow to reach the big trout standard. There are many others with trout that come within a pound or two.

Brad Kerr, a fishery biologist in Oregon who designs and builds big trout ponds and lakes professionally, describes a typical high desert, man-made pond. He starts with the cold winter environment when few insects are active and the trout slow down their metabolism in response. Rainbow trout typically spawn in these ponds from February till June, depending on water temperature and genetics.

In most big trout stillwaters there is no natural spawning, which artificially controls the population. Even if the trout can't spawn, they will still produce the gametes and must either reabsorb them or drop them in an unsuitable habitat. After this reproduction, their condition is at the lowest point in their lives, and they must find forage to grow stronger and rejuvenate in order to ward off bacterial infections and death. Spring feeding will be on whatever they can find. Early in the season, leeches, scuds, sowbugs, water boatmen, and prey fish may be the only food sources available. Anglers need to adjust their offerings to these off-season prey items.

Later, as the water warms, caddis and *Callibaetis* become more important, and in the fall, snails become a significant part of their diet. During the summertime, the water temperatures become higher, there is less oxygen, and too much oxygen depletion by bacterial decomposition that can make the pond a stressful environment. Often the trout will sulk in the deeper waters, uninterested in feeding. The richer the environment, the lower the temperature tolerance for trout. Ponds with an area suitable for active feeding over more of the year will often have larger fish. As the waters cool, the trout will go on the feed again and start to fatten up for the winter. You will have to watch the fish in your local water to determine the temperature curve for best fishing.

Large, Nutrient-Rich (Eutrophic) Reservoirs

The second type of stillwater is an impoundment, formed by damming up a river or creek. Many of them are large bodies of water with surface areas of tens of thousand of acres. Often, the prey fish were planted to sustain the growth of the trout or the trout were planted to control the prey fish. The first plantings of trout often result in state records. In the western region of the United States, the top producers of big trout are these high desert, nutrient-rich reservoirs. These reservoirs are publicly managed resources that regulate the size and quantity of trout that can be taken. There are other types of western stillwaters where excess brooder trout are planted. They are not listed in this book, but can be found by contacting local state fish and wildlife departments.

Crane Prairie Reservoir in central Oregon has gained national attention as a productive big trout fishery and is easily recognized in photos by its standing timber. The reservoir is over 4,000 acres, sits at 4,445 feet above sea level, and has an average depth of 11 feet, with a maximum depth of 20 feet. It opens for angling on the fourth Saturday in April, when the larger rainbow trout are in a post-spawn recovery mode and on the feed. The big trout will key in on three-spined sticklebacks but take other easy meals that cross their path, including an abundant supply of aquatic invertebrates that are estimated to be over 100 pounds per acre.

At ice-out the rainbows start their feeding in the warmer shallows on the sticklebacks, leeches, and active invertebrates. The sticklebacks will be focused in and around vegetation and on the bottom where they feed on small insects and zooplankton. As the waters warm, more biofilm (such as algae, fungi, and decayed matter) and phytoplankton will develop and spread the food production into other areas of the reservoir. Some portion of the sticklebacks will remain near shallow water during the late spring and summer months where they spawn. Crane was once a prairie that had three major tributaries running through it (the Quinn, Deschutes, and Cultus Rivers) that originated from the east slopes of the Cascade Mountains. When the area was flooded, the cool creeks entered the reservoir and flowed along the bottom of the submerged channels. There are also springs that percolate up from the bottom of the reservoir.

During most years, the beginning of July will be a turning point, when the waters warm and big trout look for cooler oxygenated waters. The big rainbow trout congregate near these cooler flows where they are more comfortable. Based on spawning redd counts, biologists from the Oregon Department of Fish and Wildlife estimate that there are over three thousand large trout in Crane, most of which hold over springs in the three major channels. A small proportion will congregate in other spring-fed areas. There might be three or four areas of springs in each channel that cover an area of 40 by 100 yards. Some of these springs flow as low as 42 degrees Fahrenheit, in contrast to the surface temperatures that can reach upwards of 80 degrees. The springs also serve the purpose of keeping the blue-green algae in the upper water separate from the clearer water below. If an angler can locate one of these springs, the nearby cooler water may hold hundreds of rainbows over 8 pounds.

In 1994, Crane was devastated by low water and the fishing was shut down because the trout became too concentrated. Down on the bottom, the rainbows feed sporadically on *Chironomidae* and sticklebacks. The cooler water lowers their metabolism so that they do not need to feed often or aggressively.

The next turning point for the system occurs in early September when the water temperatures start to decline with the cooler evenings. The trout move from the springs and channels to forage on sticklebacks wherever they are present in the reservoir. The sticklebacks will most likely be feeding just below the surface on the abundant zooplankton on the downwind shores. The fishing season closes on October 31.

Deep, Unproductive (Oligotrophic) Lakes
The third type of stillwater is a natural, deep lake with inflow and outflow rivers. Many of the top, super-trout stillwaters in North America are of this type. They include waters such as Bear Lake in Utah, Quesnel, Eutsuk, Shuswap, and Kootenay Lakes in British Columbia, Lake Pend Oreille in Idaho, and Lake Iliamna and Naknek Lake in Alaska. Understanding how to fish them requires knowledge of the movement of the trout and their prey.

Quesnel Lake in the Cariboo region of British Columbia is a large body of water with a length of 120 km (75 miles). It is the deepest and longest fjord lake in North America (almost a small sea). It holds numerous fish species, including lake trout, Dolly Varden, sockeye, kokanee, and its unique stock of rainbow trout that grow into the high 20-pound range. The younger and smaller rainbows, from two to four pounds, feed on invertebrates, but the trophy hunter will concentrate on the large mature fish. The alternative is much like I told a hunting companion that was chasing blacktail deer on a bowhunting trip for elk. "You don't stick a doe when there are big bulls around."

From late March until April, the rainbows spawn on their beds in the Horsefly and Mitchell Rivers. The females return to the lake quickly after spawning, while the males hang around to fertilize other eggs. By early May they are all back in the lake and on the feed. From the last two weeks of April until the first week of May, the sockeye yearlings start to migrate to the outlet of the lake and the trout concentrate on them.

Other big rainbows are in open water at the north arm of the lake. This is a highly productive area where zooplankton grows, a primary food for sockeye and kokanee. During the day, the zooplankton, the sockeye and kokanee, and the trout that feed on them are found in the top 30 feet of the water. At dusk, they all move to the surface. This light to dark transition period is when the predators become very active.

From the middle of June until the second week in July, the sockeye fry migrate from the streams into the lake. They are visible against the shore in tight schools. The 3- to 5-pound class rainbows and a few big trout will be back and actively feeding on these easy meals. This is due to their recent spawning activity and resulting hunger, and the lower density of food in open water. This mostly takes place in the junction and north arm of the lake.

From the middle of July until the first week of September, the lake will form a thermocline, the middle layer in a stratification of layers where the trout find a balance of oxygen and adequate temperatures. The big trout will hold on the bottom side of the thermocline, about two to three yards from the surface. The kokanee and sockeye will be in the same zone with the smallest individuals highest in the water column. The trout will feed on all of them, but they prefer fish about one-third their own length. Starting in the middle of September, some of the adult kokanee will stage to spawn in streams, such as the Mitchell River, and the big trout will stay with them. The kokanee will be stressed and easy to capture. By the early part of October, the shoal-spawning kokanee will be on their redds and become easy meals for the big rainbows. By November, the trout will move off the shoals to open water to feed on the yearling sockeye and two-year-old kokanee.

Large, Fertile (Mesotrophic) Lakes Where the Trout Cannot Spawn Successfully
The fourth type of stillwater is a self-contained lake fed by springs, rainwater, or snowmelt. They do not have in- or outflows and the trout do not have spawning habitat. They must be replanted with juvenile trout in order to maintain a viable fishery. Oregon's spring-fed East Lake, which was formed within a volcanic crater with Paulina Lake, falls into this category. Pyramid Lake in Nevada, where the inflows to the lake are dammed, also falls into this category. The behavior of the brown trout in East Lake, as described below, is probably similar to how they live in many reservoirs along the east coast.

East Lake covers 1,044 acres and sits at an elevation of over 6,000 feet above sea level. The maximum depth is 180 feet and the average depth is 67 feet. Due to its high elevation, the ice does not come off until the early to middle part of May, depending on the severity of the winter. At ice-out the big brown trout will be scattered in the deeper waters during the day and will feed in the shallows during the early mornings and evenings. The southeastern shoreline of the lake is extremely popular among anglers, due in part to the hot springs that breathe life into that portion of the lake much earlier than the cooler areas. Most big trout are caught during this period because they are feeding aggressively after a long winter. Also, low angling pressure up to this time results in an undisturbed feeding pattern.

Their primary food source is the large concentrations of tui chubs. There are other foods in the lake, including kokanee, but they will play a minor role in the large trout's diet. The deep-by-day resting and shallow-by-low-light feeding patterns of the large browns will continue into and throughout the summer when the lake stratifies thermally. The chubs spawn in the shallows from the middle of June through the middle of July and feed on small insects near the shore and on zooplankton swarms. In addition to the chubs, an occasional odd brown trout may happen into a school of stocked rainbow fingerlings. This was demonstrated by one angler who gutted an 8-pound brown that had a half-dozen 4-inch rainbows partly digested in its stomach.

The next major transition for the browns occurs in October when they prepare to spawn. The browns cannot spawn in East Lake as there is no suitable habitat for them, but in October they cruise the shorelines early and later in the day, looking for spawning sites. The stock of the East Lake browns is from nearby Wickiup Reservoir. The angling season closes on October 31.

Northern Latitude Brook Trout Lakes
Another type of stillwater is a shallow, productive water with a short growing season. These are typical of the brook trout lakes in Labrador, Quebec, and Ontario, where the ice is off at the end of May and on again during the beginning of November. They often have frost on the shores as late as the middle of June and as early as August. The weather in these regions can be harsh and unpredictable, even during the summer. Labrador, for example, is surrounded by three major bodies of water: Hudson Bay, Ungava Bay, and the Labrador Sea, which brings in storms almost continuously. When planning your trip to this area, leave two to three days on each end for delays.

Osprey Lake in the Eagle River watershed of Labrador sits at an elevation of almost 1,200 feet and is roughly 2,200 acres. The average depth of the lake is 6 feet and the maximum depth 10 feet at full pool. Aboriginal people named the lake "Island Lake" due to the dozens of islands that dot it. There are also many more submerged boulder fields that are coated with biofilm and the aquatic invertebrates that feed on it.

Osprey Lake has three species of fish—northern pike, brook trout, and a bottom-feeding fish that is possibly a white sucker. The pike appear to range from just a few inches to over 20 pounds. The smallest brook trout in the lake are about 3½ pounds and a few go over ten. The average size of the brook trout is just over 5 pounds. The upper reaches of the creeks that feed the lake are full of sexually immature brook trout that have not ventured down to the lake.

The primary food sources for the trout in the lake appear to be aquatic invertebrates such as water boatmen, diving beetles, *Chironomidae,* scuds, caddis, and mayflies. They may also be eating small pike, other brook trout, suckers, and lemmings when available. Osprey Lake is usually clear of ice in late May and opens for fishing from the third week in June. The water is a cool 48 degrees Fahrenheit during this period, but the brook trout will go on the bite to regain their energy after a long winter.

This is also an ideal period to take a trophy fish as they are unpressured and an abundance of insects will be active and in their metamorphosis period. The brook trout will be feeding on the rocky areas around the islands where the insects feed on the periphyton and near the mouths of small streams. This pattern will continue until the middle of July. As the days get longer, the lake warms up considerably, reaching the 70s by the middle of August. The trout will become more lethargic during this period and hold near the inlets and spring heads. Some time between mid-August and the middle of September the brook trout will prepare to spawn in the inlets and outlets. Large colorful brook trout are caught during this period, although fewer than during the early part of the fishing season. Labrador brook trout fishing season closes September 15.

Tailwaters

Trout in most tailwaters and rivers on this continent fall into the drift-feeding resting model during the daytime. In some of the big trout waters this model is also applicable such as the opossum shrimp drifts on the Colorado tailwaters and the scud/cressbug drifts in the Little Red River. It is not applicable to the White River and Nipigon River tailwaters, where sculpins and crayfish are the primary food sources. The trout in these latter waters are primarily roving hunters. Roving hunters tend to have one or more home ranges (bases of operation), where they rest during the day and hunt during the lower light periods. When the trout have more than one home range they will usually migrate between them at night (Clapp, et al.). Numerous studies have shown that big trout in moving waters are also structure-oriented. Local fishing lore always has a big trout that seems to sit under the same log for generations. It isn't the same trout that has lived in this location, but rather a super-productive site that served as a resting or feeding zone to many big trout.

In rivers, feeding and resting zones can be affected by water flows. Heavy water releases raise the level of the river and concentrate fish near the banks and on the tail ends of islands

and push them away from the bases of the dams. The opposite extreme, low water, concentrates the fish in pools and at the bases of dams. Regardless of the water flow, the feeding zones must be associated with where the trout's food is available. For example, there are two tailwaters where the locations of the trout were identified by electro-fishing surveys conducted separately by John Stark and Tom Bly of the Arkansas Game and Fish Commission.

Tailwater 1 in the illustration below is a eutrophic river with dense vegetation and the brown trout feed on scuds and cressbugs in the behavioral drift or on other trout that become active with the increased drift. During daytime low water flows, they will hold within or under vegetation. Anglers will have an extremely difficult time reaching these trout, as they are hiding, resting, and digesting until the evening feed. During high water flows, the strong currents will push the trout from the main current to safer areas along and under the banks. If the water flow is heavy during the evening, they will continue to hold in these zones and feed when water visibility is acceptable. When water flows are low at night, they will hunt around the vegetation, where the scuds, cressbugs, and small fish are feeding.

The flow of water in tailwaters such as the Frying Pan heavily influences where trout will be holding.

The flow in a tailwater can dramatically change in just a few minutes, while such a change in the flow in a river such as the Beaverkill would only occur after something like a hurricane. Geography is not as much an issue as the types of water and their changes in flow. You will find these feeding and holding patterns in nutrient-rich streams everywhere.

In tailwaters like Tailwater 2, where trout feed on sculpins and crayfish, their areas of activity will be a little different. During low water daytime flows, we will find them at the bottom of the pools, holding near structure such as logs and boulders. They will rest and digest in these zones. During heavy flows, they will be pushed to the edges of the current, just as we saw with the trout in the eutrophic tailwater. Under low water evening flows, they will migrate from the pools to the riffles where their prey (the sculpins and small crayfish) are feeding. (I have observed this horizontal migration for a wide range of trout sizes in smaller freestone streams such as the West Branch of the Delaware, as well.) Reduced illumination at dusk will usually be the trigger for this resting-to-feeding-zone migration. The duration

Tailwater 1

Conditions

Low water day

High water day & evening

Low water evening

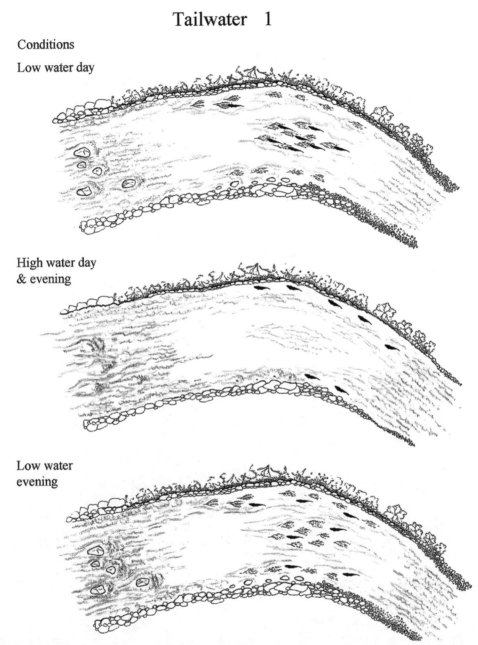

This is a good example of how trout will hold in highly eutrophic, heavily vegetated tailwaters and rivers. In this situation, the food source is within close proximity to the trout's resting zone (under the mats of weeds). Note the difference in their daytime and evening and high water positions.

Tailwater 2

Condition

Low water day

High water day
& evening

Low water
evening

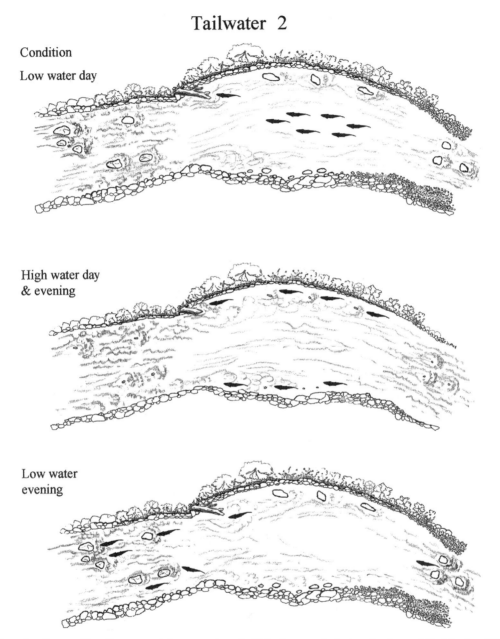

Trout in oligotrophic tailwaters and freestone rivers hold in deep pools during the day and feed in the riffles at night, where the invertebrate life and other prey for the trout are more plentiful.

of the hunt will be dependent on available light and if and when they become tired or satiated.

There are moving waters other than the types of tailwaters previously discussed where big trout reside. On some free flowing rivers, spring creeks, and other tailwaters, a few trout make the shift from feeding on drifting invertebrates to small prey fish and other trout early in life and grow to the big trout standard. Anglers will often spook such large trout from a hidden lair on these streams when wading to smaller trout feeding in the drift. The daily resting and feeding positions of these trout will usually be similar to those in the tailwaters just covered, and the angling tactics and flies for tailwaters would apply in catching them. These waters are not listed here as the quantities of big trout are often fairly low and the waters that hold them are few and far between.

Case Study

The White River is oligotrophic with limited productivity. The two species of trout in the White River are naturalized browns planted over 30 years ago and hatchery rainbows that are stocked yearly. The river has been shown to support as many as 266 brown trout over 20 inches per river mile. The present population is somewhat less, largely due to overharvesting by anglers. Current estimates are about 180 brown trout in the 5- to 7-pound range, or about 24 inches, per river mile. The browns become sexually mature at 3 years of age and often live to over 13 years. They make the shift from small crustaceans and insects to sculpins and crayfish at about 13 inches. As they get larger, they shift to small trout.

The brown trout in the White River have one major migration to their spawning grounds just below the dam. The migration is from the home ranges of the browns, which can be as far as 35 miles away—often traversed in just two days. This migration occurs from the early part of October into December.

After the trout spawn, they may remain near the dam to take advantage of the threadfin shad die-off. This shad kill usually occurs from the early part of January when the temperatures in the reservoir drop to below 40 degrees Fahrenheit. The threadfin shad were introduced from a more moderate climate and cannot withstand these lower temperatures. Many threadfin shad are swept through the turbines and fed to the waiting trout below. This high-protein food source is critical to the quick post-spawn recovery and continued growth of the trout. A brown trout of 16 inches may grow 1.5 inches and gain almost a half-pound per month during this period. The threadfin shad kill will usually last until the first part of April, but may terminate earlier in the case of an extremely cold winter.

Large brown trout in the White River primarily feed on crayfish, small trout, and sculpins. A crayfish that is too large for the trout may roam about in pools during the afternoon, but the more easily captured and handled ones will be hiding under the rocks in the riffles.

When the threadfin factor ends, the trout will return to their home ranges. Based on radio telemetry studies, the big brown trout in the White River do not hunt far beyond a 60-yard home range circle. During the day, they will hold under cover such as in clusters of boulders, along rock ledges, around root wads, and under overhanging trees. At dusk, they move into the shallows to feed. This tailwater has a wide range of water flows, from 210 cfs to 24,000 cfs, which sometimes makes angling difficult and unpredictable.

Migratory Trout Rivers

My definition of a migratory trout river is one that seasonally holds large fish. These trout live in a large body of water and move into rivers and streams to spawn, feed, or find more comfortable water temperatures. Some lakes may be as large as Lake Ontario, which holds big brown trout before they climb New York's Oak Orchard Creek and Oswego River and Ontario's Credit and Ganaraska Rivers. There are also many other good migratory rivers that feed Lake Superior and Lake Michigan. Other waters, such as the brackish Great South Bay, provide ample food for browns, rainbows, and brook trout that are caught as they climb up the Connetquot River on Long Island. Another large stillwater, Upper Klamath Lake, supports Oregon's Williamson River rainbows. The trout in the Babine and Mitchell Rivers in British Columbia spend most of their lives in Babine and Quensel Lakes, respectively. There are also cases where trout survive during high water temperature periods by taking refuge in cooler tributary streams. One could also consider the trout in lakes without an in- or outflow stream as migratory, but they are included in the stillwater section. One such case is Pyramid Lake near Reno, Nevada, where an underwater discharge from the hatchery seeps into the lake and entices the fish into and along the shoreline.

In most migrating trout rivers where these fish are big, the residence time in the river is rather short, perhaps only a few months. There are exceptions, such as in some of the Alaskan watersheds where small populations of rainbow trout seem to be spending alternate years over-wintering between the larger rivers and lakes. After they spawn in the spring, at the end of May through the beginning of June, they tend to congregate at the lake outlets in anticipation of the sockeye smolt salmon movements. Later in the summer, they key into the sockeye eggs. In most of the Alaskan rivers, the upstream movements of sockeye adults are the most significant event, which is soon followed by the migration of chum, pink, and silver salmon. King salmon migration tends to have little effect on the movements of trout (Meka).

During the year 2000, over 19 rainbow trout measuring 30 inches or better were caught by guests at one Kvichak River lodge. A 30-inch rainbow trout in this river will range from $8\frac{1}{2}$ to $13\frac{1}{2}$ pounds, depending on girth. Only two fish were post spawners caught in June; the remainder were caught after the 20th of August. One fall-caught fish, with a length of 33 inches and a girth of 20 inches, was estimated to be $16\frac{1}{2}$ pounds. This is the period when they are drawn by the sockeye eggs and the prime time to fish for them.

The timing of the maturation cycle in brook trout is regulated by the normal seasonal changes of day length (Henderson). There is no reason to believe that the true trouts do not have spawning rhythms related to the seasonal photoperiod, as well. Most rainbows spawn some time between January and June; however, their migrations into the rivers can be during the later autumn months. Wild rainbows tend to move in small groups or pairs, while hatchery-reared spawners tend to pod in larger groups as they come up the river. If one fish is taken in a hole, a few more usually follow within a few minutes.

Browns typically spawn during November, although in some regions the range can be from October until January. Most begin their movement up the river to spawn as early as September, triggered by shorter day lengths. Those browns that come up in the spring and early summer feed in the river until their spawn. Despite such large movements of big fish, the rivers and streams will seem undisturbed and the fish invisible. Browns are the masters of stealth and often hold in the shadows of overhanging banks and under logs and mats of weeds. I once watched a brown of over 12 pounds hold in a heavily fished section of river for weeks without being detected, or at least without being taken home by another angler.

I studied the holding patterns of migratory trout in a number of rivers across North America and noticed that they are somewhat similar regardless of the species. To start with, trout that are migrating to spawn do not all actively feed. Thus, there will not always be feeding zones. There will be resting zones, which most anglers call "holding water." Those fish that migrate to feed will position themselves in relation to the food source, mainly spawning salmon. This is their feeding zone. The various angling approaches that fly fishers use to catch trout migrating for all of the above reasons are strictly a function of compensating for water clarity, velocity, and depth, regardless of whether or not they are feeding. Anglers can target brook trout during the early fall months and rainbow and cutthroat trout in the late fall, winter, and spring around the mouths of the creeks and feeder river.

The migratory trout river illustration describes trout moving up to spawn. This river is characteristic of some of the Great Lakes tributaries, where good numbers of big brown trout migrate from the lakes into the rivers to spawn. The angler should focus his efforts to catch fish in the main channel, where the trout swim through hard structures that break the current for them to rest, and seams along pools allow them to position themselves to swim up through the next series of riffles and runs. Note the unconventional structure made by the pillars on the downstream end of the bridge. This is an often overlooked spot for big trout. Migrating trout will often hold in holes created by small boulders, logs jammed into the bot-

MIGRATORY
TROUT
RIVER

MAIN
CURRENT
FLOW

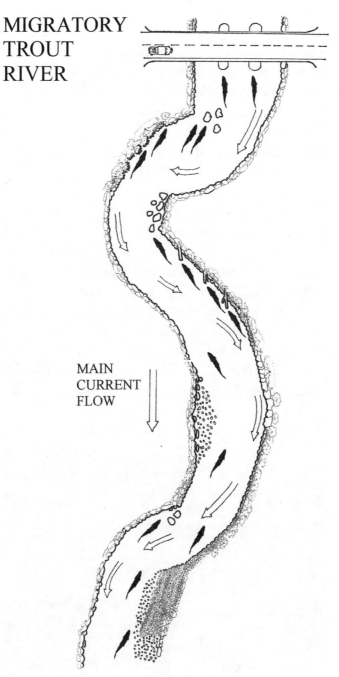

Target areas where trout are holding between upriver movements.
Consider both natural and man-made structures.

tom, and undercut banks and seams of the currents, much like steelhead, and in softer currents that feather out.

Some anglers are averse to fishing for trout that are migrating to spawn. I am not. I also fish to migrating steelhead and salmon, as do most anglers that cast to them in rivers. Does the process of playing, hooking, and releasing trout seriously harm them and inhibit them from reaching their spawning beds? Scientific studies have found that hooking and releasing an upstream-migrating steelhead, without inflicting gross injury, has no apparent effect on its ability to reach the target spawning stream (Reingold).

There is certainly a human influence on fishing success in many of the migratory brown trout rivers. Some of these are located along the Great Lakes within an hour's drive of Rochester, Buffalo, or Chicago. I think Rick Kustich of the Oak Orchard Fly Shop put it best when he told me that the people are going to be there when the fish are running. Also, when they are running, they are moving through quickly and will cover a lot of water. If you stake out a position, be considerate of others around you and accept that there are other people sharing the river. You might even find some good conversation between hook-ups. Most anglers will respect your need to move along the bank of the stream when you go chasing after a fish on your line.

If you really want to get away from people, go for a walk a few minutes up or downstream to find your solitude. Many anglers also tend to hang near the bridges, where they see other fishermen catching fish. Other than the softening of the current on the downside of the bridge, trout don't know the bridges are there.

CHAPTER 5
STUDY THE WATER

Chance favors the prepared mind.
Louis Pasteur

Not long ago over a business lunch, a woman asked me what I did for fun. The question was innocently posed from an elegant older lady who just wanted to make polite conversation. I replied that I fish and hunt. She then commented that it surprised her as the two are nothing alike. It seems that she had grown up in a household where they did both. The hunting consisted of studying the terrain, watching the habits of their prey, and sometimes going through hell to reach them. The family fishing outings were usually afternoons lounging in the sun while waiting for the fish to swim by and suck down their baited hooks. She was correct, the ways that her family hunted and fished were nothing alike. But the successful big trout angler needs to approach his prey much like the big game hunter. He researches the area, how the trout feed, where they rest, what affects them, and then he goes to where they are expected to be. If they are not there, he moves to other expected areas.

Trout behavior and their reaction to environmental factors is an incredibly complex puzzle that takes into account more variables than I have discussed in these chapters—or even understand. The only mistake you can make is to think that you have it figured out. This would be much like having a scheme to clean up in Vegas and then dropping your life savings on a roll of the dice. We do know that big trout are not widely distributed, even within areas of rivers and stillwaters. They are in the prime feeding grounds and most hospitable and safest areas. Not because they know these areas have the most food, but because zones with the most food produce the biggest trout. Their behavior is predictable, to some degree, and you can find the productive zones. You have just two options: hire someone who knows where they are, or figure it out for yourself with the assistance of available information. Let's look at how to choose a guide before focusing on taking big trout the old fashioned way—earning it.

Guides

There is nothing more valuable for finding places where the fish are present at a specific time of year than hiring a guide who spends a great deal of time on a local water. I usually start my guide selection based on references from friends, books, the Internet, or reputable magazines. I then call the guide and start the questioning process. Guides can be hardworking and good listeners, but they are certainly not mind readers. Express to your guide what you intend to achieve from the trip—primarily a big trout. He or she may inform you that your choice will mean passing up a lot of good fishable water on your way to that trophy. I also ask the guide when is the best day of the year to catch a big fish in that river or stillwater and why they think so. What is the triggering factor? Triggering factors for all of the big-trout waters discussed in this book are listed in this chapter.

Few guides have a scientific perspective on the water systems. Much of what is written in these pages may be completely unfamiliar to them. You may have a guide who thinks you should use gear other than a fly rod. Another may tell you that whenever he wakes up in the morning is the best time to fish. You are paying the guide for his service so the final decision, unless there are safety considerations, is yours. All of the places that have big trout may not have fly fishing guides available. You may need to put your expectations in writing. I also suggest that you not commit to the transaction until your conditions are met. This is sometimes difficult to arrange with a lodge, where the fishing hours are based on the cook's schedule. I once presented my trout feeding rhythms slide program at a lodge that was on the cook's schedule. The first question from a guest was why they were not fishing at the prime times of the day. The manager quickly answered that he had tried to fish at those times to no avail and that they were better off with a hot meal. The guest was unconvinced. Ask the lodge manager the question and, again, get your answer in writing. It is also a good idea to request a guide who has an open mind to technologies such as fish finders and who is willing to work with you. The following is a sample query to a guide/lodge asking what the best time to fish for big brown trout would be.

I am planning a trip to your lodge to catch a brown trout over 10 pounds. Your website states that early spring (March and April) is the best period to catch a trophy. I am guessing that ice-out and the opener (unpressured fish) are the reasons. What week do you expect that to be? I understand that this is variable. I would like to fish until 10:00 P.M. or start before sunrise in the morning. Is this acceptable? I plan to use fly-fishing equipment. Are there any types of fly lines or flies that I should bring? Can you suggest other equipment? Do you have experience guiding fly fishers? I look forward to your response. Thank you.

Knowledgeable guides and fly shops provided much of the fishing destination information in this book. Most of them would be more than willing to guide you for a day or find someone who will. In addition to fly shops, there are bait and tackle shops and boat ramps nearby or associated with every body of water that holds big trout, but they may not be fashionable establishments sporting the finest bamboo rods and embroidered hats. They will have big stuffed fish specimens on the walls and plenty of guys sitting around stoking the fire

A professional guide such as Ed Miranda, Sr. will position you on the river and point out the most productive drifts. This photo was taken on Oregon's Williamson River. Note that the guide is standing next to the angler coaching him along and not lounging on the bank.

who, if asked politely, may be willing to tell you the details of the catch. Ask them where the big fish are taken, the time of day and year, weather conditions, etc. Look at the dates on the photos tacked behind the counter. Research the time of day, point in the lunar cycle, and weather. If it happened once under these conditions, the chances are that it will happen again. One of these fellows might even guide you around just for kicks.

The Internet/Magazines

Just a few years ago, one might not have considered the Web to be of much value in researching anything. Today, if you are not on the Web, you are not achieving your full business, educational, or recreational potential. I developed a website during the course of writing this book to condense all of the details that I needed on a regular basis. This website, www.bigtroutbook.com, includes the weather forecasts, reputable guides and outfitters I have worked with, and links to other sites that I often frequent. Each big trout water in this book is listed with links to other resources, including guides, lodging, maps, and other services.

During the course of my research, I used the Web to find new and out-of-print books, find people I wanted to interview through the online white pages, and research academic journals through search services. I find it much less intrusive to email someone—or receive—a two-line question than to call someone who may be busy. A great number of fly shops and outfitters are listed on the Web with information about their services, the waters they cater to, the equipment you need, the flies to purchase, and how much it will all cost you (one of the best is The Virtual Fly Shop at www.flyshop.com).

State and provincial tourism departments have sites that also list guides and outfitters. Many offer maps of the regions and places where you can stay for a night. Some Websites have bulletin boards where anglers relate all of the details about their experience on a body of water for a specific day and time. Many local fly fishing clubs also post the latest happenings on their waters. The McKenzie Flyfishers in Eugene Oregon, for example, offers almost up to the day images of the major passes over the Cascade Mountains that are downloaded from the Oregon Department of Transportation. Great Lakes' anglers tune into postings on their club boards to track the movements of brown trout into the tributaries. Some Websites provide professional guide reports.

Magazine publishers are rapidly developing Websites that carry feature articles unique to the Internet in addition to reprints from earlier issues. Although Websites and magazines are quickly merging, the advantage of searching for information on the Web is that data is stored for a longer period of time. The shelf life of a magazine is only a few months, and back issues are difficult to come by, even if you can figure out which article was in which issue. In contrast, Web articles may be there for eternity and can be located easily with a variety of search engines.

Maps

A few years ago, I watched Larry Dahlberg, on his ESPN television program *The Hunt for Big Fish,* searching out some exotic species on a lake in Africa with a contour map of the lake in one hand and the controls of a fish finder in the other. The guide was steering the boat. Dahlberg seemed to have complete confidence in his strategy and resources, and he did catch the fish he was after. Most anglers start and end their research with a state road atlas or a guidebook that shows the location of the boat ramps and camping areas. A better place to start is with a map like Dahlberg's that shows the entire drainage and the contours of the lake's bottom.

Many of the top big-trout stillwaters have a man-made dam that is regulated by a civil authority. That organization has a map, called the bathymetry, which shows the depth of the lake, and rivers, and streams that connect to it and its dam. Some states and provinces have compiled books that show the bathymetry for most of their important reservoirs and lakes. A number of angling guidebooks also include such maps. (Refer to the bibliography for a listing of resources.) I print such maps from my computer on waterproof/weather synthetic papers such as the Topographic Immortality available at www.lat26inc.com. For hard copies, you can use the compass on your GPS or fish finder to coordinate the map to your position.

Information about free flowing rivers can be just as easy to come by. Buy a river map and look for islands, the confluence of creeks and other rivers, big bends (potential resting zones), and try to estimate where the riffles, runs, and pools will be. Take a walk along the shoreline to get a feel for the water, figure out a strategy, and then put your waders on.

Determine What the Trout Are Feeding On

There are hundreds of different species of prey fish on which big trout feed that can make understanding where they hold in the water column and imitating them daunting at times. I categorize prey fish into three groups that primarily indicate where and what they feed on and further describe their sizes as adults and primary foods. There are many types of prey fish that fall within each type. For example, I have counted six types of sticklebacks in North America. Their physical characteristics are fairly close and habits similar. There are many other prey fish present in North American waters that are not listed. If you are unfamiliar with the prey fish in your area or how they hold in the water column refer to *Peterson Field Guides: Freshwater Fishes,* where you will find detailed descriptions and geographic distributions for them. Most states also have a more comprehensive guide to their fish. Typical titles are *Fishes of Arkansas, Freshwater Fishes of Canada,* and so forth. They are fairly expensive when new, but you can usually purchase them at cheaper prices through secondhand bookstores, either locally or on the Web.

I originally sought to list the coloration of the many prey fish represented in the waters that we fish, but after careful research I learned that many prey fish have the ability to change colors. This is a camouflaging technique that helps the prey to hide from trout and other predators. Prey fish typically have greater coloration at night and lighter coloration during the daytime (Emery). This change may be partly due to the melatonin release that affects coloration, both through uptake in the blood and via possible diffusion through the skin (Hafeez and Quay).

Trout also camouflage themselves. I once caught a brown trout that had been feeding in the drift with half of its body in a dark area and the other half in the sun. Upon close observation of the fish in the net, the forward half of the trout was light amber while the rear section was a porter brown. These changes also occur with depth (less light) but are difficult for us to see as the coloration of fish quickly changes as we pull them out of the water into the sun. When we consider the colorations of our flies or lures we should take these issues into consideration.

Group I: Open Water, School Fish

These prey fish typically have deep sides, thin backs, large metallic scales, and big eyes. Their physiology helps them to swim quickly in open pelagic waters to avoid predators and catch prey. These fish are usually in stillwaters, and sometimes large rivers, and have daytime colors that are mirror-like to hide them in the open water, or pelagic, zone. In stillwaters, the principal food sources for these prey fish are zooplankton and *Chaoboridae,* and opossum shrimp where they occur. Examples of these prey fish are alewife (6 inches), cisco (10 inches), shad (5 inches), kokanee (8–10 inches), sticklebacks (2–4 inches), and smelt (6–10 inches). Ideal imitations for them are the Stinging Bucktail and Stinging Hair flies.

Group II: Solitary or Small-Group Free Swimming Fish

These prey fish have long, oval bodies that derive their color patterns from close proximity to the sides and bottoms of streams and stillwaters. These near-bottom-dwelling fish are typically colored in shades of brown, green, and black and sometimes have silvery or amber flanks. In the shallows they will primarily consume cressbugs, scuds, and small insects on the bottom, or zooplankton, *Chaoboridae,* and *Chironomidae,* farther up in the water column. At nighttime (when there is not enough illumination to see), they often rest on the bottom and take on reddish colors to blend into this environment. A few examples of this group are chubs (4 inches), shiners (3 to 4½ inches), sticklebacks (2 to 4 inches), minnows (3 to 5 inches), and small trout. Note that the sticklebacks may be pelagic and benthic feeders. My Stinging Bucktail and Stinging Bunny are ideal fly imitations for this group.

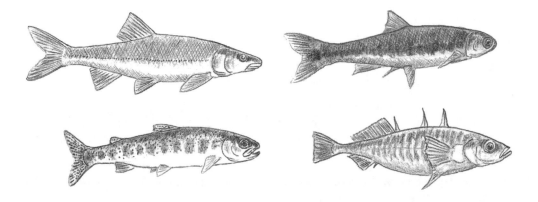

Group III: Individual or Small Group Bottom-Dwelling Fish

These prey fish have compressed bodies and wide bellies that display intricate back and side color patterns to camouflage them on the stream or lake bottom. Common prey fish in this group are sculpins, darters, and suckers. The daytime and night colorations will be fairly similar as they feed and rest on the bottom in the darkest areas of the water column. Sculpins (2 to 8 inches) do not have swim bladders and have no choice as to what level in the water column they can feed. Ideal fly patterns to imitate these prey fish include my Stinging Sculpin series.

 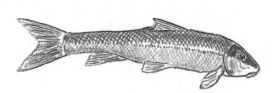

State and Provincial Fish and Wildlife Agencies

The first stop for researching anglers should be the state or provincial fishing synopsis. Look for waters that have daily limits of one or two fish, those that are "catch and release," or that require barbless hooks. Clearly, ones that limit the catch size to over 20 inches will be key targets. These regulations are generally aimed at allowing trout to grow big and minimize the mortality of large spawners. If you can find the data for *Total Dissolved Solids* (TDS) in your intended waters and tie them to the regulations you will have a base of information to build on. The TDS is a measure of the relative productivity of water. The greater the number, the more productive the water is. The upper limit for an oligotrophic lake would be 75 parts per million (ppm), while the lower limit for a eutrophic lake would be 75 to 100 ppm. Lakes within the 200 to 400 range are very productive and have the capability to maintain healthy populations of trout (Chan). Unproductive waters with late-maturing trout, such as the Bear, Quesnel, Eutsuk, and Kootenay Lakes mentioned earlier, can also have big trout.

Table 5-1 shows the TDS and the trout sizes for a few stillwaters in British Columbia. All of these waters are capable of producing big trout, but the goals of the fishery biologists are not always to grow large specimens. Some fisheries are managed for larger numbers of fish.

Table 5-1: Potential Trout Growth, TDS, and Special Regulations for Rainbow Trout in the Kamloops Region of British Columbia

Stillwater	Total Dissolved Solids (ppm)	Max. Size of Trout (pounds)	Special Regulations
Stump*	1220	14	NSR
Pennask	27	2	FO, BB
Lac Le Juene	176	4	NSR
Paul	212	6	NSR
Knouff	184	10	DQ-2
Community	256	4	BB, DQ-2
Hatheume	265	8	FO, BH, DQ-1
Leighton	310	4	BB
Tunkwa	248	5	NSR
Pass	182	12	BB, FO, DQ-1, ML 20 inches (2)
Island	263	8	FO, BB
Lac Des Roche	153	12	NSR
Shuswap**	75	30	DQ-1, ML 20 inches

Source: British Columbia Ministry of Fisheries
*Windy lake that few anglers choose to fish
**Unproductive lake with late-maturing race of rainbow trout
Key: BB - Bait Ban; FO - Fly only; DQ - Daily Quota; ML - Minimum Length; NSR - No Special Regulations

There is no group of people more concerned about the welfare of a body of water than the federal, state, and provincial fish and wildlife biologists. Their livelihoods depend on stable and productive fisheries. They are often an untapped resource for the angler, as they usually only get calls from inquiring outdoor writers. This book would not have been as complete without their assistance. Their jobs are being paid for by your fishing license dollars and you have the right to ask, politely and preferably by letter or email, for information about the waters you intend to fish. Often, the information is contained in a report that they are more than happy to send you, or they may refer you to a library that has one. All of the state wildlife agencies can be found on the Internet. Many of them list the state game fish records, the waters they came from, and the date they were caught. Anglers can also find local contacts for each state with their email address. Some of the key questions that you can ask your fish and wildlife agent, or try to determine from other sources, are:

- What bodies of water have big trout in them?
- Are there any written reports for these waters?
- Which waters have a high TDS?
- Are there oligotrophic waters with late-maturing trout?
- What waters have special regulations for big trout?
- What do those trout feed on, and when and where? If prey fish, what do they look like? When and where do these prey fish spawn?
- Where might the big trout's resting zones be?
- What methods do anglers use to take the largest trout and why?
- On stillwaters, how do the trout move throughout the seasons (ice-out, summer heat, fall turnover, etc.)? What is the depth of the thermocline?
- For migratory rivers, when are the peak of the runs and what type of water do the trout hold in?
- For tailwaters, how is the water released and how do the releases affect the trout? Is there a phone number that you can call to get the scheduled releases?
- What are the legal fishing hours? Does the finishing time mean that is when you have to pull in your line or be off the water?
- Can you fish with more than one hook on the fly? Can you fish with more than one rod or fly?

Arriving at the Water

Although a great deal of preparation may be made before you leave home, close observation once you arrive at the water will help to complete the puzzle and put your research into perspective. When I arrive at my intended fishing destination, I first go to an elevated position where I can take a good look around. I often carry binoculars, and I always wear a wide-brimmed hat and sunglasses. I look for landmarks to correlate to my maps and scan the water for signs of life. I note the wind direction and the transitional zones where the waves break off to quieter waters. I might even walk or drive around a stillwater to see it from a few different perspectives. I look at the surrounding hillsides and try to determine how and where the light will be hitting the water. On a river, I will drive a road that either crosses or runs along it.

I then go down to the water, turn over a few rocks, and sift my hand through the weeds. While out on the water, I look at what the birds are doing. Diving sparrows key me into *Chironomidae,* mayfly, and caddis hatches. Pelicans, diving ducks, loons, osprey, eagles, herons, grebes, and kingfishers can signal prey fish or small trout. I also watch the surface of the water for activity. Surface slaps are often trout or other fish keying in on duns. A porpoising trout will make me think of pupae just below the surface, and dimples might be trout or other fish sipping midges and spinners. I generally do not tie on a pattern to imitate the insects, but I will consider what size trout I am looking at and where the bigger ones might be in relation to them. I find that where there are little trout, no big trout are present; thus, identifying the location of smaller trout will help me to find the ones I am after.

Schooling

Out on the water we often observe schools of prey fish. Conventional angling strategy suggests that we fish the schools. But schooling has many functions for the prey fish, and an understanding of the different schooling formations is critical to estimating the trout's position in relation to the prey and to putting the fly in the right zone. Just casting to a school doesn't guarantee that a big trout will see your fly.

The following illustrations show the structure of schools under different scenarios. Recognizing them may give you an indication of the resting or active state of the trout and where the trout may be holding when they are active.

Traveling: Typical of when prey fish migrate to and from feeding and resting zones.

All-around coverage: The fish are slightly mobile and turned in different directions, which provides all-around coverage. This is typical of resting prey fish.

Defense: The school's defense as a unit displays maximum maneuverability to elude a predator. Note the positions of the trout; they are outside the school.

Feeding. The school has broken up to feed on zooplankton or other small aquatic invertebrates. This is often characterized by dimpling in the film when the food source is on or near the surface.

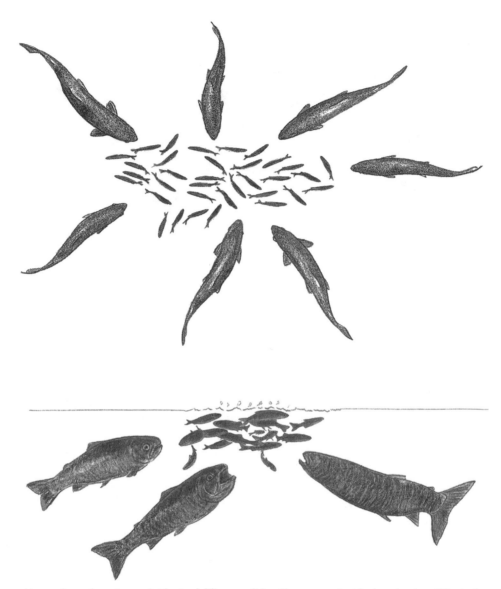

Trapped by predators (top view and side view): The prey fish will try to stay inside the school until limited oxygen forces them to the outside. The key to fishing for trout attacking schooling prey fish is to target the periphery of the school. These prey fish will be breaking water in a slow globular side-to-side movement. To reach these trout with your fly you will need to have your fly line penetrate to the bottom and outside of the school. Sometimes the school can be a few feet deep and it will take some patience. If you start your retrieve too early, your fly will be hidden from the trout in the school. If the school is moving rapidly, try a sink-tip fly line. The splash is probably not going to alarm the frenzied trout.

CHAPTER 6
NORTH AMERICA'S BEST BIG TROUT WATERS

For everything there is a season, and a time for every matter under heaven.
Ecclesiastes 3:1

I have fished on many waters over the years and been told too many times that I should have been there the previous week or month when the fish were heavily feeding or concentrated in places that I could reach them. While trout feed in daily rhythms, they may not be accessible to anglers throughout the year. Stillwaters may be in a spring turnover or migrating trout have not yet come into the river or a river's water flow may be too high and murky from a seasonal run-off to fish or the fishing season may be closed.

In the previous chapters, the types of waters that have big trout were identified and feeding/migrating patterns for a select few were discussed. The next step is to identify what periods will provide us with the greatest chance of catching these trout. The reasons are varied and based on environmental conditions, trout behavior, and the activity levels of insects, crustaceans, and prey fish. There is also what I call "the human factor." I once asked a steelhead guide on a heavily fished river: "What are the two best days of the year to catch a steelhead?" "That's easy," he responded. "Christmas, because everyone is home with their kids and the pressure is off the fish." He even offered to guide me on Christmas Day. I booked him on Thanksgiving—the second best day.

Waters may have more than one peak period. During the course of researching this book, I interviewed over a hundred guides, outfitters, fishery biologists, and local experts about the prime periods to fish their home waters. Often two knowledgeable anglers will have different periods when they consider a water to be at its peak. I included both and the reasons supporting their views. I also rechecked most of the guide and outfitter sources with a third party.

Considering that few of the guides, with the exclusion of the remote fishing camps, actually live on these waters and have the opportunity to fish them every day, there are probably more windows of opportunity to be found. I surveyed many other waters that are not included in this book due to the number of pages they would take up. I have put many of them on my Website at www.bigtroutbook.com. I did not personally meet all of the guides and outfitters noted with each entry and do not necessarily recommend them. I also do not advocate some of the ones that I listed. I have a separate list on my website for the ones I have experience with and do recommend. This information was not included in this book as phone numbers and email addresses often change. The Internet is a better medium for these rapidly changing sources of information.

I have included the nearest town and GPS coordinates for most of the big trout waters. The location of the town will help you to find a place to stay for the night. The GPS coordinates are much more useful. They can help you to actually find your launching point, the stretch of river to fish, or the parking lot to access them. Another use of the GPS data is to help you determine the sunrise/set and moonrise/set data for your targeted destination. You can plug the GPS coordinates into the U.S. Naval Observatory website, and download information for the days you intend to fish. The U.S. Naval Observatory data does not cover Canada, but you can use the longitude figure to position a point on the U.S. border that will get you fairly close.

Stillwaters

Big trout anglers will improve their success on western stillwaters if they can pinpoint the periods of the year that fish are concentrating. Opportune periods when the trout are concentrated are when they are drawn to food sources and hold over springs and at the mouths of tributaries during the hot summer months. Other periods are when they are preparing to ascend a river or creek to spawn or feed, or at ice-out when the trout go on feeding binges after a lean winter. Whatever the factors may be, research what they are for the targeted body of water and try to determine the periods when they affect the trout.

The sizes and numbers of trout in many stillwaters tend to be cyclical, based on changes in water levels and temperatures, populations of trout, and the availability of food. Always check with a local contact when planning your trip. There are hundreds of other stillwaters in North America that have a few big trout that meet my standard, but the ones listed here may be the most stable.

Some of these stillwaters are huge bodies of water. Lake Michigan is a good example. I do not provide exact places to fish this lake as the brown trout travel along the shorelines of the lake. Again, check with a local shop or outfitter for the latest conditions. I have included a local contact for most of the waters.

During the course of writing this book I did not have the opportunity to research the many reservoirs that feed the cities on the east coast. Anglers often fish the tailwaters of these reservoirs and a few cover the larger bodies of water. Most of the hypotheses and techniques that I discuss for oligotrophic and mesotrophic stillwaters will apply to catching brown trout in these reservoirs. The waters may not be well-known for big trout, but one should not conclude that they are not present. Start your research by identifying the type of trout in the lake and what type of prey fish are there. Then, study the stillwaters in this chapter for analogies that you can apply to them.

Assinica Lake/Broadback River
(Assinica Preserve, Quebec—50 degrees, 54′30″ North, 74 degrees, 37′10″ West)
The Broadback River is rather short, and anglers should consider both Assinica Lake and the river, as one wouldn't travel here to fish just the river. Some large brook trout hold in the deeper pools throughout the summer, although the river is basically a hatchery for small trout and a place where they can avoid the big pike in the lake. The mouths of the tributary streams fish well at ice-out (around the first week of June) when the big brook trout feed on the eggs of spawning suckers. The lake fishes well throughout the short summer from the middle of June until the middle of August. (Bob White, Square Tail Lodge)

Awesome Lake (Labrador)
This high elevation lake is ice-free about the end of June and fishing is consistent throughout July into the middle of August. The 25-mile English River exits Awesome Lake, providing excellent river angling in numerous pools. The only resource in this entire watershed is resident brook trout that commonly grow to over four pounds by feeding on smaller brook trout. (Len Rich, Awesome Lake Lodge)

Bear Lake
(Garden City, Utah—N 39 degrees 38.485'/W 106 degrees 24.895')
During the month of December the Bonneville whitefish come into the shallows to spawn and this is the time to catch the largest Bonneville cutthroats (Bear Lake stock). Fish in the 8- to 12-pound class are commonly caught. Other opportune times are during the month of January into the second week of February when the cutthroats prey on Bonneville ciscoes in shallow waters, and then again during the months of May, June, and July when some of the cutthroats are spawning and their co-horts prey on their eggs. Anglers target the river mouths during this period. Repeat spawning for Bear Lake cutthroats is rare (less than 4 percent), so these anglers are not targeting spawning fish. (Jim Stone, Bear River Basin Outfitters)

Big Minipi Lake (Labrador)
Big brook trout may be best taken from the middle of June until the middle part of August. These trout are primarily invertebrate feeders. (Jack Cooper, Cooper's Minipi Camps)

Crane Prairie Reservoir
(Sun River, Oregon—N 43 degrees 47'53"/W 121 degrees 45'29")
July through August offers great fishing over springs and in the river channels where the water is cooler. (Bob Gaviglio, Sun River Fly Shop) The primary foods for the big trout are three-spined sticklebacks and the nymph forms of insects such as large dragonflies and damselflies. (Steve Marx, Oregon Department of Fish and Wildlife)

Davis Lake
(Sun River, Oregon—N 43 degrees 35'46.5"/W 121 degrees 50'9.7")
Fish in the Odell Creek Channel and near the lava flow when the ice and roads clear around April 1, and in the lava flow area from late September into early October as the rainbows fatten up for winter. These are native redbands that originate from Odell-Davis Lake with a small number of Upper Klamath Lake redband strain. Their primary food source is tui chubs. (Bob Gaviglio, Sun River Fly Shop)

Dragon Lake
(Quesnel, British Columbia—N 52 degrees 55.93/W 122 degrees 24.87)
The Premier and Blackwater strains of rainbows feed best on *Chironomidae* hatches after ice-out during the first three weeks of April, and during the end of September into early October when the *Chi-*

ronomidae become active again and the trout feed on anything to bide them over the winter. (Doug Brautigan, Cariboo Fly and Tackle)

Duck Lake
(Babb, Montana—N 48 degrees 51.54′/W 113 degrees 21.01″)

Kipp Lake
(Browning, Montana—N 48 degrees 33.72′/W 112 degrees 50.84′)

Mission Lake
(Browning, Montana—N 48 degrees 33.857′/W 112 degrees 38.027′)

Mitten Lake
(Heart Butte, Montana—N 48 degrees 18.237′/W 112 degrees 59.202′)
Fish at ice-out at the end of April (lasting until the end of May) when the fish congregate into a fake spawn and then again during the latter part of October when the water temperatures become cooler and more conducive to active feeding. During both periods the weed growth is down, which makes it easier to land the big rainbows. (Joe Kipp, Montana Star Outfitters)
For the brown trout, fish during the end of September into early October when they go into a fake spawn. Both the rainbows and browns primarily feed on scuds. (Dave Parsons, Cutbank Creek Outfitters)

East Lake
(La Pine, Oregon—N 43 degrees, 43′54.2″/W 121 degrees, 11′47.1″)

Paulina Lake
(La Pine, Oregon—N 43 degrees, 42′45.9″/W 121 degrees, 16′25.3″)
Both lakes have small populations of rainbow trout, but the bigger fish are the browns. In Paulina, the browns feed on an abundance of kokanee and tui chubs. In East Lake, the tui chubs are their primary food source. In both lakes the browns also feed on stocked rainbow trout when available. Both lakes also have a thermocline. (Steve Marx, Oregon Department of Fish and Wildlife)
The best time to fish for the big browns is at ice-out, which occurs some time around Memorial Day weekend, depending on the weather; then again in late September into October when the warm summer water temperatures recede and they move into shallower waters. The trout become territorial and aggressive as they approach their spawning period and cruise the shoreline. East Lake closes on the last day of October. (Bob Gaviglio, Sun River Fly Shop)

Eagle Lake (Labrador)
Eagle Lake lies at the top of the world-famous Eagle River, some 60 miles to the southwest of Goose Bay. It thaws in late May, making June and July prime for big brook trout fishing. Prolific hatches of mayflies, stoneflies, and caddis provide an abundant food source throughout the summer months. (Len Rich, Eagle Lake Lodge)

Eutsuk Lake

(Richmond, British Columbia—53.15 degrees N/126.30 degrees W)

Fish during the month of June when the large late-maturing rainbow trout tend to hold closer to the surface and feed heavily after their spawn. (Todd McPherson, Eutsuk Lake Lodge)

Fir Lake

(Williams Lake, British Columbia)

Fish the middle two weeks of June when the fish feed heavily on *Chironomidae, Callibaetis,* and caddis hatches. (Brian Chan, co-author of *Morris & Chan on Fly Fishing Trout Lakes*)

Forest Lake

(Williams Lake, British Columbia—52 degrees 17.70 N/122 degrees 02.85 west)

Fish the middle two weeks of June when the Quensel Lake-strain rainbows feed heavily on *Chironomidae, Callibaetis,* and caddis hatches. (Brian Chan, co-author of *Morris & Chan on Fly Fishing Trout Lakes*)

There are few private pay-to-play lakes in North America where there are big trout that are not fed or planted when they are already large. Bueker Lake at Grindstone Lakes in Oregon is one of the few that meets the big trout standard. The managers achieve trout that go over 10 pounds by limiting the numbers of trout in this pond.

Grindstone Lakes
(Paulina, Oregon—N 44 degrees 8.03′/W 119 degrees 57.68′)
Fish during the month of May as the lakes start heating up into the low 60s and the *Chironomidae* and *Callibaetis* hatches are at their peak. Bueker Lake, on this private ranch, is the place to take the largest rainbows. Some pass the 11-pound mark. There are other lakes on the ranch where anglers can catch larger numbers of smaller trout. At the time of this writing, Bueker Lake was washed out; however, the managers are developing another trophy trout lake at the ranch. (Bill Beardsley, Grindstone Lakes)

Heart Lake
(West Yellowstone, Montana)
Fish the last two weeks of July and the first week in August for cutthroats in this Yellowstone National Park backcountry lake. (Craig Mathews, Blue Ribbon Flies)

Hebgen Lake
(West Yellowstone, Montana—N 44 degrees 48.24′/W 111 degrees 13.27′)
Hebgen Lake fishes well for big browns cruising the shoreline as the ice comes off (early May) and fishing lasts until the end of the spring turnover (first week of June). Big browns are also available in the fall as they stage to run up the Madison River to spawn. This highly productive water has brown trout up to 15 pounds. The major prey fish for the big trout is the Utah chub. Whitefish are also available to the trout. (Pat Byroth, Montana Department of Fish, Wildlife and Parks and Craig Mathews, Blue Ribbon Flies)

Henry's Lake
(West Yellowstone, Montana—N 44 degrees 40.08′/W 111 degrees 23.49′)
The big cutbows are most readily caught from the last weekend in May until the second weekend in June when the water is just starting to warm, vegetation is still down, and the fish are often feeding near the shorelines. For the big brook trout, focus on the mouths of the tributaries where these fish start to congregate. (Jeff Dillon, Idaho Department of Fish and Game and Craig Mathews, Blue Ribbon Flies)

Island Lake
(Logan Lake, British Columbia—50 degrees 10.18 north/120 degrees 29.65 west)
Fish during the middle of June when the triploid rainbows are getting stirred up by the heavy *Chironomidae* hatches and then again during the last two weeks in September when they chase water boatmen on the surface. (Steve Jennings, Kamloops Fly Shop)
Fish between ice-out during the middle to end of May and just before the lake turns over; then again just before the lake ices up at the end of September. There is also a major caddis hatch during the middle of June that stretches into early July that stirs the fish up. (Carlos Tallent, Gone Fishing with Carlos)

Island Park Reservoir

(Ashton, Idaho—N 44 degrees 25.21'/W 111 degrees 29.06)

The best times are between July 1 and 20. During this period the damsels are emerging and they bring larger trout to the surface near the shorelines. (Craig Mathews, Blue Ribbon Flies)

From late May until the middle of June, the rainbows congregate and cruise along the shoreline on the south side of the west end, called the "fingers." These rainbow trout primarily feed on aquatic invertebrates. (Jeff Dillon, Idaho Department of Fish and Game)

Kootenay Lake

(Balfour, British Columbia—N 49 degrees 37.46/W 116 degrees 57.61)

The Gerrard-strain rainbows in Kootenay Lake prefer water temperatures about 50 degrees Fahrenheit. These conditions occur on the surface around the first week of December and last until the middle of April. The hottest period is usually during the first two weeks of January. Another period is from the middle of April to the end of May in areas where there is a lot of run-off from feeder creeks and rivers that push black ants out into the lake. Kootenay Lake also has an introduced rainbow trout from Penask Lake, B.C. This smaller trout grows up to ten pounds and is most efficiently caught in the west arm of the lake during June when the insect hatches are most prolific. (Dale Williams, Screaming Reel Fly and Tackle/Frank van Neer, East Shore Charters)

Lac Des Roches

(Kamloops, British Columbia—51 degrees 30.27 north/120 degrees 36.78 west)

The Gerrard and Blackwater redband trout become active at ice-out on about the 10th of May and during a strong *Chironomidae* hatch, which peaks about the first week of June. The lake ices up just before Christmas and the fishing can be hot at that time, as well. The last two weeks in June and the first two weeks in July are good for big damselfly hatches. (Carlos Tallent, Gone Fishing with Carlos)

The last two weeks in June and the first two weeks in July for the *Callibaetis* mayfly hatch. (Steve Jennings, Kamloops Fly Shop)

Lake Anne Marie (Minipi, Labrador)

Big brook trout can best be taken from the middle of June until the middle part of August. These trout are primarily invertebrate feeders. (Jack Cooper, Cooper's Minipi Camps)

Lake Michigan

(Shorelines near all of the tributaries in the state of Michigan)

Fish the first three weeks in May when the big brown trout feed on prey fish in the shallows. This is just after ice-out and the first pulses of the lake's production are being stimulated in this region. (Kelly Galloup, The Troutsman Fly Shop/co-author of *Modern Streamers for Trophy Trout*)

Lake Nipigon (Nipigon, Ontario)
The best time to fish this lake would be the last three weeks of June and the last week in August. The first period has optimal water temperatures (52 degrees Fahrenheit) for the brook trout, and the second has them becoming more aggressive and territorial just prior to spawning. (Scott Earl Smith, author of *Ontario Blue-Ribbon Fly Fishing Guide*)

Lake Pend Oreille
(Hope, Idaho—N 48 degrees, 13.770'/W 116 degrees, 16.682')
The best time to catch the big Gerrard-strain rainbows, locally called "kams," is from the second week in October when the surface water temperature is about 56 degrees until the second week in November when it drops to 42 degrees. Most of the rainbows over 25 pounds are caught during this period and 80 percent of the big rainbows are caught within 10 days of Halloween. Most people book this time a year in advance. From March 1 until the second week of April is another good period, as the trout start staging to spawn at the mouths of the Clark Fork and Pack Rivers. (Ed Dickson, Diamond Charters)

Lake Superior Tributaries (Nipigon, Ontario)
The best timing for coaster brook trout (migratory brook trout that live in Lake Superior and spawn in tributary streams) is during the first three weeks in June when the lake hovers around 52 degrees. (Scott Earl Smith, author of *Ontario Blue-Ribbon Fly Fishing Guide*)

Little Shuswap (British Columbia)
During the first two weeks in June the sockeye smolts come out of the Adams River into the lake and then head into the Little River on their way to the ocean. At this time, small sockeye patterns can be particularly effective near the mouth of the Adams River. (Steve Jennings, Kamloops Fly Shop)

Lower Pond (Witless Bay, New Brunswick)
Find tidal water, sea-run brown trout at ice-out, some time during the month of April and continuing for about a month. (Scott Chafe/Ian Gall, Sea Run Outfitters)

Mistissini Lake (Mistissini, Quebec)
Following ice-out during the last week of May through the month of June when the big brook trout go on the feed in shallow waters. Again during the last week in August and the first week in September when the brook trout ascend the rivers to spawn. (Emily Shecapio, Camp Louis Joliet and Mike Tremblay, Osprey Excursions)

Omak Lake
(Omak, Washington—N 48 degrees 19.31'/W 119 degrees 25.83')
Fish the north end of the lake from early February until the end of the month for concentrating pre-spawn Lahontan cutthroat trout. (Dan Beardsle, IGFA world record-holder).

Ian Forbes playing a big cutthroat trout on one of the Powell Forest Lakes in British Columbia. The Powell Forest Lakes fish best at post-spawn in April. The main food items for these fish are three-spined sticklebacks and kokanee.

Osprey Lake
(Labrador—N 52 degrees 45.179'W 58 degrees 35.011)
Osprey and nearby hike-in lakes have ideal water temperatures for feeding and growth from the middle of June until the middle of August. Brook trout in the 8-pound class are taken on mayfly, caddis, lemming, and fish imitations. (Jeff Lewis, Osprey Lake Lodge)

Lake Ontario
(Shorelines near all of the tributaries)
Fish from the middle of April into early May as the shallows near the shore warm and in early October into November near the mouths of the tributaries as the fish position themselves to make their spawning run. (Rick Kustich, Oak Orchard Fly Shop)

The Powell Forest Lakes (Powell River, British Columbia)
Nanton
Ireland
Dodd
Inland
Khartoum

Lois

These lakes fish best during the month of April when the lake-resident cutthroat (of coastal origin) have just completed spawning. They feed heavily on sticklebacks and kokanee. Another opportune period is from the middle of October until the middle of November when the cutthroats are keying in on spawning kokanee and boosting up stores for the winter. The larger trout will be caught at this time. (Karl Bruhn, author of *Fly Fishing British Columbia*)

Pyramid Lake

(Reno, Nevada—N 39 degrees, 56′4.4″/W 119 degrees, 35′4.6″)

There are two key periods to take a Lahontan cutthroat trout. The first is from late February until the second week in April when they are cruising the shoreline for spawning areas. The second period is from the second week of November to the second week in December. The older fall spawners generally run larger than the first year spring ones. The main prey fish for Pyramid Lake cutthroat is the tui chub. These trout also feed on aquatic invertebrates. (Terry Barron, Reno Fly Shop and author of *Terry Barron's No-Nonsense Guide to Fly Fishing Pyramid Lake*)

Quake Lake

(West Yellowstone, Montana—N 44 degrees 50.05′/W 111 degrees 25.45′)

Quake fishes best for big browns cruising the shoreline on the northeast shore from the old boat launch up to the mouth of Beaver Creek when the ice comes off (early May) and lasts until the end of the spring turnover (first week of June). Earthquake has a great deal of standing timber and sees little angling pressure. (Craig Mathews, Blue Ribbon Flies)

An ideal time and place for the big browns is at the inlet of the Madison River from the early part of October into November when they are preparing to spawn. The major prey fish for the big trout is the Utah chub. Whitefish are also available. (Pat Byroth, Montana Department of Fish, Wildlife and Parks)

Quesnel Lake

(Horsefly, British Columbia—52 degrees 30.94 north/121 degrees 02.25 west)

During the month of April trout move through the shallows in the Wasco Bay area to spawn. In the first two weeks of July the big Quensel strain redbands will feed on sockeye moving out of the Mitchell River. Try again over the month of September when the big rainbows are congregating near the mouth of the Mitchell River to feed on chinook and sockeye eggs. (Pete Carlson, Elysia Resort)

Fish early to mid-October when the rainbows are keying in on kokanee holding on the shoals. (Bob Dollighan, B.C. Ministry of the Environment)

Sheridan Lake

(Lone Butte, British Columbia—51 degrees 32.54/120 degrees 54.26)

Fish during the middle two weeks of June when the rainbows move over the shoals to feed on three concurrent emergences of *Chironomidae, Callibaetis,* and caddis. The caddis (a.k.a. "Traveling Sedge") is a size 6, 2x-long fished dry on the surface. (Brian Chan)

This late-maturing 13½-pound rainbow was caught in Quesnel Lake, British Columbia. The rainbows in this lake go into the 20-pound class. Quesnel is probably the most underfished big trout fishery in North America. There are also a number of smaller lakes near Quesnel with big trout that are best fished for with a pontoon craft or small pram. (Photo courtesy of Ian Chesterton.)

Try the last two weeks in June and the first two weeks in July for the *Callibaetis* mayfly hatch. (Steve Jennings, Kamloops Fly Shop)

For rainbow trout, ice-out late April until about May 24th and then again late June until about the 15th of July when major hatches come off. Another period is from about September 15 until November 1 when the big rainbows concentrate in the shoal areas. (Bob Leith, Sheridan Lake Resort)

Shuswap Lake (Sorrento, British Columbia)
Fish during the middle two weeks of July when the sockeye and chinook smolts are moving to the Little Red River from Shuswap Lake, and again during the month of September when the big rainbows congregate near the mouth of the Little Red River to feed on chinook and sockeye eggs. (Brian Chan, co-author of *Morris & Chan on Fly Fishing Trout Lakes*)

Spinney Reservoir
(Hartsel, Colorado—N 38 degrees 59.10/W 105 degrees 39.68)

Eleven Mile Reservoir
(Hartsel, Colorado—N 38 degrees 56.06′/W 105 degrees 30.11)

Both reservoirs fish well for big rainbows and cutthroats when the trout look for spawning grounds along the shoreline. Eleven Mile Reservoir fishes best from the end of March into the first two weeks of April, and Spinney at ice-out from the middle of May for about two weeks. (Rick Typher, Denver Angler)

Stump Lake
(Quilchena, British Columbia—50 degrees 22.58 north/120 degrees 20.99 west)
The best fishing is at the north and south ends of the lake during the last two weeks of May when the *Chironomidae* hatches are at full bloom, and then again during the last two weeks in June and into the first two weeks in July as the damselflies are migrating. Beware of heavy winds that make for unsafe fishing in float tubes, pontoon boats, and small prams. (Steve Jennings, Kamloops Fly Shop)

Upper Klamath Lake
(Ft. Klamath, Oregon—N42 degrees, 98', 20.9"/W 122 degrees, 5'18")
Fish near the mouths of the creeks and over springs in the Outer Banks in the Pelican Bay area from the middle of July into the third week of August when the big trout gravitate towards cooler oxygenated water. Try again at the mouth of the Wood and Williamson (at adjacent Agency Lake) Rivers during the latter two weeks in August. (Denny Rickards, Crystal Creek Anglers/author of *Fly Fishing Stillwaters for Trophy Trout*)

Wickiup Reservoir
(Sun River, Oregon—N43 degrees, 40'42"/W 121 degrees, 43'27")
Fish early in the season from the fourth Saturday in April through the month of May when big browns move into shallow water near the dam. Many will hold there through the summer. Try again in the Sheep Bridge area during the last two weeks of August when the kokanee come up to spawn. The brown trout feed on sticklebacks and juvenile kokanee (3 to 5 inches long). (Bob Gaviglio, Sun River Fly Shop)

Tailwaters

When I first started researching this book I assumed that most of the big trout tailwater fisheries were in the West, namely the Green, Colorado, Beaverhead, San Juan River, and Kootenay. I also figured on the Upper Connecticut and Androscoggin Rivers in New Hampshire and the Delaware in New York. After researching them further through interviews with fishery biologists and guides, I found that there are few big trout (that meet the standard of this book) in these waters. It takes a great deal of easy food or large food items to grow big trout and few tailwaters have them.

There are two primary food groups for big trout tailwaters. For a few of the Colorado tailwaters it is the opossum shrimp coming from the reservoirs. The farther from the dam, the

Western stillwater guru Denny Rickards with a big redband rainbow trout on his home water—Upper Klamath Lake. Denny typically fishes this lake in the latter part of the summer when the trout hold around springs and at the mouths of creeks and rivers entering the lake.

smaller the trout become, due to the smaller numbers of this food item. For the others, sculpins, crayfish, and stocked trout are the main courses.

Although many of the famous tailwaters are not in the same class as the ones I list in terms of big trout, they are mostly outstanding trout fisheries. For more information on the New Hampshire waters I recommend Hickoff and Plumley's *Flyfisher's Guide to Northern New England.*

Blue River

(Silverthorne, Colorado—N 39 degrees, 37′31.2″/W 106 degrees, 3′56.7″)

Fish here in early June when the post-run-off is at its peak and larger numbers of opossum shrimp are in the river. The stronger flow pushes the fish down from below the restricted area at the base of the dam and spreads them throughout the upper river. During late September, the reservoir turns over and the opossum shrimp come down heavily again. The optimum flow for the Blue is around 200 cfs. (Trapper Rudd, Cutthroat Anglers)

Frying Pan River

(Basalt, Colorado—N 39 degrees, 21′49.7″/W 106 degrees, 49′20.0″)

Fish in early April to the middle of March when the rainbows are spawning, in a post-spawn mode, and in accessible areas of the river. The big brown trout are often taken during the first two weeks in December for the same reasons. (Tim Heng, Taylor Creek Fly Shop)

Little Red River

(Heber Springs, Arkansas—N 35 degrees 30.62′/W 91 degrees 59.68′)

Target the middle of October until the middle of December when the big brown trout move away from the mats of vegetation to spawn on the shoals below the dam. (Tom Bly, Arkansas Game and Fish Commission)

Nipigon River (Nipigon, Ontario)

Fish during the last two weeks in June when the water reaches about 52 degrees Fahrenheit and the fish become active. The primary food sources for the brook trout are mottled and slimy sculpins. (Scott Earl Smith, author of *Ontario Blue-Ribbon Fly Fishing Guide*)

Taylor River

(Crested Butte, Colorado—N 38 degrees, 48′52.2″/W 106 degrees, 36′, 43.7″)

The last week in April and the first two weeks in May offer the greatest opportunity to catch a monster rainbow on the Taylor River. The reservoir flows are increased and the fish, with more room, seem to throw caution to the wind. The spawning rainbows also become more aggressive and some fresh, unpressured spawners will move up from the private waters downstream. Look for browns in November when they move into their spawning mode and the opossum shrimp are drawn from the reservoir in heavy numbers. The optimum flow is between 300 and 500 cfs. (Rod Cesario, Dragonfly Anglers)

White River

(Mountain Home, Arkansas—N 36 degrees, 21.293′/W 92 degrees, 35.662′)

Norfolk River

(Mountain Home, Arkansas—N 36 degrees, 14.818′/W 92 degrees, 14.593′)

In a typical winter, threadfin shad wash through Bull Shoals and Norfolk Dams from around January 1 until the beginning of April. The big trout feed almost exclusively on the shad through this period. However, during last two weeks of March the volume of shad starts to slow down and the bigger fish become more desperate and susceptible to anglers. The fishing is usually better when the water is rising, as the shad are just being pushed through the dams, and the fish are hungry. During high water, or receding flows, the big trout may be full. The optimum flows for the White are between 4,000 to 6,000 cfs and between 1,000 to 2,000 cfs on the Norfolk. Dam flow information can be found by calling 870-431-5311. Another time to take the biggest browns in these Ozark tailwaters is from the end of September until the middle part of December when these fish move up below the dams and into the tributaries to spawn. The runs are from the middle part of October until early November. A section of the White River is closed just below the dam for spawners from November 1 until February 1. Dry Run Creek below the dam at the Norfolk is open during the month of October to kids ages 16 years and under. This is prime spawning area for big browns. (Dale Fulton, Blue Ribbon Flies/Fulton's Lodge)

Migratory Trout Rivers

A number of years ago while I was on a business trip near Racine, Wisconsin, I decided to wet my line for an evening. A local tackle shop told me that the Root River had been hot for browns and I would have my best chances there. Upon arrival at the river I found it to be de-

void of anglers and fish. I learned my lesson, and since then I have been cautious about get-ting the right information and making sure I'm there at the peak of the runs. When you hear about big trout in rivers, the line "You should have been here . . . " is often followed by ". . . when the fish came up to spawn."

When trout leave lakes or the salt, their movements can be predictable, and the farther up the fish go, the narrower the rivers become—and the trout more concentrated. Few anglers catch steelhead, Pacific, or Atlantic salmon in fresh water during periods other than when they are migrating to spawn. Many anglers fail to target browns, cutthroat, and brook trout during their migrations. Some states prohibit angling for trout during the spawning period. The reason is clear: Spawning migrations are one of the periods when trout are most vulner-able to anglers. I am not advocating fishing for trout on their spawning beds. I have seen people fish this way, and this book does not cover those techniques. I am angling for trout on the way to their spawning beds. There is a difference.

Spawning migrations are not the only periods when trout ascend rivers. Cooler and more oxygenated waters are also draws for some migrating trout. In a number of British Columbia and Alaskan rivers the rainbow trout migrate up into rivers from lakes to feed on the salmon eggs and/or overwinter.

Alagnak River (Katmai National Park, Arkansas)
Fish the last two weeks in September when double-digit rainbows migrate into the upper river to feed on the sockeye eggs and overwinter in the river from Kukaklek and Nanvianuk Lakes. (Brett Chaffin, Katmai Lodge)

Babine River (Kispiox, British Columbia)
Big rainbows reside in Lake Babine and move into the river to feed. Important feeding periods are the last ten days in May and the first week of June when they are keying in on salmon fry, the last ten days in June and the first ten days in July during the height of the mayfly and stonefly hatches and

mid-September into mid-October when the sockeye and coho eggs are available. (Pierce Klegg, Babine Norlakes Lodge)

Betsie River
(Karlin, Michigan—N 44 degrees 34.68'/W 85 degrees 46.99')

Manistee River
(Manistee, Michigan—N 44 degrees 14.94'/W 86 degrees 18.99')

Pere Marquette River
(Baldwin, Michigan—N 43 degrees 53.96'/W 85 degrees 51.09')
Try from the middle of October until the middle of November when the brown trout migrate up the rivers to spawn. (Kelly Galloup, The Troutsman/co-author of *Modern Streamers for Trophy Trout*)

Brooks River
(Katmai National Park, Arkansas—N 58 degrees 33.23'/W 155 degrees 46.75')
Fish during the middle part of September into early October when rainbows in the 10- to 12-pound class migrate up from Naknek Lake to feed on sockeye eggs. This is a chance for anglers to wade for big migrating rainbows in classic fly water. (Pete Raynor, Kulik Lodge)

Chilko River (Alexis Creek, British Columbia)
Horsefly River (Horsefly, British Columbia)
Fish during the month of July when the golden stoneflies come off and the big trout come out of the lakes to feed on them, and during the months of September and October when the adult sockeye are moving up to spawn and the rainbows feed on their eggs. (Ian Forbes)

Connetquot River at the Connetquot River State Park
(Oakdale, New York—40 degrees, 44.98 north and 73 degrees, 09.05 degrees west)

Nisseaquogue River at Caleb Smith State Park
(Smithtown, New York—40 degrees, 51.12 north, 73 degrees, 12.50 west)
For big rainbows, try February and March when they move up from the Great South Bay to spawn. The browns are best from the middle of September into the middle of October after heavy rainfalls. The largest brook trout move early to mid-October. The Connetquot River State Park closes to the public after October 1 with the state trout-fishing season, but private bookings can be made for the section of river within the park. The Nisseaquogue receives all of its brook and rainbow trout, and many of its browns, from the Connetquot. (Gil Bergen, Connetquot River State Park)

Credit River (Georgetown, Ontario)
Fish during the last week in October and the first two weeks in November as the browns come up the river to spawn. (Scott Earl Smith, author of *Ontario Blue-Ribbon Fly Fishing Guide*)

The Connetquot River on Long Island, New York is an outstanding brook, brown, and rainbow trout fishery. The size and number of fish in the runs of each species rival those of the best rivers in the world. What is most extraordinary about this fishery is that it is in a heavily populated suburban community less than 50 miles from New York City. The success of this fishery is largely a result of the foresight of the original owners and Park Manager Gil Bergen.

Ganaraska River (Port Hope, Ontario)
Fish during the last week in October and the first two weeks in November as the browns come up the river to spawn. (Scott Earl Smith, author of *Ontario Blue-Ribbon Fly Fishing Guide*)

Kewaunee River
(Kewaunee, Wisconsin—N 44 degrees 27.51′/W 87 degrees 29.94′)

Menominee River
(Marinette, Wisconscin—N 45 degrees 6.24′/W 87 degrees 37.54′)

Root River
(Racine, Wisconscin—N 42 degrees 43.779′/W 87 degrees 46.990′)
Seeforellen brown trout arrive in these rivers from Lake Michigan during the latter part of October. The prime fishing lasts into the first two weeks of November. The Menominee attracts and sustains the older of these fish and can have the largest. (Steven Fajfer, Wisconsin Department of Natural Resources)

Rick Typher from the Denver Angler with a nine-pound-plus cutthroat trout taken from the South Platte. (Rick Typher photo)

Kvichak River
(Katmai National Park, Arkansas—N 59 degrees 17.858′/W 155 degrees 59.091′)
Fish the first three weeks of September when the big rainbows come out of Lake Iliamna to feed on the spawning sockeye eggs and flesh and overwinter in the river where they will spawn in the spring. (Alaskan Sportsman's Lodge and Jack Holman, No See Um Lodge)

Mitchell River (Horsefly, British Columbia)
Fish from early September to mid-October when the sockeye enter the river to spawn and the big rainbows come out of Quesnel Lake to feed on them. Also, try from late March through April when the Quesnel Lake rainbows are spawning. (Brian Chan, B.C. Ministry of the Environment)

Naknek River
(Katmai National Park, Arkansas—N 58 degrees 38.9′/W 156 degrees 27.1′)
Angling for the big rainbow trout starts in late August and gets better until freeze-up. The best window to catch the largest trout in the crystal-clear Naknek River would be late September into the second week of October. The larger rainbows from Naknek Lake have entered the river by this time to feed on the salmon eggs and overwinter until they spawn in the spring. (Dan Dunaway, Alaska Fish and Game; Lodging contact: Diedre and Patrick O'Neill, Rainbow Bend Cabin & Boat Rentals; Outfitter contact: Scott Ruprecht, Sportfishing Worldwide)

Oak Orchard Creek and nearby Lake Ontario tributaries
(Albion, New York—N 43 degrees 16.47'/W 78 degrees 19.76')

Oswego River
(Oswego, New York—N 43 degrees 22.05/W 76 degrees 26.18')
Fish during the last week in October and the first two weeks in November as the browns come up the river to spawn. Oak Orchard Creek is a tailwater with a regular flow, but the nearby creeks are dependent on seasonal rainfall and/or draining from Erie Canal. (Rick Kustich, Oak Orchard Fly Shop/co-author of *Fly Fishing for Great Lakes Steelhead*)

South Platte Between Eleven Mile Reservoir and Spinney Reservoir
(Hartsel, Colorado—N 38 degrees 58.19'/W 105 degrees 36.40')
The prime time to catch big cutthroats is when they begin their spawning run, from early to mid-March. (Rick Typher, Denver Angler)

North and South Rivers
(St. John's, New Brunswick)
Fish for tidal water sea-run brown trout at ice-out during the months of March and April and again in the latter part of September into early October. (Paul Smith, guide)

Williamson River
(Chiloquin, Oregon—N 42 degrees, 31'26.9"/W 121 degrees, 53'5.7")
The Upper Klamath Lake redband rainbows move into the river from late August into the end of September 1, triggered by the warming of the lake and spawning urges. (Steve Hilbert, Lonesome Duck)

CHAPTER 7

BE FLEXIBLE WITH YOUR FISHING TECHNIQUES AND FLY SELECTION

You have to find a strategy that works and then work the strategy.
Keith Snyder, Lake Pend Oreille guide

One of the slide programs I present to fishing clubs and clinics, *Stillwater Trophy Trout Tactics,* is just about catching big fish. There is no discussion of dry flies or a detailed look at hatches. I recommend avoiding small fish if big trout are your game. This often means ignoring rising trout—a difficult thing for most fly fishers to do. Casting a dry fly to rising trout on a picturesque river is a rewarding experience and can be productive. There are certainly places where trout feed on bugs that appear in numbers sufficient to bring large trout to the surface, such as during the Green Drake hatches on the Labrador brook trout lakes or the super caddis hatches (Traveling Sedge) on the Cariboo Lakes in British Columbia. But if you want to take big trout consistently, plan to carry a fly box with large streamer patterns.

Matching the Hatch

Breaking away from the dry fly rage is often difficult to do. Angling literature, movies, and Madison Avenue bombard us with images of the well-clad angler casting a mayfly imitation on a mountain stream. Sometimes these anglers catch trout whose sizes are ecologically out of place with the productivity of the water. But these are the sirens that attract many anglers to the sport. I have seen many a fly fisher walk into a shop and ask the proprietor what will be hatching that day. The man behind the counter pulls a few dry flies from the case and, as they are exchanged on a one to two basis with dollar bills, both are confident that they are on the right track.

The "match the hatch" approach dates back to the foundations of fly fishing. The book often credited to Dame Juliana Berners, *Treatise of Fishing with an Angle,* published in 1496, presented twelve flies; although not dry flies, all were imitations of natural insects. John Waller Hill's 1971 book, *A History of Fly Fishing for Trout,* chronicled the evolution of fly fishing as follows: "There are four great landmarks in fly fishing. The first is imitation, the copying of the colour and shape of the natural insect. The second is presentation, when action as well as colour and shape is copied, and the fly is cast in such a manner as to come over the fish in the same way that the natural insect does. The third, the practice of casting over individual rising fish, is presentation also, to a higher degree. And the fourth is both imitation and presentation in their highest forms; the copying of shape and colour, the copying of motion, and individual fishing, all combined in the use of the floating fly."

Hill's synopsis is the generally accepted idea among fly fishers and non-anglers alike about the sport of fly fishing. I agree with his chronology, but I would suggest that few anglers copy the colour of the fly, as it appears to the trout underwater, especially in the depths of stillwaters. Hill's synopsis pertains almost exclusively to drift feeding trout—the classic view of fly fishing.

By the late 1800s, anglers started to find success with colorful flies that attracted the trout rather than imitated insects. Mary Orvis-Marbury wrote in her 1892 book, *Favorite Flies and Their Histories,* that "fancy flies (colored) are more numerous than the imitations, especially since their introduction as a lure for black bass." In her words, "In America the majority of flies are the creation of fancy, without an attempt to imitate any known insect, and are named according to circumstances." The anglers of her day knew that flies could be tied to imitate naturals but preferred these colorful flies. Somehow they still caught big trout. In Orvis-Marbury's text, one letter from an angler who fished the Nipigon River area for big brook trout noted that ". . . (anglers) have invariably found the usual trout flies to be of no use to catch the large fish. On most of the rivers small salmon flies were the most taking. On the Nipigon the large salmon flies were the most taking."

What this angler had accidentally uncovered was that the big Nipigon brook trout he was pursuing were piscivorous and preferred larger food items. These larger trout were no longer invertebrate feeders.

Active vs. Inactive Trout

If the average angler doesn't fish during the transitional light periods when big trout are most active and presents patterns that do not imitate what these fish actively hunt, then, in most cases, he is probably catching them incidentally. This is easy to verify if they are catching big trout with other size classes, which is not usually the case if big trout are being specifically targeted. Most angling techniques and approaches are geared towards trout in general, when big trout are not in an active feeding mode (daytime drift feeding), and when there is little competition with the naturals (also day drift feeding).

A Word on Fly Patterns

Different techniques and patterns that catch big trout are profiled in the following section. Each pattern is categorized as trolling, casting, sitting, or drifting. The trolling and casting flies are generally for actively feeding fish, as the trout has to move to the fly. The sitting and drifting flies can be either for feeding or inactive trout, with a slant towards the latter, depending on the water and time of day. For example, in the Blackfeet Reservation lakes the trout actively feed on scuds during periods with lower illumination. Scuds do not travel far so I call flies that imitate them sitting patterns. In some of the Colorado tailwaters the trout actively feed on opossum shrimp in the drift when they are caught in the dam outflow. I call the mysis patterns that imitate them drifting flies.

The occurrence of both these activities is highly time dependent, and these invertebrates are the primary food items for the trout. However, in most other lakes and rivers, big trout inactively feed on drifting invertebrates in resting zones during the daytime and actively feed on prey fish or crayfish in feeding zones during the transitional hours.

For each pattern presented there are guidelines for how the naturals act in the water or how the pattern can be best worked as an attractor. There are thousands of other patterns available to anglers and dozens of techniques to fish them. The patterns listed here should by no means complete the angler's repertoire or discourage him or her from experimenting. They are simply the flies and techniques I have found most useful in catching big trout.

Table 7-1: Big Trout Patterns by Water Type and Approach

Pattern	Trolling	Casting	Sitting	Drifting
Stinging Bucktail	Stillwater	Stillwater		
Stinging Bunny		Stillwater		
Bloody Chironomidae Pupae			Stillwater	Tailwater
Bloody Scud			Stillwater	Tailwater
Stinging Hair	Stillwater			
Stinging Crayfish		Stillwater/Tailwater		
Tim's Mysis				Tailwater
Bloody San Juan Worm				Tailwater
Stinging Sculpin		Stillwater/Tailwater		
Bloody Egg				Migratory
Alaskan Beads				Migratory
Teeny Nymph		Stillwater		Migratory

Patterns and Techniques for Stillwaters

My five primary patterns for big trout in stillwaters are from my Stinging: Bucktail, Bunny, and Hair and Bloody series (Chironomidae Pupae and Scud). The Stinging Crayfish and Stinging Sculpin, covered in the tailwater section, will also work well under many stillwater situations.

The basic body forms and movements of all these flies, with the correct retrieves and lines, can imitate most big trout meals. The Stinging Bucktail and Stinging Bunny are casting flies. The Stinging Hair and Stinging Bucktail are trolling flies. These flies are best used during active feeding periods. I categorize the Bloody Chironomidae Pupae and Bloody Scuds as sitting flies. They are best worked during low feeding periods in the trout's resting zones or in active feeding zones on stillwaters where they are the main food item for the trout.

Stinging Bucktail (Created by Bernie Taylor)

		Blue Water Day	Green Water Day	Green Water Day	Green Water Day	Blue/Green Water Night
Base Hook	TMC 811S or Mustad 34007 Sizes 6 to 1/0					
Stinger Hook	Mustad 92553 or VMC9299 RD Sizes 4 to 1/0					
Stinger Mono	25–30 lb. test					
Streamer Fin	Size small for casting, larger for trolling	Silver	Silver	Silver	Silver	Silver
Thread	3/0 Monocord	Black	Black	Black	Black	Black
Underbody	Lead wire	Optional	Optional	Optional	Optional	Optional
Upper layer of wing	Dyed Bucktail	Black	Green	Black	Brown	Black
Lower layer of wing	Dyed Bucktail	Gray or Blue	Orange	Olive	Tan	Black
Body	Chenille or Diamond Braid	White	Yellow	White	White	White
Bead	4 or 6 mm	Red	Red	Red	Red	Glow
Throat	Any poly fiber	Red	Red	Red	Red	

The perfect fly doesn't exist, but we can incorporate some of the major stimuli (color, sound, movement, shape, size) into a pattern to attract big trout and make them strike. The Stinging Bucktail series is my best attempt so far to imitate a wide variety of prey fish. First, it has the horizontal contrasting colors of prey fish. You can change the color combinations to match the water conditions simply by altering the chenille (or diamond braid) body and bucktail.

All Stinging Bucktails for daytime use have a red bead set just above the stinger hook. I use a glow-in-the-dark bead for the darker hours. This fly also utilizes a silver streamer fin that sends pressure waves out to attract big trout, making it ideal for fishing under low light, at night, and in murky waters. It is not going to attract trout from all over the lake, but the signal will be sent farther and louder, without startling the fish, than a typical streamer fly. Size small streamer fins should be used with a size 2 mm bead for casting. You can use a larger bead and streamer fin for trolling. The smaller streamer fins will send out less intense vibrations, but since you are casting to fish and not trying to attract them from longer distances (trolling), a louder fly is not necessary. The backside of the streamer fins will reflect the coloration of the beads and make them appear much larger. Consider tying on a ball-bearing swivel a foot or two up the leader to limit twisting of the line when trolling. (I find that a ball-bearing swivel is not necessary for casting.)

The Stinging Bucktail can be tied with one or two hooks, but clip off the forward one if local regulations require that you only use one. The stinger hook can either be tied up or down for this fly.

The Stinging Bucktail can be used as both a casting and trolling fly. However, it is most effective as a trolling fly, as it will attract big trout from fairly long distances and make them strike. Casting is a technique to cover water that brings your fly to the fish, thus the fly will only help to make them strike, which isn't such a bad thing. One trolling tactic is to pull a full sinking fly line (90 feet of fly line into first few feet of backing) with elongated "S" patterns at a quick pace with a trolling motor. I don't advocate trolling on shallow lakes to catch big trout. When I do, I am usually hunting for fish and keeping my line in the water while I am reading structure below the surface with my fish finder.

When trolling, I am trying to determine how the fish are holding in the water column (bottom/mid-depth/surface) and what types of soft and hard structure they are gravitating towards. Two rods with different density full sinking fly lines or a floating fly line will increase your odds of the fish finding your fly. (British Columbia regulations allow two lines in the water if there is only one angler in the boat, but only one line per angler if there is more than one person fishing. In Idaho, your fishing license buys you one line in the water per angler, but you can pay for one more.)

I will usually start trolling with Class I and III full sinking fly lines. I will also use a floating running line rig if I am fairly certain that the fish are feeding up on top, as during the dusk/dawn transition hours. I am not going to be casting, so the wider diameter of the weight-forward section is a burden to my retrieve ratio and limits the amount of backing I can hold. Anglers will also get a faster reel-in-retrieve if they have their reels filled to capacity.

When trolling, the drag should be set so that the spool turns over during the strike, but not so loose that the resistance of the water alone will pull out line. Combining a higher drag setting with your cruising speed and the weight of the line in the water can result in break-offs. If a trout hits and misses when you are trolling, slightly reduce the speed of the trolling motor and drop the rod back to give the fish a second chance. The trout will often come back for the kill.

"S" patterns are a good way to cover water as this movement will help you to hook into trout that may have moved aside as you were trolling over them. I tend to have the most hook-ups on the turns. I also see fish following my fly when the fish finder is aimed behind me, so the turn may be inciting the trailing trout to react. On narrow shoals, narrow the "S" pattern and on wider shoals widen it. This will allow you to better cover more water. When the water is flat, troll off the shoals, and when the water is choppy you can cruise closer to shore.

Check your line frequently for debris when trolling, as it may deter the trout from taking your fly when you are passing through good numbers of them. If you are seeing significant numbers of large trout in your fish finder, check your line, change to a different fly color and/or trolling rate. It is also useful to have another rigged rod at hand in the boat so that you can cast in front of trout following prey fish to the side of your craft without having to reel in your trolling lines. Again, check local regulations before trying this. I do not advocate trolling from a float tube as it is difficult to vary your speed and direction. A float tube also isn't going to help you cover much water.

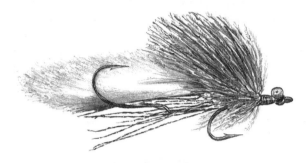

Stinging Bunny (Created by Bernie Taylor)

		Green Water Night	Green Water Day	Green Water Day	Green Water Day	Brown Water Day
Base Hook	TMC 811S or Mustad 34007 Sizes 6 to 1/0					
Stinger Hook	Mustad 92553 or VMC 9299 RD Sizes 4 to 1/0					
Stinger Mono Head	25–30 lb. test 2 Connected Gold Bead Chain Eyes $^1/_8$–$^3/_{32}$ or $^5/_{32}$ ounce Dumbbell eyes					
Thread	3/0 Monocord	To Match Collar	To match Collar	To Match Collar	To Match Collar	To Match Collar
Body	Dyed rabbit hair strips tied on top of Krystal Flash	Black	Olive	Brown	White	Chartreuse
Collar	Strung Marabou	Black	Olive	Brown	Red	White
Underbody	Krystal Flash	White	Red	Red	Red	Red

After seeing both of my stillwater slide presentations, a student told me that he was starting to fill his fly box and asked me the first three types of flies he should buy for the Oregon high desert lakes. Before I could answer, he added, "I hear that *Callibaetis* emergers work great." I then asked him, "What do you want to catch?" He responded, "Big trout?" So my reply didn't include the brief metamorphosis stage of this small insect.

"In my opinion, the first fly should be a leech pattern. My second choice would be a leech pattern of a different color. For the third, find a leech pattern of another color and size." Why leech patterns? Because they catch fish and not because the trout take them for leeches.

I asked Ron Newman to delve into his research and come up with a number on leeches as a proportion of food from the stomachs of trout sampled. His answer was that they are insignificant. One would immediately assume that the lakes he fished were devoid of leeches, but I saw a leech swimming around when I fished with him. If I saw one swimming leech there had to be a lot more there. I checked his findings with those of scientists who recorded stomach samples and the results were the same.

Leeches are prevalent in many of the waters that hold big trout and there is a general direct correlation between leech abundance and lake productivity (Wetzel). However, high densities of leeches do not necessarily translate into more predation by trout. One study on Henry's Lake in Idaho, where the concentration of leeches in the bottom fauna showed that this food item could have accounted for 33 percent of the potential food for the trout, showed that as a percentage of stomach content they were almost non-existent (Irving).

The conventional wisdom is that trout take leech patterns because they feed heavily on leeches. This makes me think about a largemouth bass lure patterned after a Budweiser beer can. An analogy to leech patterns would be that largemouth bass take the beer can lure because they like to drink Bud, or at least chew on the can. Egg-sucking leeches probably fall into the same category, but they can still be effective.

An interview with Steve Marks from the Oregon Department of Fish and Wildlife uncovered that leeches are sometimes significant for larger trout during the months of April and May, or later depending on water temperature. The trout appear to key in on them in waters where and when few prey fish are available and before the insects become active. Leeches are typically found in water less than six feet deep and these areas warm faster in the spring, which may partly explain their early seasonal activity. Leeches usually spend much of their time in the sediment, so they may also be available when wave action stirs them up. Other food sources may also be limited until production increases later in the spring.

One explanation why leeches are not prevalent in the stomachs of trout is that the swimming activity of this creature in search of food is primarily nocturnal, when the trout cannot readily see them. Leeches have a daily rhythm similar to the aquatic invertebrates. Leeches are more prevalent in turbid waters, especially in heavily silted areas, which may help to hide them from predators. Leeches also undergo changes in coloration in response to light levels. Individuals become dark when exposed to incidental light, and blanch when exposed to darkness. The full response is fairly rapid, taking 15 to 30 minutes to achieve, and is sustained indefinitely under constant conditions (Sawyer). This is possibly a more efficient cloaking mechanism than that of prey fish. Thus, the prey fish may seem to be preferred, although they may just be more accessible.

Why do leech patterns work so well when available but not an active part of the trout's diet? My hypothesis is that the fish are attracted to the movement and/or color, or strike out of aggression. I have done well fishing an olive Stinging Bunny in waters with fathead minnows, which also have a green tint. Gary Borger may be on the mark in his book *Designing Trout Flies*. Borger ties his leech, minnow, tadpole, and crayfish patterns with rabbit strip fur.

Master angler and fishery biologist Brian Chan from British Columbia caught this fine rainbow trout while fishing a *Chironomidae* pattern over resting fish. (Philip Rowley photo.)

If we look carefully at the leech patterns we fish with and the way they move, we have to consider their similarities with these other fish foods.

The Stinging Bunny is a good casting fly pattern because it is relatively light and slim. I primarily fish the Stinging Bunny with a Class I, II, or III full sinking fly line. I use the bead-chain eye version for shallow waters where I do not want it to sink rapidly and the dumbbell one for greater depths. I strip it along with two different retrieves. One is a long, slow pull with pauses and the other a quick two-inch strip. The best places to present the Stinging Bunny are hard structures, such as close to reeds, in channels formed by weeds, and just above submerged weedbeds. The angler can fish it with either one or two hooks. If regulations prohibit two hooks on one fly, clip the forward one off at the bend. This set-up, whether with one or two hooks, will triple your hook-ups on big trout.

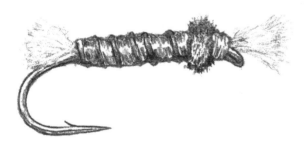

Bloody Chironomidae Pupae (Created by Bernie Taylor)

		Green Water Day	Green Water Day
Hook	TMC 3761 sizes 14–16		
Thread	6/0	Red	Red
Tail	Translucent Fibers	White	White
Rib	Fine Wire	Silver	Gold
Abdomen	Floss	Black	Reddish-Brown
Thorax	Peacock Herl	Peacock Herl	Peacock Herl
Gills	Translucent Fibers	White	White

In my sophomore year in college a friend's grandfather took us trout fishing on a pond in Pennsylvania. We had absolutely no success that day, and upon returning to the boat ramp a man approached us with a plastic bubble and a little plastic box with five flies neatly lined up in a row. He guaranteed us each a fish on our first cast. We were a bit skeptical about his sales pitch and asked him to demonstrate how his flies worked. Sure enough, he caught one right off and made three sales in the process. I asked him what the flies imitated and he replied that he didn't know, only that they worked. A few years later someone presented me with the same flies. At first I thought that the fellow in Pennsylvania must have been quite the salesman, but I was soon told that they were *Chironomidae* imitations.

Earlier in this book I stated that big trout anglers should not focus on insects unless they are the only food source available. I stand by this statement, even with *Chironomidae*, but I discuss them here as an effective fly when trout do not have a prey fish food base, when they are in a resting mode, or when they are holding on or near the bottom. An almost satiated trout may not feel up to chasing a big tui chub, but a few *Chironomidae* dangling in front of its nose may be tempting. This is not much different than your feeding habits after a big Thanksgiving dinner. You may find room for a chip or two, but another turkey leg is not likely. A big, satiated trout will not travel far for its food, and you will want to place your *Chironomidae* imitation in the paths of trout casually feeding on them or instinctively grabbing them while lounging. Just as a double-digit trout isn't going to stray far from its feeding path for one stray bug when there are millions of others floating around, he also isn't going to chase around small bugs when his stomach is full.

My best *Chironomidae* pattern is the Bloody Chironomidae Pupae, tied in black with silver ribbing, red thread, and reddish brown with gold ribbing. One has to ask how such a small fly catches big fish. The answer is in the numbers of *Chironomidae* present in some lakes. The bottom samples of some white marl shoals in British Columbia lakes have been measured with over ten thousand *Chironomidae* per square meter, equating to almost two per square inch. Before you can start to even figure out how far a trout will travel in a minute, he has already swam past or consumed a lot of midges.

One study on the highly productive Henry's Lake showed that as many as 670 larvae and 730 pupae were found in a single stomach (Irving). Ron Newman's stomach samples of trout caught in the lower Kamloops area of British Columbia over a twenty-three year period showed that midges were the second most important invertebrates consumed by trout. He found scuds to be number one and caddis number three. He also found that 95 percent of the *Chironomidae* samples were in the pupae stage, while on Henry's Lake the surveys found the larvae and pupae samples to be almost equal in both studies, indicating feeding on or close to the bottom.

Three elements in the design of a midge pattern are size, shape, and color. Newman found that the most frequently occurring color of *Chironomidae* pupae in the stomachs of trout was black and the second a reddish-brown. However, some colors change after being killed (Ibrahim and Huntingford), so we have to be careful how to interpret these observations. Anglers present other colors to the trout, but they probably appear black (or reddish-brown) to the trout because of the low light color shifts. Red *Chironomidae* larvae have been found to be preferred over pale-colored ones, probably because the contrast with the blue or blue/green environment makes them more conspicuous under certain illuminated conditions. As such, I use red thread to set them off.

Chironomidae larvae that were presented straight were also more frequently fed on than rectangular or globular ones. Thus, I tie my Bloody Chironomidae and Bloody Scud patterns on a straight hook.

British Columbia anglers have a number of methods to work midge patterns into the path of feeding trout or in front of lounging ones. One floating line technique is to set the indicator, the bigger the better, at a distance equal to the depth of the fish and let it bob up and down in the ripples. Some anglers use their fish finders to determine the depth that fish are holding. Be sure to compensate for the depth of the diode on the fish finder when setting the length of your leader.

If trout are holding shallower than ten feet, you may not be able to see the fish below the water as the cone on some fish finders may be too narrow and the fish may not be cruising just below the watercraft. When fish are located in an area but not taking, change flies or start working your way up to the surface by shortening the length of the leader from the fly to the indicator. Some anglers anchor their crafts and fish their midge patterns downwind. Others use the same set-up and either hand-twist retrieve the fly line in or slowly troll it around through a targeted area.

A common type of strike indicator is a corkie with a toothpick to hold it in place. The toothpick through the corkie tactic can be tricky if the water is deeper than ten feet, as the angler must release the corkie by pulling out the pin as he is playing a fish in order to reel in the line. While I do not advise using this tactic, it can only be done in a boat as the angler has to stand up to pull the pick out of the corkie. My personal opinion is that sticking the corkie over the loop on the fly line is a better idea, as the corkie will release itself when bringing in the line. Your casting is limited, but if you are on top of the trout, you don't need to throw the line far. You will need to look for slight twitches in the strike indicator, another reason not to cast out too far. Another toothpick-less corkie tactic is to let the weighted midge pattern drag the leader down through the corkie to the required depth and then slightly twitch it up.

There are a number of big trout stillwaters that do not have prey fish or large crustaceans. In order for those trout to grow big there must be another major food source for them. In some locations, such as the Blackfeet Reservation lakes, gammarids have met that requirement. There are many types of gammarids; however, fly fishers tend to lump them all into

Bloody Scud (Created by Bernie Taylor)

		Green Water Day	Green Water Day	Green Water Day	Green Water Day
Hook	TMC 3761 sizes 14–16				
Thread	6/0	Red	Red	Red	Red
Dubbing	Hare's Ear/ Antron Blend	Green	Red	Orange	Tan
Shellback		Clear Plastic Film	Clear Plastic Film	Clear Plastic Film	Clear Plastic Film
Weight	.010 Lead wire				
Rib	Silver fine wire				

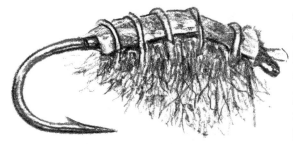

one group called "scuds." Studies have shown that scuds can be as dense as 10,000 per square meter (Penak). While this is an extreme, in productive waters scuds can provide a great deal of energy for trout. As noted earlier, Ron Newman found scuds to be the number one invertebrate food in the stomachs of trout. The difficulty with angling to fish keying in on scuds is that there are so many of them and your imitation has to compete with a multitude of naturals.

Crustaceans usually take on the color of their surroundings (Ghidalia). Scuds typically feed on biomass around surfaces of plants, on rocks and wood debris, and in mats of weeds. They are typically not open water animals, although you may find some dead samples floating in the film. So when feeding around green weeds, they will have a greenish hue, and if feeding on the bottom in a reddish-brown environment, they will take on this coloration. Both of these tones serve to camouflage the scuds in their environments during the day and when they feed at night. Red is a highly conspicuous color in blue and green environments. When these reddish-brown shrimp are dislodged from their bottom feeding they will become easy prey for trout, as the color of this food item will contrast with the environment. I use a red thread on my scuds to differentiate them and elicit a strike. I also tie them on a straight hook, as they are instinctively more likely to take this form than a rounded one.

The Bloody Scud should be presented in and around where scuds are naturally present. In such shallow vegetated waters, this can be with either a floating line (with or without an indicator) or a Stillwater Class I full sinking fly line. You can also use the *Chironomidae* techniques discussed earlier. Rig as many Bloody Scuds as the local law permits to maximize the chance that the trout will see, and be tempted by, your offering. Most scuds can swim, although they

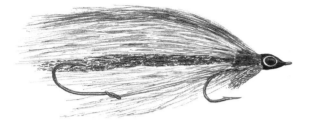

do this infrequently, and their intended movements are usually crawling or burrowing. Your retrieve should be slow. When used with a floating line, be sure that your Bloody Scud has a little weight in it so that the fly stays in the trout's feeding zone. A slight ripple on the water should provide all of the movement you need when using a floating line.

Stinging Hair (Created by Bernie Taylor and Dale Williams)

		Blue Water Day*	Blue Water Day*	Blue Water Night
Base Hook	VMC 1/0–3/0 9255 Nickel or Mustad 34007			
Stinger Hook	VMC 1/0–3/0 9299 Nickel or Mustad 92553			
Stinger Mono	25–30 lb. test			
Body	Diamond Braid	White or silver	Purple	White
Flanks	Krystal Flash	Blue/Green	White	Silver
Upper Back	Yak Hair	Black	Aqua Blue	Black
Mid-Back	Yak Hair	Dark Purple	Black	
Lower Back	Yak Hair	Dark Green	Red	
Belly	Yak Hair	White	Purple	White
Gills	Any synthetic fiber	Red	Red	None
		Blue Water Day*	**Blue Water Day**	**Blue Water Day**
Base Hook	VMC 1/0–3/0 9255 Nickel or Mustad 34007			
Stinger Hook	VMC 1/0–3/0 9299 Nickel or Mustad 92553			
Stinger Mono	25–30 lb. test			
Body	Diamond Braid	Silver	White	White
Flanks	Krystal Flash	Pink	Pearl Red	Minnow Blue
Upper Back	Yak Hair	Aqua Blue	Black	Black
Mid-Back	Yak Hair	Light Gray	Herring Black	Smolt Blue
Lower Back	Yak Hair	Red	Gray	Gray
Belly	Yak Hair	White	White	White
Gills	Any synthetic fiber	Red	Red	Red

*Dale Williams patterns

Big trout are solitary predators and I often see them through fish finders in large lakes at over 100 feet apart. Open-water prey fish, such as kokanee, feed on the move, and I do not believe that any angler can effectively imitate their movements from a stationary position. In shallow, eutrophic reservoirs you may sometimes find groups of trout holding over springs, but in deeper oligotrophic lakes you have to cover water to catch them. As my Kootenay Lake guide Frank van Neer puts it, "The more miles you pull, the better your chances."

The most productive method of reaching open-water feeding trout is to troll. When targeting cruising trout on open oligotrophic waters, any shallower than 15 feet on your fish finder should be considered surface fish because trout can see the prey fish from this distance. Since the trout will be looking up at your fly, you should design it from the bottom up, as that is how the trout will see. Dale Williams and I tie the Stinging Hair with yak hair. This material has a translucency that almost glows when backlit. We also use the two-hook stinger system where allowed. If a two hook set-up is prohibited, clip off the main hook at the bend; this hook holds and balances the body.

When trolling Stinging Hairs, the movement of the boat jerking the fly and the flowing movement of the yak hair should create the action—not manipulation of the line or rod. For most flies to swim properly, including the Stinging Hairs, they need to be tuned. They generally do not come tuned out of the vise, regardless of how good a tyer you are, and must be checked in the water. There are four steps to checking if a fly is properly tuned: 1) Drop the fly in the water with about 4 feet of leader; 2) Jerk the fly forward and parallel to the boat; 3) Confirm that the fly is swimming in a rocking/wobbling fashion and not twisting or running too much to one side; 4) If the fly is running properly, leave it in the water and slowly let out line. Do not do this in the prop wash, as the flow of water can tangle the hook with the line. If you noted that the fly was not running properly, pull the fly out of the water and into the boat. Comb the hair back so that all of the fibers are straight and then bend the hook in the direction that the fly was running improperly (just like an arrow in archery). Repeat steps 1 through 4. If the fly still doesn't run correctly, take a small piece of lead and pinch it to the shank of the hook. The lead will act like a keel and keep the fly upright.

The trolling angler handles a great deal more line than the casting one and needs to think about efficiency when retrieving line so as not to pull any arm muscles. It is not uncommon to have 200 feet of line out that has to be pulled in every half hour to check for clinging debris. Here are a few tricks to conserve your energy for the battle with the fish: 1) Do not strip off line when letting it out behind the boat. Set your drag on a minimum setting and let the resistance of the water pull it off as the boat is moving. 2) When retrieving line to check or change flies, flip the reel up so that you retrieve the line in with the hand that normally holds the rod when you fight the fish. 3) Use a wide-arbor reel that gives you a maximum retrieve ratio and fill the reel to its capacity.

When targeting surface/near surface-feeding trout, use a running line as your fly line (as suggested with the Stinging Bucktail). The running line is especially critical for open-water trolling, as you will need to run 30 feet or more of backing with your 90 feet of running line and then another 60 feet of level leader. You have to position the Stinging Hair away from the boat while still keeping 300-plus feet of backing on the reel for the trout's initial run when the boat is still moving and a minimum of another 300 feet on the spool to make sure that something is left to play the fish. You will not be able to get this much backing on your reel with a weight-forward fly line. As you will not be casting, go to a narrower running line.

Patterns and Techniques for Tailwaters

The food sources most common for trout in tailwaters are aquatic worms, scuds and cressbugs, *Baetis*, caddis, and midges. In tailwaters where we find big trout, their diet and growth is also strongly influenced by opossum shrimp, threadfin shad, wild and stocked juvenile trout, sculpins, and crayfish. A water-specific mix of these two groups will produce the biggest trout at different times of the day. Big tailwater trout will usually be roving hunters during the evenings or drift feeders when resting during the day or when the opossum shrimp are present. The roving hunters will be looking for flies that fit into my swinging flies category (Stinging Crayfish and Stinging Sculpin) in feeding zones, while the drift feeders will be searching out food items that are caught up in the current (Bloody San Juan Worm and Tim's Mysis).

In either case, the trout know how their prey moves. Your most important decision for both swinging and drifting flies is how to weight or not weight your fly, fly line, or leader. Add to that whether or not to use a strike indicator for drifting flies. In slow-moving waters, the trout will have plenty of time to look at, and sometimes lightly taste, the fly. In such cases, a strike indicator is often necessary. In faster waters, the trout must react more quickly while the angler must keep the fly on the bottom. A strike indicator drifting on the more rapidly moving surface often makes this maneuver difficult. High-stick nymphing with a split shot positioned a foot or so above your fly will help you to put the fly in the trout's feeding seat at a fairly natural drift when the water is moving rapidly.

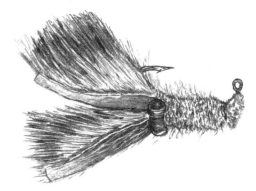

Rod Cesario from Dragonfly Anglers drifts his fly on the bottom of a run on the Taylor River.

Stinging Crayfish (Created by Bernie Taylor)

		Green/Blue Water Night	Green/Blue Water Day	Brown Water Day	Green Water Day/Night	Green Water Day/Night
Thread	3/0 Monocord	To Match Body	To Match Body	To Match Body	To Match Body	To Match Body
Hook	Mustad 32760 sizes 6 to 4					
Body	Furry Foam	Rust	Tan	Brown	Olive	Moss
Claws	Zonker Rabbit Strips	To Match Body	To Match Body	To Match Body	To Match Body	To Match Body
Weight	Dumbbell Eyes 5/32 ounce	Red	Red	Red	Red	Red

Crayfish are an important food source for large trout in many rivers and stillwaters. Anglers realize this and present a variety of imitations of this crustacea to the trout. Coloration of crayfish will vary with the location and environment, much like scuds, but they will generally be much lighter colored after a molt, gradually darkening as sediment and other debris coat their exoskeleton. The timing of the molt varies by species and the environment.

Throughout this book I have written that bigger is usually better. However, this is not the case with crayfish imitations. Game fish prefer smaller crayfish for ease in handling, and I recommend tying a crayfish pattern no longer than two inches. I am not suggesting that trout will not strike a larger crayfish imitation, but the chance of their taking a smaller one is greater.

I use Mustad 32760 hooks, size 6 to 4, that have an eye at a 90-degree angle to the shaft. This design allows the fly to jump slightly off the bottom when retrieved and remain snag-free. The dumbbell eyes should be tied in just before the bend in the hook so that when the fly is retrieved the tail section comes up first. This design will also help to limit hang-ups. The body is tied with Furry Foam and the claws with rabbit strips that give a lifelike look. The rabbit-strip claws should be tied in on the sides so that they slightly flare out. When you strip the pattern in they will hang back.

Before you tie on a crayfish pattern, check the water temperature in the zone where crayfish are present. Crayfish are temperature sensitive and prone to burrowing in the silt when the temperatures drop. At about 40 degrees Fahrenheit, they become almost inactive (Prins et al.) as do the trout.

Three key elements of the Stinging Crayfish are that the fly pulls the claws back on the retrieve, the hook is placed to the rear and up, and the fly is weighted so that it sinks to the bottom. Crayfish crawl to feed and migrate and swim in short bursts to escape predators. The escape burst is a backwards swimming motion that helps the ani-mal to move along quickly, but at the same time leaves it vulnerable to fast-swimming predators as the crayfish's claws are down and back. Most escape movements are not more than a few feet and your retrieve should have a pause after each pull at this distance. In moving waters, I fish the Stinging Crayfish with a fast sink-tip fly line such as the Teeny 100 to 400 series or the SA 150 to 450 series, with a density that will reach the bottom and stay there. In stillwaters, I use a full-sinking fly line.

Mysis relicta, the opossum shrimp, is an open water/stillwater crustacean that feeds on zooplankton. When resident in some reservoirs, they get swept into the outflows of reservoir dams. Most of these tailwaters are in Colorado, and Tim Heng from the Taylor Creek Fly

Tim's Mysis (Created by Tim Heng)

Hook	TMC 200R
Thread	White 6/0
Tail	White Z-Lon or Antron
Wingcase	Clear Plastic Baggie
Abdomen	White African Goat or any spiky material
Ribbing	One Piece of Pearl Krystal Flash

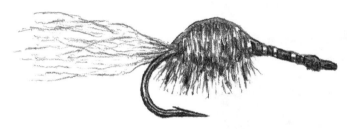

Shop in Basalt, Colorado is an expert on how to catch trout with this fly imitation. Heng developed Tim's Mysis for the nearby Frying Pan River. Developing the fly was a trial and error process for him. Over the years Heng tied many different mysis patterns. They all worked some of the time, and some of the time none of them worked. Tim finally settled on one of his own patterns that has been the most productive for him over the past six years. It is a combination of several other patterns that he tied and fished.

Tailwater fishing with Tim's Mysis is typically performed with a floating line and varying types of right-angle nymphing systems. When blind drift fishing, trophy hunters use a strike indicator, but when working runs where they know fish are lurking or have spotted big trout, they present the fly without an indicator. Sight fishing can be a great advantage when nymphing, and some anglers do not put their line in the water unless they see the fish. The trick to the dead drift is to present the fly in a drag-free state that appears natural to the trout. Your hook-up ratio will increase by proper manipulation of the fly and your ability to detect light takes from the trout. The opossum shrimp are dead when floating down the rivers, and anglers fish imitations weighted on the bottom or floating along on, or just below, the surface. The Stinging San Juan Worm and all of the other drifting flies are fished on or near the bottom. Anglers often cast these flies with a "backhand slap," which, when properly executed, takes the line in one motion from downstream to a two-o'clock position upstream where the line is drifted again. This maneuver eliminates the shadows from false casting, which can spook wary fish in shallow water.

Tim Heng from the Taylor Creek Fly Shop shows a nice Frying Pan rainbow caught on his mysis pattern. Tim fishes this fly on the surface to active fish and on the bottom with a split shot to inactive fish. (Greg McDermid photo.)

Bloody San Juan Worm (Created by Bernie Taylor)

		Brown Water Day	Brown Water Day	Brown Water Day	Blue/Green Water Day	Blue/Green Water Day	Blue/Green Water Day
Hook	2–10 TMC 200R						
Thread	6/0	Red	Red	Red	Red	Red	Red
Body	Six Strand Floss	Fluorescent Orange	Fluorescent Red	Fluorescent Pink	Brown	Orange	Red
Rib	26–32 gauge wire	Silver	Silver	Silver	Copper	Copper	Copper

If I could have only one fly in my box for tailwaters, the Bloody San Juan Worm would be it. The so-called "San Juan Worm" is actually an aquatic annelid (worm) that is prevalent in many waters. There are many San Juan Worm patterns out there. One popular version uses chenille tied on the shank and dangling off both ends. This is a great attractor pattern, but it sometimes results in misses from trout that grab the ends. The Bloody San Juan Worm is almost all hook, so it sinks well to the bottom where the annelids live. The slightly bent hook shape gives the illusion that the worm is flexible, much like when you wiggle a pencil up and down while holding it between your thumb and index finger. An added bonus is that

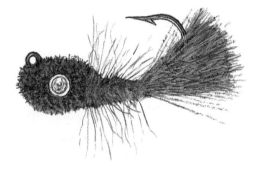

since it is so simple to tie, you don't have to worry about losing flies on the bottom. You can tie up a dozen replacements in a few minutes. I tie these patterns in three natural colors (brown, orange, and red) and in three high visibility colors (fluorescent orange, fluorescent red, or fluorescent pink). I use the natural ones in clear water, while in murky waters I go with high visibility patterns.

Stinging Sculpin (Created by Bernie Taylor)

		Green/Brown/ Blue Water	Green/Brown/ Blue Water	Green/Brown /Blue Water
Hook	Mustad 32756 sizes 4 to 2			
Thread	3/0 Monocord	Red	Red	Red
Body	English Mohair	Black	Dark Olive	Brown
Head	Lamb's wool	To match body	To match body	To match body
Weight	Dumbbell Eyes 5/32 ounce	Red	Red	Red
Tail	Rabbit Strip	To match body	To match body	To match body
Dorsal Fin	Palmered saddle feather	Orange	Orange	Orange

Sculpins lack the swim bladder typical of most swimming fishes. As a result, they stick
close to the bottom. Their imitations should be presented in the same zone.

The first time I saw a live sculpin was in my crayfish trap, which had been set under a bridge
in a muddy creek. That's the kind of place where sculpins hide during the day (also under
boulders in the riffles and in deep pools). They generally don't swim in shallow or clear waters
during the light of day, and when they do move it is in the silt, dredging up *Chironomidae* larvae. Sculpins lack the swim bladder typical of most swimming fishes. As a result, they stick to
the bottom like rocks. Their imitations should be presented under the same conditions.

Sculpins seem to have the characteristics of a chameleon, using different colors to blend
into the substrate. Combinations of browns, blacks, and dark greens are common. I tie the
Stinging Sculpin with the Mustad 32756. The vertical section below the eye is slightly
longer than the Mustad 32760 used for the Stinging Crayfish. This longer section gives the
tyer more room to work the lamb's wool. I add dumbbell eyes just behind the forward bend
in the hook. I also tie in an orange saddle feather palmered forward and trimmed to a quarter of an inch to represent the orange tinting that is characteristic on the dorsal fin edges of
many sculpin species. The hackled feather gives the pattern the impression of movement.
Some species of sculpins grow larger than five inches, but I generally tie my patterns between two and three inches in length. This distance is measured from the front of the hook
to the tip of the tail.

The most important aspect of the presentation of a sculpin fly is that it should be worked along the bottom. This may mean that you need a Teeny 400 or S.A. 350-grain sink-tip fly line to place the Stinging Sculpin in the strike zone. The weight of my sink-tip is directly related to the depth of the water I need to reach and the intensity of the current.

Scott Smith, author of *Ontario's Blue Ribbon Fly Fishing Guide* and a guide for big brook trout on the Nipigon River, describes the delivery as being reminiscent of casting an apple on a rope. "You must keep your back cast on a sidearm plane and the forward cast on an overhead plane, all the time keeping your rod fully loaded with maximum tension on the fly line. Casting a heavy sink-tip fly line is as easy as a quick pick-up, one false cast to change direction, and then let it fly."

The Stinging Sculpin should be cast/flung to the targeted area, such as in the riffles during the evening where they will be feeding and the trout will have an eye out for them. Throw a few mends into it so that the fly has time to catch up to the sink of the fly line tip. A short 3- to 4-foot leader should be used to minimize the sinking time between the two. This is generally a night-fishing technique so trout probably cannot see your fly line anyway. During high water flows when trout are holding near the bank or when trout are feeding on sculpins out in the riffles, drifting from a boat and casting to the banks or riffles is the most efficient approach. In either case, the fly should be swung downstream of the boat and then stripped in. Sometimes a trout will follow. If so, Smith suggests not stopping the retrieve. His observation is that the fish will stop as well and slowly turn away because something in his natural-prey memory chip tells him that fleeing prey fish don't stop and wait for him to catch up. Smith recommends keeping a constant retrieve or even speeding it up if you notice a trout following your fly. If you can manage it, he also recommends a change in the direction of the fly, which will often invoke a strike.

Patterns and Techniques for Migratory Trout Rivers

Most migratory trout patterns fall into two categories—drifting flies and swinging flies. Drifting flies are primarily used when an identified food source, such as salmon eggs or flesh, is floating through the water (usually on the bottom), and the trout are feeding on them. Swinging flies are primarily used for attracting trout, whether by aggression or triggering an instinctual reaction to something they once ate. The Teeny Nymph is a swinging fly, while the Bloody Egg and Alaskan Beads are drifting patterns.

Bloody Egg (Created by Bernie Taylor)

		Brown Water Day	Brown Water Day	Blue Water Day	Blue Water Day
Hook	TMC 2457 sizes 8–12				
Thread	6/0 tied around hook	Fluorescent red	Fluorescent red	Fluorescent red	Fluorescent red
Stabilizer	Pair of gold bead chain-eyes sizes $^1/_8$ to $^3/_{32}$				
Body	Glo-Bug Yarn	Baby Pink/ Oregon Cheese	Light Roe/ Chartreuse	Blue/White	Red/White

		Blue Water Day		Blue Water Day	
Hook	TMC 2457 sizes 8–12	Fluorescent red		Fluorescent red	
Thread	6/0				
Stabilizer	Pair of gold bead chain-eyes sizes $^1/_8$ to $^3/_{32}$				
Body	Glo-Bug Yarn	Deep Dark Red/Peach King		Light Roe/Oregon Cheese	

Most egg patterns, including the Bloody Egg, are tied with Glo-bug yarn. There are dozens of colors to choose from, and a combination of two contrasting colors should stimulate the trout to take. Glo-bug yarn flies are ideal for migratory trout rivers, as they can be tied cheaply and easily. When you lose a few on the bottom—where you should be drifting—it isn't going to set you back much in time or money. I tie my Bloody Egg with a fairly sparse amount of yarn. A sparsely-tied fly will wick up water much better than a more compact one and look more like an undulating egg. Eggs tied with pom-poms will not have the same effect. The sparsely-tied fly will also compress in the trout's mouth when picked up, giving the angler a better chance for a hook-set. I also tie my flies with a pair of bead-chain eyes that sit on top of the hook. In the water, the weight of these eyes, much like a Clouser Minnow, will flip the fly over and allow it to run virtually snag-free.

My Bloody Egg is fished at a dead drift in the same manner as the tailwater flies. Just as important as the drift is the method of approaching the fish. In many small migratory streams and rivers, sight casting to big trout can be helpful. In larger rivers, you may not be able to see the trout, but you can find them by analyzing the structure and holding lies. To the benefit of anglers with good memories or catch records, large migratory trout, especially browns, tend to hold in the same lies year after year—assuming that there have not been any major changes to the rivers. Spawning salmon will hold in the same places every year, as well, and the trout that feed on their eggs will be in the same spots.

The best method for locating these spots is to put your rod down and look for them or watch where other anglers are catching them. In clear waters, they can sometimes be seen from an elevated position such as a tree or a steep bank. When there is heavy vegetation or submerged brush, you can flush them out from their lairs by walking through this structure. Big browns and rainbows usually return to their original lie after being frightened, so an angler can rest the area until the trout feels secure and comes back. Your return approach should be slow and cautious, from downstream of the fish.

Polarized sunglasses and a wide-brimmed hat are necessities. It is rare to observe the full length of a big trout, especially browns, as they will take on a darker camouflage pattern or spawning colors soon after entering the river. An opening white mouth, a slow-moving shadow under weed growth, the flash of a tail, or a whirl of mud on the bottom are more visible signs.

Alaskan Beads

During the latter part of August into September the big Alaskan rainbows appear to be keying in on drifting sockeye eggs. For years anglers have worked patterns that look something like the eggs and others that do not resemble them at all. When the salmon are in Alaskan rivers, egg patterns are unbeatable. The attraction to the trout is their high nutritional value. The eggs have the highest fat content of any part of the salmonid's body. They become accessible to the trout when sockeye move into an existing redd with eggs and kick them up and into the current.

Not long ago, a clever angler came up with the idea of presenting something that

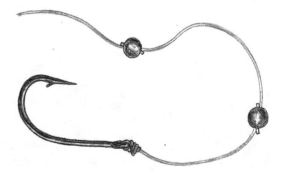

looks almost exactly like the sockeye eggs. Guides call them beads, bead patterns, or egg flies. I call them Alaskan Beads. The concept is simple. There are two 6 mm beads on the leader. The first is placed 3 inches above the Mustad 9174 hook (in size 4 or 6) and the second 5 or 6 inches farther up. Split shot are placed another 18 inches up the leader. The beads are held in place by inserting a toothpick in the bottom hole and pinching the tag end off with a pair of pliers.

The Alaskan Beads are either fished with a sink-tip fly line or a floating one with a strike indicator. It is critical that the beads are drifted right along the bottom. Real eggs don't swim around. Alaskan Bead fishing is primarily a daytime technique for rainbows resting behind sockeye and picking up eggs in the drift. When the illumination diminishes to a point below where the trout can see colors, this technique is not as effective. The beads should be drifted through areas on the downstream end of spawning sockeye. Depressions just behind the sockeye or undercut banks seem to hold the most fish. You can either work these areas by wading or from a boat. Nymphing with a strike indicator will alert you to the most strikes; however, it is sometimes hard to cast such a line in high winds or see the indicator in the chop. Under such conditions a sink-tip fly line is recommended.

What color should the beads be? Each guide seems to have about a half-dozen favorite colors that he keeps closely guarded. Some are natural tones of the sockeye eggs and others are unlike anything that exists in the river. Some have a dab of opaque nail polish to give them a natural effect. All catch trout under crystal clear and slightly murky water conditions. Most of the beads are shades of red and orange, both of which are highly visible colors. Some of the beads, such as the fluorescents, are not natural, especially in chartreuse. So does the trout take the bead just because he can see it or because his genetic programming tells him that it is a sockeye egg? We may never know the answer, but certainly if the trout cannot see the bead it cannot take it. The beads do not have a smell and sound would be minimal. Thus, visible colors that are not intimidating will be the most productive. I suggest reds and oranges for clear water and fluorescent oranges and reds for murky waters.

If I am reincarnated I hope that I come back as Jim Teeny. (If this isn't reason enough to convert to Buddhism, I don't know what is.) My first encounter with Teeny was through his videotape *Catching More Steelhead with Jim Teeny*. I had just returned from a long, cold, and unsuccessful January steelhead trip on New York's Salmon River, and I wanted to learn more about this aspect of fly fishing. Teeny's video and tactics came highly recommended.

As I watched Teeny glassing a pool of fifty or more summer steelhead, while dressed in a short-sleeved shirt, I asked myself, "Why don't I live there?" I researched where Teeny shot

Teeny Nymph (Created by Jim Teeny)

		Green Water Day	Green Water Day	Green Water Day	Brown Water Day	Blue Water Day
Hook	Jim Teeny Custom Hooks sizes 2–10					
Thread	3/0 Monocord	Black	Black	Black	Black	Black
Body	Pheasant Tail	Brown	Black	Ginger	Flame Orange	Insect Green

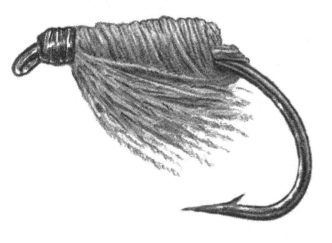

the footage and that's in the region where I now reside. The steelhead aren't as numerous in Oregon as they were during Teeny's video filming, and now he travels to other destinations, including New York, in search of big trout.

Teeny has demonstrated the value of his flies, lines, and techniques on almost every species of fresh and saltwater fish across four continents and in three oceans. His hypothesis is that fish are attracted to basic sizes, shapes, colors, and movement, and that thousands of different patterns are unnecessary. He ties his Teeny Nymph in seven sizes and ten colors. Exact appendage counts may sell more flies and make good copy in magazines but are not required to catch fish, especially big trout. If I could only fish with one fly for big trout on all waters (tailwaters, migratory rivers, and stillwaters), the Teeny Nymph would be a strong contender.

One has to understand that Teeny's techniques are not designed for the Beaverkill and other trout rivers with small insects. Teeny's techniques were designed for big trout, although the smaller sizes may at times work in these freestone streams. He is not what you would consider a "dry-fly man."

Teeny's flies were developed on Oregon's East Lake for the cruising brown, rainbow, and brook trout that primarily feed on tui chubs. There are also aquatic invertebrates in this stillwater, but they are somewhat smaller than his nymphs, which go up to two inches. The big trout in the waters where Teeny uses his fly probably consider the Teeny Nymph to be a prey fish, as these meat eaters don't consume many invertebrates. This is especially the case when Teeny uses them for salmon and steelhead. While the Teeny Nymph could fall under any of the water-type categories in this chapter, I am placing it where I have seen it used most productively—on migratory trout rivers.

The most important aspect of how Teeny fishes his flies on migratory trout rivers is that they are positioned perpendicularly to the trout so that the fish can see the full length of the fly, or its silhouette, with binocular vision. A sideways and downstream drift is not the natural swimming motion of a healthy prey fish, so the trout may also be thinking that the fly is wounded—a more easily obtainable meal. Teeny positions the fly with the Teeny series sink-tip fly lines and a short nylon monofilament leader. He casts the line quartered upstream, lowers the rod tip to let the line pull the fly down, and follows the line downstream with the rod tip. The line generates the action of the fly and establishes its depth and speed of drift. This method is not difficult, and Teeny's system has been used by thousands of anglers to catch more and bigger fish.

CHAPTER 8
HONE YOUR SKILLS

You can't buy fishing success.
Doug Stange

A professional athlete needs to be at the top of his or her game. Timing must be perfect, all steps in place, and concentration unwavering. The difference in winning or losing a match can be as quick as the blink of an eye, whether receiving a serve or catching a high fly ball. The margin of error for the big trout angler is no less intense. It is so small that a fraction of an inch on your drag setting left or right can make the difference between talking about losing the fish of a lifetime and bringing one to the net.

In both business and sports, people who pay attention to the details, but are not consumed by them, generally exceed those that do not. In some cases, we do not have all of the data or may not even recognize all that we should be looking for. Given the time and resources, each one of us could figure out how to catch big trout on any water. We could also independently learn how to cast farther, play big fish, develop better stealth techniques, and improve our other angling skills. But, for most of us, the time is not available and our resources are better spent elsewhere—where our spouses think we should spend them.

These pages cover the details that may make the difference between the big one that got away and a well-deserved trophy fish. This chapter also explains why two anglers in the same boat with the same equipment, presentation, and flies can catch dramatically different numbers of trout. Finally, it covers how trout can be admired and released for another angler to enjoy.

Leaders and Knots

I consider the leader to be the most important link in the system. Not so much for the taper, but for the right products and types of material for the anglers' targeted species under different fishing conditions. Few anglers consider these factors because it requires knowledge of polymer science and processing techniques not usually covered in a fly fishing book. The most common material used in the construction of leaders is nylon.[20]

Nylon monofilament comes out of a machine, called an extruder, much like homemade spaghetti. The material once extruded is stretchy by nature. The technical term for stretchy is elongation, and manufacturers can manipulate monofilament to have more or less elongation. The more stretch the manufacturer takes out of the line, by pulling it under heat, the more closely aligned the molecules will become and the stronger the line will be for its diameter, technically described as the tensile strength. Most of the fly fishing tippet materials on the market have a fairly high tensile strength, as the average fly fisher believes that he needs a super fine line to fool the trout. I usually use 200-yard spools of monofilament line developed for the conventional fisherman who thinks that he needs a line with more elongation and is willing to give away a little in tensile strength.

For anglers, it is important to know how diameter affects trout: Can they tell the difference between a leader rated 5X versus one rated 6X? While at Pure Fishing, Paul Johnson conducted a series of tests to determine the shyness of largemouth bass to varying diameters of nylon monofilament fishing line. The tests were conducted in super clear water at a depth of 15 feet and where Johnson could see horizontally at up to 75 feet. His results were that the bass approached and often took his lure if the diameter of the nylon monofilament was less than .005 of an inch, or about 4-pound test. The bass turned away from his offering at a distance of six feet from the lure if the diameter is greater.

The short-range vision of trout is also highly acute, but in green and murky waters the visibility of fish is much lower. This gives anglers the opportunity to utilize heavier leaders. My observations under green and brown water conditions is that the trout can't see the difference between .005-inches (6X/3-pound) and .008-inches (3X/6-pound) during daylight conditions, and even larger diameters during the morning and evening transitional light periods. The increased strength between these two diameters is significant and will allow the angler to bring the trout in much faster.

There is another type of monofilament available today called "fluorocarbon." Fluorocarbon consists of fluorine, a common element that is chemically bonded with carbon, another common element, to create a polymer. Fluorocarbon can be extruded in a fashion similar to nylon to make monofilament. This process has been available in Japan for many years, as this is where the fluorocarbon monofilament manufacturing techniques were developed. Most fluorocarbon leaders, with the exception of Berkley Vanish, are distributed by companies that import their products from Japan.

The primary advantage of fluorocarbon is that the base material has a lower refractive index, meaning that it reflects less light. The less light that an object reflects, the less visible it is under brightly lit and clear water conditions. Fluorocarbons are not invisible, though. When processed, the difference between water and the monofilament can increase. Scientists in the Pure Fishing lab set up a series of grids under simulated daylight conditions and found that the fish were more likely to bump into the fluorocarbons than the nylon monofilament.

Visibility of an object can also be measured by how it contrasts or blends into the environment. Thus, a green leader material in a eurotrophic lake (green water) should be less visible than a fluorocarbon product, and a brown monofilament line should be similarly effective in murky rivers. Time of day and the illumination from the sun are also determining factors. There should be no measurable effect on fishing success using a fluorocarbon leader during low light conditions, as little light is penetrating below the surface. Therefore, the usefulness of fluorocarbon leaders is a function of the environment and not the fish. During my travels I did see one situation where fluorocarbon leaders definitely provided an advantage to the angler. This was on crystal clear tailwaters in Colorado where anglers were fishing during the daytime drifts.

Another attribute of fluorocarbon leaders that may be of importance to the angler is their excellent wet strength, as the base material does not absorb water and weaken like nylon monofilament. Fluorocarbon also has a greater density than nylon, allowing leaders made from this material to sink faster, and they have lower stretch than nylon, making them much more sensitive.

Table 8-1: Refractive Indexes of Water and Fishing Line Materials

Base Material	Refractive Index	Difference
Water	1.33	0.00
Fluorocarbon	1.42	0.09
Nylon	1.55	0.22
Polyester	1.64	0.31

The base fluorocarbon material has a lower refractive index than nylon, making it less visible during the daytime in clear water.

Leader Types

The decision to use one leader design or another should be determined by looking at the complete fishing system. As a starting point, let's examine the general types of nylon monofilament leaders for big trout. Level leaders provide the simplest and strongest method of connecting the fly line to the fly. They require two knots: one knot that connects the fly line to the leader and the other from the leader to the fly.

Knotted tapered leaders are constructed from two or more leader sections with different diameters. The leader section closest to the fly is called the tippet. The section nearest to the fly line is the butt. The butt should have a wider diameter than the tippet section to transfer the fly line's energy to turn over the fly. This category of leader requires at least three knots. The first is between the butt section and the fly line. Another connects the butt and tippet section. The final one is between the tippet section and the fly. Anglers can add more sections between the butt and the tippet sections to give the leader a more gently sloping or tapering effect. These sections are the body of the leader.

Knotless tapered leaders are extruded in one piece from machines in a factory. They have butt, body, and tippet sections. Typical butt and tippet sections are one to two feet each. The butt is soft with a higher stretch or elongation. The tippet has lower stretch and is stiffer. The body has a graduated taper, softness, and elongation that are achieved during the manufacturing process.

Some anglers feel the stiffness of spooled leader materials and then construct their leaders based on this property. Stiffness should not be a factor when choosing a leader material, regardless of what the label on the box and magazine advertisements promote. All nylon monofilament leader materials become soft after being emerged in water. This is a basic property of the material. Laboratory tests have found the differences between leader materials of the same diameter to be indiscernible.

There are two questions that big trout anglers must answer to determine the usefulness of each leader type: Do I need a tapered leader or is a level leader satisfactory for my purposes? (A level leader will be the strongest and the advantage achieved may help you to catch that trophy fish.) If I need a tapered leader, does a knotted tapered leader have any advantages or disadvantages in comparison to a knotless tapered leader, or vice versa?

Many fly fishing situations do not require a tapered leader, while others demand leaders with finely tuned lengths and tapers. For most stillwater, tailwater, and migratory trout river angling with either sink-tip or full sinking fly lines, level leaders are adequate. I also prefer heavy level leaders for my floating fly line nymphing and for casting heavy streamers, as I would rather accept a less delicate casting presentation over the possibility of having reduced leader strength from a knot that connects the main body to the tippet. In the odd situation that I need some tapering effect, one piece will be added to the body of the leader with a triple surgeon's knot. I also use a level leader when trolling, as there is no casting involved.

Under most moving water nymph and streamer situations, limiting drag from underwater currents is the most critical part of the presentation. While we cannot eliminate drag completely, wider diameter butts and body sections will have greater resistance to the current than lighter tippets, increasing drag. Long and fine leaders are designed for dry fly angling that requires a tapered leader for a delicate turnover of a light fly and an accurate presentation. Most weighted or waterlogged flies won't be turned over by a tapered leader. The fly's own weight will carry it to the end of the leader and sometimes jerk the leader out a bit like a rubber band.

Knotted vs. Knotless Leaders

As a general rule, line-to-line knots decrease the strength of a leader, regardless of the tier's ability. Knotless tapered leaders, by their description, are not constructed with knots and are thus stronger than those constructed with knots. Knotless tapered leaders also form a straighter line. The two major drawbacks of knotless tapered leaders are their cost and versatility in design. Nevertheless, although knotless tapered leaders are not adjustable, many manufacturers offer specialty knotless tapered leaders for fishing spring creeks, nymphing, and other situations.

Typical strengths (as a percentage of the total leader strength) of section-to-section knots for 6X nylon monofilament leaders are as follows:

- Blood Knot (4 barrels)   79.3%
- Blood Knot (6 barrels)   91.2%
- Triple Surgeon's Knot   98.3%
- Surgeon's Loop   96.6%

When I first presented this data in a *Fly Fisherman* magazine article in the mid-1990s, many anglers were surprised to learn the true strengths of these popular knots, especially the blood knot. Each knot has a place in a knotted tapered leader system despite their obvious differences in performance. For example, the blood knot makes a good straight connection between two sections of line; however, it is weaker than other knots. Thus, it can be used for tapering sections within the body of the leader (except for the body section that connects to the tippet). It is unlikely that the heavier sections within the body will break before the knot that connects the body

Blood Knot

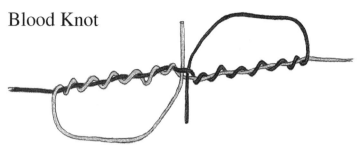

to the thinner tippet section. Anglers should note that a six-barrel blood knot is much stronger than a four-barreled one, although some books suggest using the weaker version.

The triple surgeon's loop has greater strength than the blood knot and offers a stronger connection between the body to tippet sections. The only drawback of the triple surgeon's loop is that it veers off to a slight angle.

Triple Surgeon's Knot

The effect is insignificant if it is only used once in the system. The surgeon's loop also has its place. This knot has the advantage of being tied quickly and easily, even in the dark. Under difficult lighting conditions it can be a lifesaver as a body-to-tippet knot. The knot is also ideal for connecting the butt section to a loop attached to the fly line. Whenever two loops are interconnected, anglers should use a square knot to prevent the loops from cutting into each other.

Square Knot

Crucial Link to the Fly

There are dozens of leader-to-fly knots described in various books and magazines. Every year, someone comes up with a new version that is professed to be the best knot ever tied. I could review dozens of different knots, but I exclusively use the Trilene and Palomar knots, both of which are easy to tie and have break strengths of 100 percent. This means that you are just as likely to break at the knot as at any other point in the

Trilene Knot

leader. Why would you need another? Part of the strength of these two knots derives from looping the line twice through the eye of the hook. This double point of impact distributes the load over a wider area.

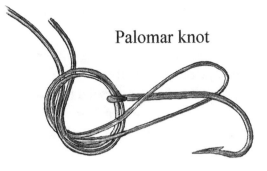

Palomar knot

Leader and Knot-Tying Tips

- When fishing light leaders, regardless of the leader type you choose, avoid leaders that are longer than the length of your rod. You will have to reel in the leader within the tip of your fly rod, putting undue pressure on it. This may be a good case for longer rods, especially for stillwater anglers in float tubes. When trolling, the diameter of the leader is less of an issue, up to a point, so the angler can and should use a longer leader—especially when a motor larger than an electric one is involved. When trolling behind a boat, I may use a 30-foot leader attached to a floating line.
- Buy a good knot book, like *Practical Fishing Knots,* by Mark Sosin and Lefty Kreh, and relearn the correct way to tie your required knots.
- It is best to practice in a comfortable atmosphere with a piece of rope or an old fly line. The large diameters of these lines will help the angler to follow the steps and inspect the finished knot.
- Never tie a knot with a frayed, nicked, or curly tippet section. Such deformities will further reduce the strength of the knot.
- Tie on a fresh leader when you first go out on the water.
- Change your leader frequently and after each big trout.
- Continually check your leader for abrasion and nicks.
- Wetting a knot with saliva or water before it is drawn tight will reduce the friction and prevent kinking.
- Trim your knot with clippers, never with a cigarette, cigar, or lighter.
- Check the knot before your first cast. Poorly tied knots will often break or slip with a minimal amount of pressure. Complete the knot by pulling the tippet tightly while it is connected to a stationary device.
- Some anglers find curls in the tippet when they close the knot. This curling results from that section of the tippet being pulled (stretched out) longer than the adjacent sections. Such a knot/tippet should be cut off and retied. For better results, try drawing the knot tight from farther up the tippet (away from the knot) to spread the load over a wider area.

Stealth and Casting

The big game hunter quickly understands the importance of stealth because he can see small animals and birds retreating from him and alarming his prey as he takes a misstep in the woods. The small-stream angler also has this unique perspective, as he can see trout darting under the banks as he waves his rod to cast to them. He learns to wear drab-colored clothing, creep up on the water, and cast his line by pulling the tip of his rod back like a slingshot or false casting away from the water.

The big trout angler does not usually have this perspective. He fishes waters that are typically large, deep, with swift currents, or full of vegetation. When the trout are feeding in shallow waters it is often on salmon eggs, and the fish are more concerned about finding the right spawning partner or what the salmon and bears are doing than the human anglers. The first concept is profile, or the angler's position to the fish, and vice versa. Anglers should take care to never move (while wading) when retrieving line, to oil their oarlocks, and to never throw an anchor out of the boat; one cast, one retrieve—don't repeatedly slap the water with your fly line. Some serious big trout hunters purchase low-glare fly rods and lines with a gray color, or remove the shine of their rods with sandpaper.

On all of the migratory trout rivers and tailwaters that I visited during the course of my research, I found that none of them required the angler to cast more than 40 feet of fly line. Mark Williams quotes Gary Soucie's two basic rules in his book *Freshwater Fly-Fishing Tips From The Pros,* and they hit the mark: "Never cast over water you can wade, or wade through water you can fish." These are truths for both moving and calm waters; however, they are of special value to river anglers.

Stillwater angling is a little different. A stillwater angler who can cast an extra ten to fifteen feet will show the fly to more big trout than one whose casts achieve less distance. The more big trout that can see the fly, the greater the chances the angler has of hooking into one. (There are limits to this, as discussed in the next section.) The angler should also assume that there is an area around his craft that is void of big trout due to their shyness of the boat. I have often observed this zone through the side finder (horizontal view) of my fish finder.

Setting the Hook

In my mid-twenties, a local angler named Joe Scandore showed me how to right angle nymph fish for trout with a short line and a strike indicator. Prior to teaching me the subtleties of the technique, Joe caught ten trout to my one and most of his were in the five- to eight-pound class. He showed me that the slightest twitch could be, and usually is, a trout. In later years, this experience has reminded me that we are probably not detecting most of the strikes that we get. Joe and I were only fishing in a few feet of water and not drifting our nymphs more than a dozen feet away on a migratory trout river. I assume that even more strikes are missed in faster and deeper waters, and where anglers are trying to set the hook at much greater distances.

Paul Johnson ran a series of tests on the angler's sensitivity to strikes in stillwaters. From a directional standpoint, Johnson found that the lure had to be pulled 30 inches from the angler to be detected. When pulled two feet to the right or left or in the direction of the angler (slack line), few strikes were detected. He also found that fewer pick-ups were detected as the distance increased. At distances of 20 feet, the angler detected 100 percent of the strikes, at 40 feet 50 percent, and at 80 feet no pick-ups were detected. Although these tests were conducted with conventional tackle, the findings should be similar for fly tackle. The fly fisher has one advantage over the conventional angler, though, in that he can watch his fly line to detect subtle strikes. Holding the fly line in your hands can also increase your sensitivity to strikes.

Detecting strikes is only half of the challenge. Setting the hook in time, and with adequate force, is another. Paul Johnson found that a new hook required 2.2 pounds of force to be set into the jaw of a rainbow trout, while a dull hook took 2.8 pounds. My belief is that most anglers, including fly fishers, do not exert this amount of force when setting the hook and that the trout are probably hooking themselves.

I ran a series of tests to determine what it takes to exert two pounds of force. I used a nine-foot, six-weight high modulus/sensitive G. Loomis GLX fly rod, a Scientific Angler's weight-forward floating fly line, a four-foot monofilament leader, and two pounds of weight placed on the ground behind a pail at distances of 30, 45, and 60 feet. At each position the line was held taut and horizontal to the top of the pail. I measured the force that it took to raise the weight off the ground by both pulling the fly straight towards me without the aid of the rod, and also by lifting the rod perpendicularly, as would be the case when an angler jerks the rod to set the hook. My findings are shown in Table 8-2.

I made six observations from these tests. 1) It takes a great deal of line pull and a high angle to reach two pounds of force. The 90-degree lift at 60 feet took the rod as far back as it could have possibly set a hook, and the 40-inch pull extended beyond what I could easily achieve. The next time you rig up your rod, try bringing in 40 inches of fly line with one sharp pull. 2) You have a much greater chance of hooking a trout if you are close to the fish. 3) The less slack you have out will increase your chances for a good hook-set. 4) You stand a much greater chance of hooking a fish while trolling, as the line pick-up is much faster and a greater length of line can be taken in. 5) In most cases, it is not likely that the angler alone is setting the hook on the fish. The trout is probably doing most of the work. 6) While long-distance casting will bring you into the reach of more fish on stillwaters, your maximum hooking distance is only about 60 feet. We should assume that these are best-case scenarios in relation to actual fishing conditions. We can expect line drag, slack, and fish running towards us to have an effect in the real world. Other modulus rods will have the same results for the pull test, as it is a function of the elongation of the fly line and leader and not the flexibility of the rod. They will also have similar results for the horizontal lift test. Note that there is a linear relationship between the pull and distance and lift and distance.

Table 8-2: Amount of Energy Required to Move a Two-Pound Weight

Distance from Rod Tip	30 Feet	45 Feet	60 Feet
Horizontal Pull	18 inches	25 inches	42 inches
Horizontal Lift	70 degrees	80 degrees	90 degrees

Do you think that you are going to break your leader with such a powerful hook-set? This may be the case for 8X leaders, but there are few instances where you should be approaching 8-pound trout with this size monofilament. I have never even broken an 8-pound test or

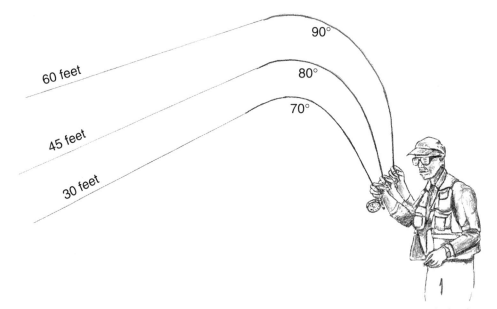

At 60 feet the angler needs to lift his rod from a horizontal position to 90 degrees to set the hook on a trout. A trout running in the opposite direction can achieve the same effect.

It is best to resharpen all of your hooks before use. I use a battery-operated hand tool for a sticky-sharp point.

greater leader on the hook-set. Also, if the trout are hooking themselves, then we must make sure that our hooks are sharp. I find that sticky-sharp points on my hooks more than double my catch rate. But how sharp do you need your hook to be? I sharpen all of my hooks at the fly-tying bench with a battery-operated, hand-held Dremel tool and then resharpen them before use. New hooks, including chemically sharpened ones, are not as sharp as advertised. They should all be sharpened again before use.

Playing and Landing Big Trout

After you've made hundreds of casts you will eventually hook into a monster trout. If you are fortunate, it will take a darting run, jump once or twice, and then fall into the net. More likely there will be a ping and a mocking tail splash from a departing fish. Sometimes, we will say that the fish was "too big to handle and broke us off." But is that really the truth? Was the correct knot used? Was it properly tied? Could there have been a nick in the leader? Did we check for one? Was it the same leader from our last trip? Were we reeling in when the fish was running in the opposite direction? Did we slowly move away from, or position our craft away from, snags and other possible hang-ups?

Most big fish do not "break off" by themselves. They are broken off by an action stemming from the angler. Rod Cesario from Dragonfly Anglers related to me that "Most people go wrong on the Taylor River because they don't understand the size of fish and instantly break them off. They hold on tight, but they should just let them go." Ideally, you want to work your gear (reel, leader, hook, and rod) to just below their breaking point. There is a delicate balance between bringing the trout in as soon as possible and letting the fish flounder until the hook works its way free.

Trout only have enough energy to run for a few minutes. Most anglers have heard about hour-long bouts with big trout, and I too have played fish for longer than was probably required. Sometimes we misinterpret "bulldogging" with resting. A trout played for an extensive period of time is also in greater mortal danger than one played quickly.

The drag on the reel should be set when you have your line extended as far as you can cast and should not be set when the fly line is fully wound on the reel. It takes greater force to turn over the spool as the amount of line is reduced. The stopping power on your reel should be measured by how little energy it takes to turn the spool from a dead start once you are down into your backing. The dash of a big trout will be most vulnerable to you at that time. On the Frying Pan, a tailwater that can receive heavy angling pressure, Tim Heng sets his drag to the lightest setting possible so as to not break off the double-digit trout on 7X or 8X fluorocarbon tippets.

A low setting is also critical for the trolling angler. The drag should be slowly tightened after the fish has been played and is brought in closer. The late "Rip" Collins, the angler who caught the 40-pound, 4-ounce IGFA world record brown trout in the Little Red River on 4-pound test line, had a good technique for checking his drag. Before getting in his boat, he tied the leader to an immobile object, pulled it back so that the line broke, then backed off a click or two on the drag again until the line came off the spool without breaking.

Here are a few tips to help you play and land big trout on any water type:

- Set your drag properly.
- Make sure you have properly tied knots.
- After the fish has made its initial run—on shallow stillwaters and rivers, this is usually after about fifteen seconds—never let the fish rest.
- Play the fish from your reel and never from line in your hand.
- "Pump and load" your rod to work the fish. The pump should be slow and gradual. Jerking your rod up will only aggravate the trout.
- Never reel in line when the fish is running.

This Oak Orchard angler is demonstrating the correct method of weighing a trout in the net. After the trout is released, he weighs the empty net and deducts the net weight from the first weigh-in.

- Drop the rod tip to lighten pressure on the leader when fish jump.
- Use a net appropriate for the size of the trout.
- Retie your fly on your leader (by changing the entire leader) after every big fish, and periodically check it for abrasion and stress.

Releasing Fish

The type of angler who spends hundreds, even thousands, of dollars on a fishing trip in hopes of catching one or two big trout typically understands the true value of such fish and releases them. This is especially true of those anglers that pursue the super trout. Releasing fish is not just a preference anymore; it is often the law. Many of our top rivers and stillwaters have become strictly "catch and release," or have regulations limiting the size and number of fish. Nevertheless, even with the best intention in mind, unless the fish is caught and released properly, it would have probably been better off in the cooler. If properly played and handled during release, trout will recover and will experience no difference in long-term growth and development than those fish that were not handled (Mason & Hunt).

The fly or lure angler is starting off on the right foot due to the nature of this tackle. Studies have shown that the hooking mortality from worm fishing is significantly higher (42%) than from the use of artificial flies (3%). The reason is that the worm-hooked fish often, although not always, takes the bait deep down into its stomach, and the propensity to cause fatal damage is greater than the artificial fly, which is almost always hooked in the jaw area (Mason and Hunt).

John Randolph, Editor and Publisher of *Fly Fisherman*, wrote an excellent piece on handling fish in the December 1994 issue of his magazine. To summarize his article, trout have a high chance of survival provided that they are not touched by dry hands, their gills are not handled, they are not squeezed or held up by their tails, that the water does not exceed 72 degrees Fahrenheit, and that they are not played for excessive periods of time or held out of the water for more than a minute or two. It is recommended that anglers fight the fish with the strongest tippet they can get away with, land the fish from behind within a soft cotton net (avoid hard nylon ones), discharge the hook with forceps, hold the fish by its wrist (the area where the tail meets the body), and revive the fish in an upright position until the gill plates are moving oxygen into its system and the fish can swim on its own. In support of John Randolph's position on utilizing forceps, researchers have found that you have a three times better chance of saving a fish whose hook is dislodged with the aid of an extraction device than when you do not use one (Mason and Hunt).

If you decide to take pictures of your trophy trout, give the fish a drink between flash recharges, hold the fish under the belly to keep it calm, and get the pictures over as soon as possible. It is best to have a loaded camera easily available at all times. Some photographers hold the fish upside down for a moment, which seems to immobilize it during the short course of the photo session.

Today's angler can purchase hand-held digital scales that can be used to weigh the trout. The trout should be weighed in the net and then the net weight, or tare, is deducted to determine the weight of the fish. There is a wide variation in the accuracy and quality of scales. A few years ago, someone gave me a steelhead net with a built-in scale that always weighed fish in at about 18 pounds. The first fish I weighed might have been about that size, but the second one—noticeably smaller—registered the same weight. I still use the net, but I only show people the scale for gags. With the knowledge of how to catch big trout comes a re-

Fish should be released right side up and given enough time to catch their breath.

sponsibility to help maintain these unique fisheries. If the fish dies, it is probably a handling issue—and your fault.

Something to Remember

Years ago, I promised my wife that I would not put any dead fish on the walls of our home. After looking at the dried-up skin mounts on the office walls of some of my business associates, I thank my wife for her wisdom. If you want a life-size replica of your trophy for bragging purposes, there are options other than stuffing the skin of a dead fish and burying it up in your attic for the moths to chew on. Painted plastic trophy mounts last longer and look better over time. Many taxidermists who do skin grafts are already using a plastic head, so the leap to a fully plastic body isn't that great. You do not need to kill the fish to achieve a decent replica. A dead fish doesn't retain its natural coloration, regardless of how quickly it is frozen. It can also cost you between $50 and $100 more for a dead fish, as you will have to ship it airfreight to a taxidermist. A few photos from different angles and measurements will achieve the same, if not a better, result. The true size of the fish varies depending on when it last ate and how much it consumed.

I also prefer woodcarvings of trout. They are a beautiful art form and fit well in most offices and dens. Another option is a trophy fish watercolor, such as those done by East Hampton, Massachusetts artist Alan James Robinson. Robinson can paint your trophy on a blank sheet or make it more memorable by incorporating it on a map of the area where it was caught and released. Similarly, you can commission artists such as Peter Corbin of Millbrook, New York, Luther Kelly Hall of Mystic, Connecticut, and Brett James Smith of Kenner, Louisiana to paint a scene in acrylics on canvas that depicts you and the trout in its environment. The painting will become a family heirloom enjoyed by anglers and non-anglers alike.

CHAPTER 9
MATCH YOUR EQUIPMENT TO YOUR INTENDED PREY

There is nothing more final than hearing the knot or line break.
Mark Sosin

About 150,000 years ago, *Homo sapiens* appeared on this rock that we call earth. He became a crafty hunter who had such confidence in his methods that he killed for both food and sport. The modern-day big trout hunter carries on the spirit of his not-so-remote ancestors. He delves into the mind of the big trout and adapts his tools to their unique environments. He equips himself with rods, reels, leaders, hooks, and a flotation device that can get him to big trout and help him handle them on the line. He jumps on an airplane that will take him to big trout when they are most accessible. He carries on some of the more spiritual rituals by placing photos and replicas of his trophies in the den. He thinks like a predator.

Although we are more intelligent than the trout, the fish's advantage has been that the underwater world was hidden from our view, and we did not always have the ability to reach them. Today, we have devices that can peer deep into the water and technologies that can help us to reach the trout at any depth and water velocity. The modern fly fisher seems to have easily adopted graphite, nylon, and GORE-TEX into his arsenal—a significant step up from the cane rods, horse-hair leaders, and cotton outerwear of the early 20th century. But has the angler really harnessed all of the technologies of our age?

Rods

For most anglers, the rod is the primary tool used to catch big trout, the one we all take the most interest in. A great fly caster can throw a fly line into the backing with a broomstick. A good fly caster can add ten to twenty feet to his cast with a high performance rod. A poor fly caster isn't going to get any more distance regardless of how much he spends. Buy equipment that maximizes your potential, but more importantly, spend the time to learn how to use it correctly.

Casting should not be the only consideration that the big trout angler should make when choosing a rod. An equally, if not more, important characteristic of the rod is how it handles line in the water and how it aids the angler in playing big fish. In my view, the first question that the angler has to ask himself is whether he needs a casting rod, a trolling/playing rod, or a big fish drifting/playing rod. They are not the same. When researching this book, I found that many of the top big trout hunters that fish waters where they drift their flies use slower rods with soft tips.

The concept is similar to that of the noodle rods used for Great Lakes steelhead. These steelheaders use the lightest tippet they can get away with on the wispiest rod and a reel at a minimal setting. The fish will stay on if it doesn't throw the hook, or as long as the angler is not reeling in when the fish is running. A guide demonstrated to me how this principal works. He walked his line about forty feet away from me and then yanked it as hard as he could. The rod bent down, as it should, and the leader stayed intact. The second time he yanked on it, he told me to reel line in. This time the leader broke. The right rod can absorb the shock if the angler is playing the fish correctly (e.g., not reeling in when the trout is running.)

But the softest rod is not always the best one to play big trout. The angler needs to balance the size and stiffness of the rod to how he'll play and handle the fish that he is after. If the rod is described in the catalog as "delicate and wispy for those discerning mountain brookies," it is probably not the best choice for trophy hunting. Safe bets for tailwaters, stillwaters, and migratory trout rivers are rod weights six and over. Long rods are also useful for the angler who is trying to manage an extended drift.

The long-line trolling angler needs a stiffer rod that will set the hook against the forward movement of the craft. When trolling on the big oligotrophic lakes, I go with an eight or nine weight. When fishing these waters you will have a minimum of 400 feet of fly line out by the time the fish reaches the end of the first run. The stretch from this much line is extensive and the stiffer rod can help you to play the fish to the boat. Remember that a trout chasing a trolled fly on open water is not going to be very leader sensitive. A 10-pound-plus leader will probably be used, which is not likely to break at the initial hook-up if the drag is properly set.

If you are going to be trolling out of a boat, most likely the rod will be kept in a holder of some sort, especially if you are fishing more than one rod at a time. Rods without fighting butts will not stay safely in most rod holders. This is especially important on boats where the rod holders stand upright and only the leverage from the butt keeps them in. I bring my own rod holders with u-bolts and wing nuts to attach to the railings when on guided trolling trips.

Fly Lines

Many introductory fly fishing books describe the floating, weight-forward fly line as the "all-purpose" line that anglers should purchase first. Today's big trout angler also utilizes many other fly line designs to meet a wide range of fishing conditions. The stillwater trolling an-

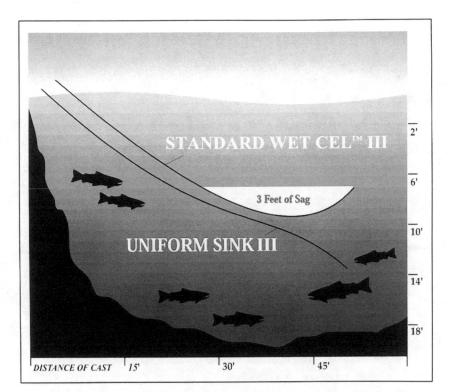

Uniform Sink, full sinking fly lines have less sag, allowing a straighter line connection to the fish during the take and hook-set. (Photo courtesy of Scientific Anglers.)

gler targeting trout near the surface can use a level running line, and the stillwater angler targeting subsurface trout has the option of six classes of full sinking fly lines to help them reach desired water depth (see Table 9-1). These subsurface lines can either be trolled when searching for fish, or a cast-and-wait method can be employed until the line reaches the targeted depth. The former tactic is for when you are searching for trout and trying to scan different depths with your line, and the latter is for when you know exactly where concentrations of trout are.

The standard length of full sinking and floating fly lines is about 90 feet. This is important to know for gauging distance when trolling. Full sinking fly lines are color-coded to indicate their densities. They are rated in Classes I through V, with the highest number being the densest with the fastest sink rate. There is also the clear "Stillwater" type of fly line with a slower sink rate than the Class I. There are two categories of full sinking fly lines on the market: Standard and Uniform Sink. The tip of the latter has a greater density to eliminate the sag. The former leaves the tip of the fly line and the leader sagging in an upward direction.

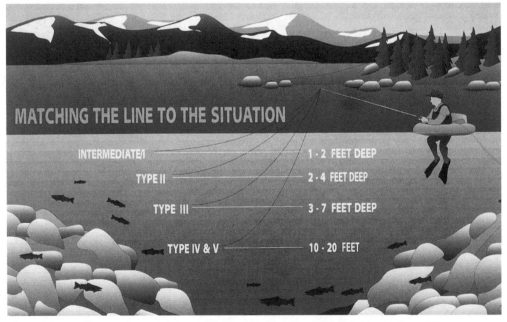

When fishing stillwaters, be prepared to reach a range of depths with full sinking fly lines. (Photo courtesy of Scientific Anglers.)

Table 9-1: Sink Rates for Full Sinking Stillwater Fly Lines

Line Type	Sink Rate Range (inches per sec)	Suggested Depth Range (Feet)	Target Depth	Estimated time to Reach Target Depth (Seconds)
Stillwater	1.25–2	1 to 2	1	9.60
Class I	1.5–2.25	1 to 2	2	16.00
Class II	1.75–2.75	2 to 4	3	20.57
Class III	2.5–3.5	3 to 7	5	24.00
Class IV	4–5	10 to 20	15	45.00
Class V	4.5–6	10 to 20	20	53.33

When Jim Teeny first started fishing for steelhead on the west coast, most anglers were approaching this fish on the surface with floating fly lines and traditional Atlantic salmon techniques. Jim reasoned that steelhead could be more easily caught if the fly was closer to them, especially when the sun peaks in the sky and the sharp light dampens surface strikes. Jim found that he could catch more trout with this idea and pioneered sink-tip fly lines for migratory trout. Sink-tip fly lines existed long before Teeny held a fly rod, but he systematized and marketed his approach so that the average angler could utilize them. His T-series fly lines are rated by their weight in grams: 100, 200, 300, 400, 500, with sinking lengths of 24 feet and floating lengths of 58 feet (the lower numbers being the lighter in the series). Teeny selects his fly lines based on the depth and speed of the water. He also has a Mini Tip, with a 5-foot sinking section and a 77-foot floating section, for shallower and slower-moving water. Instead of a guide just telling anglers to bring a sink-tip line, they usually say to rig up a 200-grain sink-tip.

Scientific Anglers also has a series of sink-tip fly lines that resemble the Teeny series. Scientific Anglers' Freshwater Express Tip are rated 150, 250, 350, 450, and 550 grains. The lengths of the sinking sections are 25 feet and the floating 65 feet. Scientific Anglers and Cortland also have a number of sink-tip fly lines with shorter tips.

All fly lines absorb microorganisms that increase the coefficient of friction on the surface as they go through the guides. Dirt is not hydrophobic and will actually cause your line to float lower in the water and perhaps even sink. This added friction is probably second only to poor casting technique as a deterrent to smooth casts. PVC-coated fly lines also dry up and crack from overexposure to the sun or bug spray, also resulting in less than ideal casts. Most modern fly lines have lubricants built into them; however, additional lubrication from conditioners will further reduce the friction between the line and guides. There are a number of

Jim Teeny was a pioneer in applying sink-tip fly lines to migratory trout. Here, he shows off a large Lake Ontario tributary brown trout. (Photo courtesy of Jim Teeny.)

good fly line coatings and conditioners on the market to clean and condition fly lines. They are inexpensive and can be easily applied to restore a smooth and flexible coating to the fly line. Anglers should avoid storing fly lines next to radiators, furnaces, or stoves. Tight spooling on the reel also should be avoided with fly lines that have a braided-nylon core, as the nylon will retain undesirable memory and coil once unspooled. Look at the manufacturer's catalog to see if the core is composed of braided nylon.

Reels

There are many types of reels on the market today. Most anglers make their decision based on the price. They say, "My budget is around $200, so I will get the best I can afford." In the course of comparing prices on your prospective reel, also take a look at the cost of extra spools. Spools are often half the price of the reel. For stillwaters, you might require up to seven additional spools for your required fly lines (weight-forward floating line, trolling, Stillwater, and Classes I–V). The tailwater angler may need weight-forward floating fly line, a Teeny Mini Tip, Teeny 100, 200, 300, or Scientific Anglers' 150, 250, and 350 lines, depending on the depth and velocity of the water's flow. The migratory trout fisherman may need a weight-forward floating line and Teeny Mini Tip, Teeny's 100 to 400, or the S.A. 150 to 550 series, also depending on the depth and velocity of the flow. All of these lines can equate to a lot of dollars in spools.

You should also consider the drag system when choosing a reel. The stopping power for a reel is not how hard it is to pull line out at the maximum setting, but how low the settings go and how smooth the start-up is. The reel should have a mechanism to prevent free spooling into a backlash. It is also important to choose a reel from a reliable manufacturer with a good warranty policy, one that has been in business for a few years. Your reel will eventually need replacement parts, and it is much easier to purchase the pieces from the original manufacturer than to machine them on your own.

The diameter of the arbor is a new area of opportunity for the angler. On most stillwaters, if you are going to be trolling from a small boat or a pontoon craft, you will have your entire fly line out and be twenty yards into your backing. When a big trout hits, you can expect another eighty feet to disappear before you can get it under control. On large lakes, where they use bigger boats, you could have 800 to 1,000 feet of line out by the time the trout stops. That is a great deal of line to bring in. A true large arbor reel will make the task easier and faster.

The larger arbor SA 5/6 LA reel on the right will give you a better retrieve rate when you are into the backing than the SA System 2 L reel on the left. Both reels hold roughly the same amount of backing.

Scientific Anglers makes quality large arbor and standard arbor reels, and I will use two of their products as examples here, although many other quality reels are available, too. The outer diameter of the spool on their System 2 5/6 L reel, when fully loaded with a fly line and backing, will be 2¾ inches and has a pick-up of 8.6 inches per revolution. In comparison, the outer diameter of the spool on their large arbor 5/6 LA reel is 3 inches with a pick-up of 9.4 inches per revolution. The engineers at Scientific Anglers point out that the real advantage of the large arbor reel is when you get close to the end of the fly line near the backing. The 5/6 L will have a 1⅝-inch diameter at that point, equating to 4 inches per revolution. The 5/6 LA will have a 2½-inch diameter providing 8 inches per revolution. Thus, when you are playing big trout into the backing, you will have roughly twice as fast a retrieve rate with a large arbor reel.

Clothing and Safety Gear

It is easy to write in the comfort of my home office about fishing at night, at ice-out, or in fierce winds on open water. I do fish under these conditions, but I am prepared to endure the elements. The trained survivalist knows that man needs two things to bear the elements in the short term: shelter and warmth. The shelter will keep him dry while the warmth from his clothing or a heating device will help keep him from getting sick, losing his wits, or going into shock. The big trout angler who is going to brave the severest weather conditions will need to be concerned with these, as well. The angler probably isn't going to die from exposure, but not being prepared will make him uncomfortable, limit time on the water, and reduce his concentration.

The clothing that survivalists wear is not much different from modern angling attire. The outer shell is of a breathable GORE-TEX-like material, a fabric coated with a plastic that makes it water repellant yet allows perspiration to flow out while keeping the warmth in. (Try to avoid white clothing as it may give trout the impression that an osprey or another avian predator is hovering over them.) Wear or carry this garment with you at all times, regardless of the anticipated weather. The next layer is synthetic fleece; actually a plastic recycled from two-liter soda bottles. This material wicks away the moisture and keeps one warm. A neck warmer made of the same material will help to keep the heat in.

Why not a cotton sweater? The survival experts say that cotton kills when wet because it has no insulating properties. You may not be hiking a long distance to the water, but even a brisk walk can build up some moisture. With cotton, the moisture will stay with you for the day and make you uncomfortable. Waders that leak or that were not properly dried out the evening before are not much better. The moisture will absorb the heat from your body, leaving you cool and wet. The layer closest to the skin, the long underwear, so to speak, is often polypropylene, another plastic that wicks away the moisture from the skin and keeps you dry. The angler can brave even the harshest weather in this outfit.

If you do get wet, quickly change to dry clothes. I always keep a second set of clothes in my rig for emergencies or just for when I get off the water. I remember a fishing trip I made with a classmate when I was in college. My friend fell into the water on a cool Easter weekend. He made his way back to camp, but his fingers were too numb to start a fire. He was in bad shape and would have been much better off had he stripped down, dried off, or jumped into a sleeping bag. Whether you are hiking a few miles from your car or floating on a river or stillwater, a safety kit with a waterproof fire-starting kit can be helpful.

Hot summer days can be equally hazardous and uncomfortable. Always wear a wide-brimmed hat and sunglasses. I wear a Tilly Hat and a GORE-TEX-type jacket without a lining to insulate me from the sun. I also wear stripping gloves to protect my hands from the sun and my fingers from line cuts. Consider a back support device if you are going to be doing a lot of bending over. You can buy them for less than $30 at a hardware store. A wading belt can be helpful in case you fall in the water.

In addition to your clothing, there are other safety precautions to remember. Always bring water with you. Cold water will keep you cool and prevent dehydration on warm days. Warm water will keep you from dehydrating and losing your heat during cooler periods. Pack a first-aid kit. It should include some hand cream for when you get off the water. (Don't apply the lotion on the water as the perfumes in it can deter the fish.) Make sure the dates of the medicines in your safety pack are current. An easy way to update them is to ask your doctor for free samples during your annual check-up.

Make your gear waterproof. One day on British Columbia's windy Stump Lake, a wave crashed over one of my pontoons and seeped into my standard camera bag. It took a week to dry all of the moisture out of the inner optics. Since then, I protect my camera gear and electronics in a soft cooler that can be carried around with me.

If you are fishing alone, a cell phone might be a good idea. Once while fishing for steelhead not far from my home, I moved upstream by jumping from boulder to boulder, grabbing deadfall to keep my balance. One branch snapped, I slipped off the rocks, landed sideways on a boulder, and passed out. The water came up in my waders. This was lucky, as the chill woke me up. A later visit to the doctor showed that I had bruised a rib. Nothing tragic, but the situation could have been much worse.

I have met more than one guide that will not allow cell phones to be used by anglers under their care. They believe that it detracts from everyone's outdoor experience. On the flip side, many of us could spend more time out-of-doors if we had cell phones at our side. Perhaps a call or two per day into the office is all that is needed. Cell phones can also be considered a part of your safety equipment. For instance, I use a cell to let my wife know that I will be coming home late—in lieu of her calling the sheriff to send the posse out to look for me.

GPS and PDA

Devices much like the tricorder from *Star Trek* have been in the hands of technicians and engineers for years. This concept has now entered the home and leisure environments, with applications that surpass the capacities of multimeters and pocket calculators. I now download 2D contour map data from my desktop computer to my Personal Digital Assistant (PDA), and a number of mapping software companies have joined with the PDA manufacturers to offer GPS attachments. While the standard road map software may be useful in finding a parking lot at your destination, these devices and software become extremely useful with 2D contour maps that allow you to chart your strategy and results in real time. Delorme offers a program in cooporation with Trout Unlimited, called *Topo USA—Fly Fishing Edition,* that allows you to keep notes in real time on locations that can be stored or transferred to your desktop. You can mark holding areas and the soft (currents) and hard (logs) structures that do not appear on contour maps.

For the night fisherman, these units can be a big help in finding your vehicle or boat launch in the dark. You can also chart a safe path to where you want to be on the river. Or, while on a multi-day drift through the Alaskan tundra when the mountains are in a mist and you can't triangulate off of them with your compass (assuming that you know how to triangulate), you can easily locate where you are in relation to the rest of the world. The GPS units also tell you at what speed you are moving, from which you can derive how long it will take to get to your destination. I use this feature to clock the speed of schooling baitfish so that I can mimic their pace with either my hand retrieve or trolling motor. The shore angler can easily keep his bearings if he can roughly remember where he is standing and what he sees in front of him. But the stillwater angler has a more difficult challenge, especially when trolling in open water. The angler can mark his spots on the GPS and come back over them on a return swing.

Sonar Fish Finders

The river angler can usually discern the feeding and resting zones of trout based on the location of riffles, runs, pools, and other structures. The stillwater angler can also figure out a few pieces of the puzzle by analyzing structures such as points, shoals, and feeder creeks, but an electronic fish finder can be much more reliable and effective. This sounds like a simple concept, and it is, but many stillwater anglers frown on digital devices. I use fish finders to determine the depth where big fish are concentrating, to better understand subsurface structure, and to monitor water temperatures. I rarely cast unless I can see fish in my fish finder, and I use a trolling motor on my pontoon boat to scurry me around the lake to look for them. Once located, I quietly position my craft within casting distance.

Most electronic fish finders utilize sonar, short for Sound Navigation and Ranging, to identify objects in the water. A transducer sends out short bursts of ultrasonic sound waves into the water and then listens for echoes to come back from objects and the bottom. Reading sonar is not an exact science, and it isn't going to find you big trout right off. Some of what you see on your screen will appear to be fish, but might be other things such as logs, submerged vegetation, rocks, and air bubbles from spring heads. Correct interpretation may take you four or five trips to different stillwaters.

Another issue that you have to be aware of is the cone angle, or the area that the sonar covers. The deeper the water, the greater spread you will have. Considering that your transducer head, where the sonar sends the signals from, may be only a few inches wide and your cone angle is probably less than 20 degrees (check your manual), your coverage a foot or two below the boat will only be a few more inches. When you get into deeper waters, 10 or more feet, the vertical view of a sonar starts to become more practical. Realizing this inadequacy, some sonar manufacturers came up with devices that look both vertically and horizontally at the same time and show you a split-screen view. These sonar devices allow the angler a wide degree of penetration and make them practical for shallow waters. You will be able to see the trout feeding on prey fish just below the surface when the zooplankton rises up at dusk. The ability to scan sideways will help you to locate trout with a greater degree of stealth. But the same difficulties that arise with vertical views are also an issue with the horizontal one. You have to practice how to use the devices under different water conditions in order to receive the most benefit from them.

I remember the first day I used a sonar fish finder. I set the device in a PVC tube that was strapped to the side of my float tube. I was fishing a high desert reservoir in central Oregon. It was mid-summer and the trout seemed to be concentrating in front of the dam, on the bottom in about thirty feet of water. All of the other anglers in the boats around me were lowering down heavy split-shot rigs with Power Bait, a form of synthetic fish food in dozens of different colors, textures, and sizes. Just about everyone was catching fish. Then some-

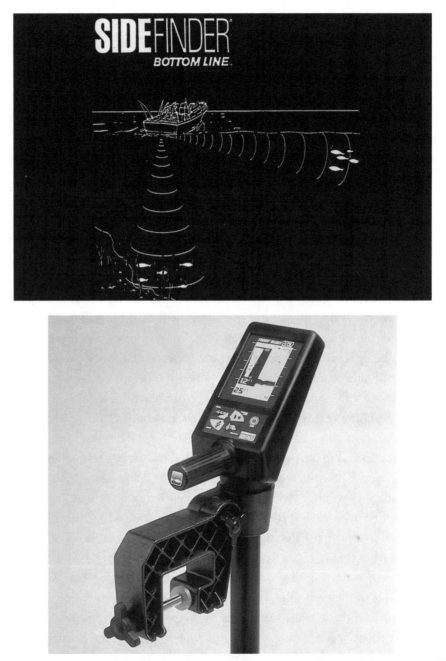

Fish finders that look both horizontally and vertically are of great benefit to the stillwater angler. The portable Fishing Buddy from Computrol can be attached to a small craft. (Photos courtesy of Computrol.)

thing changed. Through my fish finder, I could see the fish slowly rising to the surface, a foot per minute. The fishing success for the other anglers also changed. No one hooked into anything. I heard someone remark that the bite was off. The fish kept rising until they were about two feet below the surface. I could see them in the horizontal view of my fish finder. Midges began to appear on the surface but the fish didn't follow. My guess is that the turbulence of the boat traffic kept them down. I switched to a Class I/Intermediate with a *Chironomidae* pupae pattern. I used a slow, hand-twist retrieve, letting the fly line sink to about two feet, just where I saw the fish in my fish finder. Immediately, I started catching fish. It wasn't until I was driving home that I realized the power I had just experienced.

Fish finders will also help you to better understand subsurface structure. You will have the ability to locate submerged weedbeds, channels formed from old creek beds, and where shoals break off into deeper water. They are especially valuable when used in conjunction with bathymetry maps.

I remember one late fall day when I was fishing a small lake with rainbow trout that were holding where the shoals broke off to deeper water, between four and ten feet deep. It would not have been possible for me to know this without a fish finder, as the water was murky and visibility limited. I trolled along this lip with a Class II, full sinking fly line and hooked into a fish almost every minute my line was in the water. An associate followed behind me using the same technique and fly—without the aid of a fish finder. I out-fished him five to one that day. The reason was that he couldn't see the lip and thus couldn't position his fly over this structure.

Fish finders may also help you to weed out the big trout from the little ones or find where prey fish are located. A friend once related a story to me about fishing a lake and hooking into what he considered to be "hundreds of soft-taking fish." He changed patterns, hook sizes, and colors all day long but didn't land any of them, so he couldn't tell exactly what they were. He owned a fish finder that had been left at home because he thought that this lake was too small. He returned the next day armed with smaller flies and his fish finder to take a second shot at the elusive fish. Before his first cast he realized what had transpired the day before. Through his fish finder, which discerns between big and small fish, he could see masses of small fish, probably shiners, that had just been pecking at his flies. There were no big fish in the area. After a brief outburst, he regained his composure and set off to other parts of the lake in search of trout.

In addition to telling me where the fish are, I also use fish finders to tell me where the fish are not. There have been countless times when I have trolled by other anglers working dead water—an area devoid of fish. On my return to the boat ramp, some hours later, I will pass by the anglers still in the same spot. They will usually question how I did. When I respond that I caught a few nice fish, they will always ask, "What fly were you using?" A pointless question. They could have tied on the same flies I did but probably wouldn't have had any better luck in their bathtub. They were fishing areas where there were no fish.

I have to admit that I probably spent some twenty-five of my angling years fishing a lot of dead water. I will also confess that I scorned a few serious conventional anglers with their dual-engine crafts and assortment of electronics. I now realize that some of these guys know more about the habitat and biological needs of bass than I will ever know about trout. A few minutes watching *In-Fisherman* on television should humble any angler. Success for many of these anglers yields big tournament purses and advertising contracts. They don't leave it up to luck.

The prices of sonar fish finders range from about $150 into the thousands of dollars. The more advanced models can track individual fish, have higher resolution screens, read water temperatures at great depths, and record positions of fish and structure through an integrated GPS unit. There is no hard and fast rule as to what amount of money to spend or level of sophistication to buy, but a good gauge would be how much you spent on your watercraft. If you will be fishing from a float tube or pontoon boat, I would stick with a model that goes for under $250. If I ever buy a $30,000 boat, I might spend $3,000 on a unit.

I take a fish finder with me on almost all of my trips. It is best not to transport your fish finder in the bed of your truck or the bottom of your boat. I can personally attest that they will be damaged under these conditions. I fashioned a case for my Fishing Buddy by reducing the length of a big pouch, PVC-reinforced rod case down to the length of my fish finder's shaft. I have been able to fit this into the overhead storage bins on every plane that I have been on. Cases for box-style fish finders are easy to find. Both should go on the plane with you to protect the fragile electronics.

Motors

If the cliché "why walk when you can drive" makes any sense, then "why kick or paddle when you can cruise with a motor" should be of equal value. The size of the motor should be in direct proportion to your craft. I use a small electric trolling motor for my pontoon boat and more powerful motors for larger boats. The maximum speed of my trolling motor when attached to my pontoon boat is 2.1 mph, as clocked by my GPS. Your trolling motor must have a deep cycle battery for all-day use and a quick recharger so that it will be ready the next morning. I keep a second battery in my rig in case I am camping at a facility without an electrical hook-up.

Here are several reasons why you should consider using a trolling motor:

- Reduce fumbling with the line when you are starting to troll.
- Better gauge your speed of travel with the motor settings.
- When the fish grabs the fly you already have control of the line and rod and do not need to pick them up.
- If the law allows, the ability to troll with one rod without fear of having the second rod being ripped out of your hands by a fish or submerged object.
- Control a drift parallel to the shoreline and cast to cruising fish.
- Keep your hands free for changing flies, lines, and leaders while moving from one area to another.

Watercraft

Float tubes are great for getting anglers into small waters that do not have boat ramps. They can be easily portaged and hold just enough gear and food to get you through a day. When I teach stillwater clinics, I put everyone into a float tube and have them kick around a pond. I rarely fish with one these days, though. In my opinion, despite their versatility and comfortable price point, float tubes are not the ideal craft for most stillwaters.

Pontoon boats and small prams are much more versatile and can be equipped with trolling motors and oars for the angler who is moving to, or with, the trout. If you spook all of the big trout where you are fishing, or if there weren't any to begin with, you can search someplace else. An additional advantage of a pontoon boat is that you only need to deal with one anchor system in the rear of the craft as your body serves as the second anchor system in a pontoon boat. A boat requires two anchors to keep it from spinning. Pontoon boats can be easily portaged. They also tend to be quieter in the water and provide anglers with enough water clearance to cast.

There are bodies of water where the fishing grounds are separated by miles of vegetation, making them unsuitable for any craft without a serious engine. In these cases, a "real" boat is mandatory. Larger boats are also necessary to troll on bigger lakes such as Pend Oreille and Quesnel where the waves often exceed four feet in height. You don't, of course, need to buy such a large boat for your next trip if you only fish big water occasionally. If your targeted water requires something bigger than a pontoon boat, a rental will probably be available.

A boat has been developed to handle the unique characteristics of every river and stillwater in the world. The right craft for moving waters depends on the velocity of the current, the depth, and boating regulations. On the White River, anglers use long, motorized johnboats. Some Alaskan lodges portage guests in johnboats, Osprey Lake guides use 25-foot canoes, and Williamson River anglers fish from McKenzie-style drift boats. Watercraft is a broad topic and anglers should look at each water individually to determine what is the best boat and how to rig it. Tom Earnhardt recently wrote an excellent book on the topic, entitled *Boats for Fishermen.* This book is a good resource for taking that next step.

Trip Checklist

Every trip I take begins with a list. No one will ever accuse me of being the most organized person, and such a list helps me keep track of things so that I do not forget the essentials.

Equipment Checklist	Stillwaters	Tailwaters	Migratory Trout Rivers
GPS			
Bug spray/anti-itch lotion			
Suntan lotion			
Mesh bug hat/bed netting			
Mini first-aid kit			
Map of lake/area			
Flies for targeted species			
Flies for other species			
Fishing license			
Portable fly-tying kit			
Rods and reels in durable cases			
Portable fish finder in durable case with a mounting fixture			
Extra batteries for fish finder			
Fly lines for specific water conditions			
Camera, film, and batteries			
Leaders			
Hook sharpener			
WD-40			
Stripping gloves			
Waders/boots			
Wader repair kit			

CHAPTER 10
FOCUS ON CATCHING
BIG TROUT

Not all who wander are lost.
J. R. R. Tolkien

The beginner angler just wants to catch fish, plain and simple. If the angler can do it on the surface and see the rise to a personally-tied creation, he is doubly happy. The size and the species of the fish doesn't matter much. They are all beautiful—bass, panfish, trout. Assuming the angler has fished before, he probably just graduated from watching a bobber get dunked to a mayfly get munched. A certain dignity will emerge, something like new converts to a religion. This is stage one on the fly fishing road to enlightenment.

At some point, it might take one season or many, the angler will realize he or she isn't catching the fish that dreams are made of, despite spending thousands on equipment, clothing, and customized license plate frames. Warmwater fish may be scorned, depending on what area of the country the angler lives in, and trout will be king. When he thinks beyond trout, it will be steelhead or Atlantic salmon. Salmonids may not be the only fish on the angler's list. A trip to the Florida Keys for giant tarpon or moonlit stripers in the Atlantic surf may enter the fishing log.

The angler will come to one of three conclusions: 1) He isn't spending enough money and heads off to his local fly shop where the proprietor is more than willing to sell him a "finer" rod and a box of "sure" flies to boost his confidence. He will probably buy a few more angling accessories (read gadgets) on his own just to feel better, and maybe some artwork for his den or office. 2) He isn't fishing in the "right places," and starts to inquire where they are. The fly shop will often tell him these places are far away and that they can help him book the trip. The "right places" are typically north and west. He may travel to Montana for the fish of his dreams, then hear from his guide that Alaska is the place to go. After saving up the dollars for an Alaskan trip, his guide there will tell him that Kamchatka, Russia is where he will catch the biggest fish. 3) He never thought that he was going to catch any fish to begin with, and the natural surroundings relax him after a tough week at the office. Let's call this group stage two.

The first path is a dead-end. It may eventually lead to the second route once the angler buys all that can be bought, and assuming he doesn't find another expensive interest where fulfillment can be reached more quickly, and with a martini at the end of the run—like golf. I remember a comment from a new angler with a heart-attack-waiting-to-happen stressful job who frequented a stream that meandered through a closely-cut lawn with picnic tables on its banks. He said that he liked to fish there because it relaxed him. It is not much of a trout stream, but fishing is helping this angler to just stay alive and that's not such a bad thing.

It is the angler on path two that is heading in the direction of big trout. His first long-distance trip will be made with the convenience of his family, friends, and office on his mind. He will enjoy the fishing trip and catch lots of trout, although maybe not big trout. After the angler realizes that he was in the "right place" but not at the ideal time, his real-world life will begin to revolve around his fishing plans, until finally his real world is fishing and he works just to support this pursuit. He is beginning to develop the stamina and attitude needed to catch big trout. He has reached stage three. This book is for him.

You know the dedicated angler by that look in his eyes. There is a spirit of determination. He is a professional guide, has written his own book, or is the kid with a B.A. in literature or philosophy that works in an angling shop and seems to have all the answers except how to pay his student loans. There are many of them out there, some well-known and countless others who never sought to have their name in print and whose stories do not reach the larger population of anglers. I have met a few of these big trout hunters in my travels.

The Alaskan guide is the quintessential big fish hunter. He lives and breathes big trout for five months a year, enduring cramped, sweaty cabins, curious bears, rodents in his bed, infrequent showers, guests that will never appreciate his efforts, and hordes of mosquitoes that just won't quit. Needless to say, many big trout anglers have patient spouses or are divorced, remarried, divorced again, or realize early on that it would be wise to save the legal fees for fishing trips and plan to be forever single. Some have life partners that are on the same road, but these lucky couples are rare. I know of one big fish angler whose spouse had the cause in the divorce papers stated as "passionate and relentless pursuit of interests other than our marriage."

As for physical needs, a guide once responded to my question about a noontime meal with, "Lunch? It will break your concentration." True big fish anglers do just that. They keep fishing regardless of environmental extremes and human needs. The day that you take a leak while kneeling on the edge of your pontoon boat you are hooked—doubly so for women. It takes a certain dedication to succeed in anything, whether it is politics, sports, or business. Big trout hunting is no different.

And to catch big trout you do have to hunt them. You may boat one or two incidentally in a season, but the guys who catch them consistently don't do it by accident. Trophy trout take time, regardless of your timing and techniques, largely due to their limited numbers.

Dale Williams, from Screaming Reels Fly and Tackle on the shores of Kootenay Lake, considers the 8- to 10-pound Gerrard-strain rainbows to be the fishery's bread and butter. A good guide will put you into a few every day. But for sizes greater than this, he sees about one fish for each 20 rod hours, and make that 100 rod hours for a 17-pound plus fish. Similarly,

This nine-pound rainbow from Kootenay Lake in British Columbia, held by Captain Frank van Neer of East Shore Charters, is a common catch in this water.

Keith Snyder from Lake Pend Oreille estimates that you have to put in 20 rod hours for a 10-pound Gerrard rainbow on his lake, and 100 rod hours for a 20-pound fish.

An angler must be dedicated to catch these fish, and willing to focus his efforts. Anglers can reduce the number of hours per fish by hunting big trout in the right places and at the most opportune times. Most of these estimates were derived from anglers who fished over an eight-hour-plus day. Sometimes these long unproductive daytime hours on the water are necessary, as you will not have much luck trying to hire a guide to just fish the morning and evening windows.

Sometimes having your line in the water is all that it takes. I remember reading from a local small town paper as I was eating breakfast in a diner on the way to someplace else. The title read "Kid Catches Record Fish Off Town Dock." The article started off with how the kid sat diligently day after day, rain or shine, fishing on the end of the dock. The interview went into where the kid attended school, where mom and dad worked, and how long the family had been outstanding members of the community. Mom, as it turned out, made great peach pies, and dad's uncle was a local politician. It was what some journalists call a "puff piece." Trying to get back to the point of the story, the reporter asked the kid what his secret was in rigging up a worm and bobber. The kid described how he threaded his worm three times, as opposed to the two-thread local standard. But the kid had already told him the real secret. The fish was caught because the kid was there and had his line in the water. He fished through all hours of the day, weather conditions, and fish activity rhythms.

I met with the opposite extreme shortly after arriving in Oregon. As I was walking along the bank on a nearby steelhead river looking for a good place to drift my fly, I ran across another angler. He was sitting on a log beside a campfire, warming his hands with a cup of coffee. I almost tripped over his rod, which was leaning up against a rock across the path. The gentleman remarked that the fishing was slow—not just that day but the past seven years. After a little prying, he disclosed that he hadn't hooked a steelie in three years, and in his words, "It wasn't for lack of trying, as I fish every weekend in December, January, and February." I left him to his campfire and went on to fish, a little unsure about my own prospects and wondering if relocating to Oregon had been such a good idea.

I landed three steelhead that day and lost a few others. While returning to my rig, I noticed the gentleman still with a mug in hand and his rod set up against the boulder. He was cooking a can of stew over the fire this time. I thought to myself that it was no wonder he wasn't catching fish: He didn't have his line in the water.

Concentrate on waters that hold big trout. When your non-angling family wants to take a vacation, steer them to some of the serene lodges where they can enjoy the great outdoors and you can fish. Elysia Resort on Quesnel Lake, Rocky Point Resort on Upper Klamath Lake, and Lonesome Duck on the Williamson River are just a few fine family vacation retreats that you can drive to. There are many others.

Finally, don't give up. A few years ago I was fishing for migrating browns at the beginning of October and sighted a fish of about ten pounds feeding close to the bottom at the tail of a pool. I positioned myself in an ideal drifting position and dropped my fly in front of its nose over and over again for about an hour. There were no takes. I changed flies a dozen times. Still no takes. In frustration, I decided to look for another fish. I went downstream of the pool, crossed the river, and started to head upstream when out of the corner of my eye I saw the big brown splash on the surface. Would it now be interested? I positioned myself again for the ideal drift and dropped my fly in front of its nose once more. The brown took my fly this time and was landed shortly afterwards. Upon closer inspection of the fish I noticed that a large-beaked bird had taken a stab at it, piercing one eye. The wound was on the same side I was casting to for over an hour.

Sometimes I think that there is a level above actually catching big trout. At this stage, one understands the genetics, environmental influences, and behavior of trout. This angler doesn't actually have to catch a lot of fish to be successful, but he can predict when the trout will be there and when they are most likely to take a fly.

This book has discussed the daily rhythms of trout from the perspective of chemical changes—specifically the influence of melatonin—but I expect that further primary research on trout from a molecular level will be available to the angling world in years to come. This will greatly expand our understanding of this fascinating animal and our relationship with the natural world. And help us all catch more big trout.

GLOSSARY OF TERMS

Adfluvial Descriptive of migration patterns of fish species that spawn in a freshwater stream then migrate to a freshwater lake for growth.

Amphipods Crustaceans of the order Amphipoda (class Crustacea), characterized by a compressed body, first thoracic segment fuses with the head, and no true carapace.

Anadromous A fish that spawns and spends its early life in fresh water then moves into the ocean where it attains sexual maturity and spends most of its life span.

Arrhythmic No regular pattern, due to an unchanging environment.

Baetis See **Ephemeroptera.**

Barometer There are two types of barometers. One is the "aneroid." This type has a metallic surface and a pointer, with a graduated scale, and is the kind found in most homes. The other is "mercurial," which has mercury in a graduated glass tube.

Barometric Pressure A measure of the weight of air in the atmosphere measured with an instrument called a barometer.

Behavioral Drift Distinct diurnal (daytime) patterns of behavioral activity by which immature insects move at specific times to feed.

Benthic Living on or in the substrate of a stream or body of water.

Biofilm Attached heterotrophic bacterial communities. Essentially synonymous to periphyton.

Blue Water Patterns Fly colors for clear, oligotrophic lakes and rivers.

Brown Water Patterns Fly colors for murky waters such as rivers after a heavy rainfall.

Caddis See **Trichoptera**.

Casting Flies Flies, such as streamers, that are cast to fish in order to locate or attract them. The movement of the rod tip or a hand strip creates the movement of the fly.

Catastrophic Drift High-density drift movements as a result of major physical (e.g., high flow) or chemical (e.g., pollution) disturbances.

Chaoboridae An aquatic insect that feeds on zooplankton.

Chironomidae True flies of the order Diptera. Sometimes called midges.

Circadian Rhythms Such a rhythm is a basic solar-day, one whose period has either slightly lengthened or shortened in constant conditions. These rhythms can be entrained by light/dark cycles ranging from about 22 h to 26 h in length.

Coaster Brook trout exhibiting an adfluvial life history, mainly in Lake Superior.

Cone Vision The retina is made up of two types of cells: cones and rods. Cones are nerve cells that are sensitive to light, detail, and color. Millions of cone cells are packed into the macula, aiding it in providing visual detail. Cones also produce the sensation we call color. Cones contain three different pigments that respond to blue, red, or green wavelengths of light. Cones mix the color signals to produce the variety of colors we see.

Continuous Drift Simple accidental displacement of organisms from the substrata.

Copepods Small crustaceans of the subclass Copepoda, characterized by rigid, sclerotized, cylindrical segments, and a true head with five pairs of appendages.

Crepuscular Event(s) occurring twice a day, such as dawn and dusk.

Cressbugs Small invertebrates, in the subclass Copepoda. See **Copepods.**

Crustaceans Members of the class Crustacea, phylum Arthropoda; all have a hard exoskeleton, usually with a carapace and telson; includes crayfish, crabs, shrimp, zooplankton, and others.

Cycle Same as rhythm.

Daily Rhythm (cycle) event(s) occurring on a 24-hour basis. Used synonymously with diel.

Daphnia A type of zooplankton.

Diel Periodicity Twenty-four-hour pattern of behavior in plants and animals; involved with many species of stream and lake invertebrates subject to migration and drift.

Diel Vertical Migration Movements up and down that occur within intervals of 24 hours or less.

Diptera An order of insects including flies, mosquitoes, midges, horseflies, blackflies, and others; the adults are never aquatic, but many families of dipterans have members that have aquatic larvae and pupae.

Drainage An interconnected group of streams and tributaries forming a major river basin.

Drift The aggregate of terrestrial and aquatic insects drifting with the current, both at the surface and suspended in the water column. See **Behavioral Drift, Catastrophic Drift,** and **Continuous Drift.**

Drifting Flies Flies that are dead drifted in moving waters. These include nymphs, Glo-bugs, and the like.

Ecology The study of the relationship of plants and animals to their physical and biological environment. The physical environment includes light and heat or solar radiation, moisture, wind, oxygen, carbon dioxide, nutrients in soil, water, and atmosphere. The biological environment includes organisms of the same kind as well as other plants and animals.

Emergence   Metamorphosis of immature insects into flying adults; commonly called "the hatch."

Energy   Calories needed for a biological system to function or do work.

Ephemeroptera   Order of insects containing mayflies whose life cycle progression is the egg, nymph, emerger, adult, and spinner. Mayflies are among the oldest insect groups and have been found as fossils dating from about 300 million years ago.

Epilimnion   An upper stratum of more or less uniformly warm water during the summer stratification.

Eutrophic   Overly rich and productive; descriptive of a water body that is overfertilized, as with organic pollution.

Exoskeleton   Hard exterior covering insects and crustaceans, giving support to the body.

Fecundity   Number of eggs produced by a female during a breeding season.

Food Chain   Progression of feeding from prey to predators.

Food Web   Feeding pattern of predators and prey in a complex web of different forms.

Freestone Stream   Soft-water stream usually with igneous rock and cobble substrate.

Feeding Zones   Areas where the trout are active and feeding. Usually shallow areas where food is most abundant.

Full Moon   Phase of the moon when its surface as seen from earth is fully illuminated by the sun. During the full moon period, the moon rises approximately at sunset and sets around sunrise.

Gravitational Pull   See **Tides**.

Green Water Patterns   Fly colors for waters that have a great deal of surface algae, such as eutrophic stillwaters and rivers.

Hard Structure   Physical boundaries in the aquatic environment, such as the bottom, boulders, points, shoals, drop-offs, and deltas.

Home Range   Area used by an animal for all its needs, such as feeding, reproduction, and refuge from predators.

Hypolimnion   The initial temperature of the lowest stratum determined by the final movement of spring turnover.

Ichthyology   The study of fishes.

Invertebrates   Refers to any animal lacking a vertebral column, or backbone.

Kairomones   Chemical cues that animals of different species send to each other.

Kokanee   Landlocked sockeye salmon, *Oncorhynchus nerka*.

Larvae   The early, immature form of an animal that changes structurally as it becomes an adult.

Lateral Line   The longitudinal series of scales bearing pores of the seismosensory system, the system that detects pressure waves in water caused by moving objects.

Lengthy Feed   Morning and evening transitional periods when the illumination changes over a longer period of time—the zooplankton concentrate in the upper stratum of the water column and the aquatic invertebrates in rivers have a heavy behavioral drift. When this feed occurs during the morning transitional periods it starts early, after moonrise, and ends as the zooplankton slowly drop down or the invertebrate drift diminishes. Target active trout with streamers in feeding zones (shallow areas).

Life Cycle   Sequence of life stages in an animal's existence.

Life History   Series of ecological events during major stages of the life cycle.

Limnetic Zone   The region of open water in a lake away from shore extending downward to the maximal depth at which there is sufficient sunlight for photosynthesis.

Limnology   Study of the structural and functional interrelationships of organisms of inland waters as their dynamic physical, chemical, and biotic environments affect them.

Littoral   Refers to the area along the shore of bodies of water.

Low Feed   Periods when the trout cannot feed efficiently due to intense illumination or the trout are satiated after a lengthy feed. The prey fish are often tightly schooled, in dense vegetation, or low in the water column. Invertebrates will have a lower density continuous drift. If a hatch is coming off, this may stimulate the prey that the big trout feed on and excite the trout. Target inactive trout in streams by nymphing in resting zones (deep and cool oxygenated areas). In stillwaters, run a leech pattern or hang a *Chironomidae* pupae pattern just off of the bottom.

Lunar Cycle   Events occurring either at a time basis of 29.53 days (synodic month, based on moon-phases resulting from orbital positions of moon, sun, and earth) or at a time basis of 27.32 days (sideral moon cycle around earth, relative to distant stars).

Mayfly   See **Ephemeroptera.**

Melatonin   A naturally occurring hormone that is released into the bloodstream during the hours of darkness. Scientists believe this hormone (in humans) plays a role in the body's circadian rhythm. This rhythm regulates the physiological functions that occur in the body within a 24-hour period, such as sleep-wake cycles, fluctuations in body temperature, heart rate, and blood pressure.

Mesotrophic   Middle range of productivity; between oligotrophic and eutrophic.

Metamorphosis   In complete metamorphosis, a clear distinction exists between the various stages of the animal's development. In the first phase, an embryo forms inside an egg. When the egg hatches, the animal is called a larva. During the next period, the larva changes into a pupa. At the end of the pupal stage, the adult emerges. Animals that grow in this way include many fishes, mollusks, and insects.

Migratory Trout Rivers   Rivers where trout move to or from a large body of water in order to feed, spawn, or find more hospitable water temperatures and oxygen levels.

Moonlight   Sunlight reflected off of the moon that can be viewed from the dark side of the earth.

Mysis Relicta   Small aquatic crustacea, commonly called the "opossum shrimp" because juveniles are retained within the female for up to three months.

New Moon   One of the four phases of the moon, during which it is directly between the earth and the sun and invisible or seen only as a narrow crescent.

Nocturnal   Activity only during the hours of darkness.

Nymph   Immature stage of hemimetabolous insects (i.e. *Baetis,* damselflies).

Oligotrophic   Term that refers to a low level of productivity. A nutrient-poor lake characterized by low production of plankton and fish and having considerable dissolved oxygen in the bottom waters (due to low organic content).

Opossum Shrimp   See *Mysis Relicta.*

Pelagic   Open water, usually referring to lakes.

Periphyton   Film of algae and other organisms on stones and other substrates on the streambed; the principal food of many benthic insects and other invertebrates.

Phantom Midge   See *Chaoboridae.*

Pheromones   Chemical signals that animals within the same species send to one another.

Photoperiod   The daily cycle of light and darkness that affects the behavior and physiological functions of organisms.

Photosynthesis   The process by which green plants and certain other organisms use the energy of light to convert carbon dioxide and water into simple sugar glucose. In so doing, photosynthesis provides the basic energy source for virtually all organisms.

Phytoplankton   Minute plants, such as algae, which float or drift near the surface of a body of water; they are somewhat smaller than most zooplankton.

Piscivorous   Animals that feed on fish.

Pineal Gland   Small, cone-shaped projection from the top of the midbrain of most vertebrates. Photoreceptive structures linked with the pineal body are still observed in some higher vertebrates. A neural connection remains between the eyes and the gland. The functions of the pineal body in an animal are linked with surrounding light levels.

Plankton   Very small or microscopic plants and animals that swim passively or float near the surface of a body of water.

Planktivorous   Animals that feed on plankton.

Poor Feed   Periods when the natural illumination is below the visual threshold of the trout and they cannot feed efficiently on prey fish. Slowly work big and noisy streamers in resting zones (deep and cool oxygenated areas) or go home to sleep.

Predator   Animal that feeds on other animals.

Prey Fish   Small fish that big trout feed on, including kokanee, minnows, sculpins, shad, chubs, sticklebacks, shiners, smelt, alewife, and sometimes smaller trout.

Profundal   The region below the pelagic zone where light does not penetrate. It consists of exposed fine sediments free of vegetation.

Pupae   Life history stage of holometabolous insects during which larvae are transformed into adults.

Redd   Spawning nest of trout.

Reservoir   Man-made impoundment of approximately 500 surface acres or more at normal pool level.

Resting Zones   Areas where the trout rest and digest. Usually cooler regions where there is sufficient oxygen.

Retinomotor Movement   Movement of the rods and cones within the retina of the eye.

Rhythm   Periodic recurrence of an event or events. Same as cycle.

Riffle   A section of stream in which the water is usually shallower than in the connecting pools and over which the water runs more swiftly than it does in the pools. A riffle is shallower than a chute (run) and usually has at least some white-water breaking over the substrate.

Rod Vision   The retina is made up of two types of cells: cones and rods. Rods are designed for night vision and the detection of motion and objects. They also provide peripheral vision, but they do not see as acutely as cones. Rods are insensitive to color.

Salmonid   Any member of the family Salmonidae, which includes the salmon, trout, chars, whitefishes, ciscoes, inconnu, and grayling of North America.

Satiation   A point of fullness.

Scrape   Method by which some aquatic invertebrates retrieve food from the surfaces of plants, rocks, and debris.

Scuds   Aquatic invertebrates of the subclass Amphipoda. See **Amphipods.**

Sediment   Inorganic particles deposited on the streambed, ranging in size from clay to boulders.

Sexual Maturation   Age at the time of first spawning is the height of maturation. The maturation process occurs several months before spawning.

Short Feed   Morning and evening transitional periods when there is a relatively abrupt change in the illumination or periods. Target active trout with streamers in feeding zones (shallow areas).

Sitting Flies   Flies that hang from a floating fly line or strike indicator in stillwaters. Typical of this category are *Chironomidae*, scuds, and cressbugs.

Smolt   Life cycle stage of a migratory fish, particularly salmonids, when they approach leaving their natal stream for the ocean.

Soft Structure   Non-permanent boundaries in the aquatic system, such as temperature zones, currents, shade, muddy water, and the surface of the water.

Soft-Rayed Prey Fish   They have no spiney rays in any of the fins and the scales are smooth like the trout. The most common prey fish for trout are alewives, smelt, minnows, chubs, and kokanee.

Species   The fundamental taxonomic category; subdivision of a genus; group of organisms that naturally or potentially interbreed, are reproductively isolated from other such groups, and are usually morphologically separable from them.

Spined Prey Fish   Small fish that lives in salt, brackish, and fresh waters that have dorsal and pelvic fins composed of spines and soft rays. The most common prey fish for the trout are the sticklebacks.

Sporadic Feed   Periods between short and low feeds when the trout looks for food even though conditions are not optimal. Expect infrequent bites. Target active trout with streamers in feeding zones (shallow areas).

Starlight   Direct light from other suns.

Stillwaters   Ponds, lakes, and reservoirs.

Subspecies   A taxonomic category, a subdivision of a species; a group of local populations inhabiting a geographic subdivision of the species range, and differing taxonomically from other populations of the species.

Sunlight   Direct light from our sun.

Super Trout   Late-maturing, long-lived trout that grow to larger sizes. They are typically from oligotrophic lakes.

Swinging Flies   Flies, such as streamers, that are cast upstream and then swung down and across in the current.

Synchronization   To make something work at the same time or the same rate as something else.

Synodic Period   Cycle of moon-phasing resulting from orbital positions of earth, moon, and sun, each 29.53 days.

Tailwaters   Rivers whose immediate source is a reservoir.

Thermostratification   The three layers in lakes characterized by differences in temperature.

Thermocline   The plane of maximum rate of decrease of temperature with respect to depth.

Tides   The moon, being much nearer to the earth than the sun, is the principal cause of tides. Because the force of gravity decreases with distance, the moon exerts a stronger gravitational pull on the side of the earth that is closer to it and a weaker pull on the side farther from it. The world's oceans are liquid and can flow in response to the variation in the moon's pull. On the side of the earth facing the moon, the moon's stronger pull makes water flow toward it, causing a dome of water to rise on the earth's surface directly below the moon. On the side of the earth facing away from the moon, the moon's pull on the oceans is weakest. The water's inertia, or its tendency to keep traveling in the same direction, makes it want to fly off the earth instead of rotate with the planet. The moon's weaker pull doesn't compensate as much for the water's inertia on the far side, so another dome of water rises on this side of the earth. The dome of water directly beneath the moon is called direct tide, and the dome of water on the opposite side of the earth is called opposite tide. As the earth rotates throughout the day, the domes of water remain aligned with the moon and travel around the globe. When a dome of water passes a place on the earth, that place experiences a rise in the level of the ocean water, known as high tide or high water.

Transition Periods   Long transition periods occur when the moon rises before the sun sets or before the sun rises. Short transition periods occur when the moon rises after the sun sets or after the sun rises.

Trichoptera   An order of insects (caddisflies) in which the small to medium-sized mothlike adults are found near streams, ponds, and lakes; the larvae and pupae are aquatic and are found in all types of freshwater habitats. About 4,500 species of caddisflies exist worldwide with some 1,000 species in North America.

Trolling Flies   Flies, such as streamers, that are designed to be pulled behind a boat. The movement of the boat often gives movement to the fly.

Total Dissolved Solids (TDS)   Measure of the relative productivity of water. The greater the number, the more productive the water is. The upper limit for an oligotrophic lake would be 75 parts per million (ppm), while the lower limit for a eutrophic lake would be 75–100 ppm. Lakes within the 200 to 400 ranges are very productive and have the capability to maintain healthy populations of trout.

Turbidity   Refers to the decreased ability of water to transmit light caused by suspended particulate matter ranging in size from colloidal to coarse dispersions; turbidity may result from colloidal clay particles entering a body of water with runoff, colloidal organic matter originating from decay of vegetation, or from an abundance of plankton.

Waning Moon   When the moon is progressing from full to new.

Watershed   Older term often used for valley or drainage basin.

Waxing Moon   When the moon is progressing from new to full.

Zooplankton   Free-floating small crustaceans that inhabit lakes, ponds, and oceans.

ENDNOTES

1. A trout's maintenance ration is the amount of energy consumed on an average day that maintains body weight of energy (no gain, no loss). This depends on total metabolism (higher in warmer water, lower in colder water): basic or resting metabolism and active metabolism (when fish feed, or move and expend extra energy). If maintenance ration is one percent and the fish consumes ten percent of its body weight per day, then ninety percent of the energy goes into growth and ten percent is used for maintenance. At two percent consumption rate, fifty percent is used for maintenance and fifty percent for growth. The rate of growth is obviously much greater if the percentage of food used for growth is greater (Behnke).

2. Manipulation appears to be a learned behavior. Dr. Moodie observed that the first time he put hatchery-reared trout in a tank with sticklebacks they were immediately attacked and just as quickly released when the trout felt the spines. After that experience, he had to starve the trout for days before they would attack again. He reasoned that trout conditioned to eating spined prey fish appear to know how to avoid the spines.

3. According to Dr. Arthur Popper, a neuroscientist with the Department of Biology at the University of Maryland, who has a great deal of expertise on hearing in fish, little data exists on hearing in salmonid fishes. Based upon other species, he suggests that trout could detect somewhat "higher" frequencies with the ear (maybe to 500 Hz), but sensitivity is probably not great.

4. Numerous studies have demonstrated that fish can detect other species of fish with their lateral lines. However, all of the studies that I have researched place the predator and prey species within a few inches of each other and in confined quarters where the prey cannot swim away. Sometimes the predator fish would appear to bump into the prey fish while swimming (e.g. Enger et al.), suggesting that when the prey fish was not moving, no signal was released from it or it was not within the detection range of the predator. This study also suggests that the lateral line is not an efficient locating device for a roving piscivorous predator when searching for prey fish that freeze to avoid them. Freezing is a common method of predatory avoidance for prey fish (Bell and Foster). These controlled laboratory experiments also demonstrated that the

predator fish's approach is slow and cautious, and not one that could reliably catch a moving prey fish. Additionally, most spined (e.g. sticklebacks) and soft-rayed (e.g. chubs) prey fish cannot be casually engulfed by trout and must be strategically captured. Dr. Eric Moodie, a biologist with the University of Winnipeg, observed that when trout and sticklebacks were left overnight in the same 300-gallon tank (predator and prey were less than two meters apart) the prey fish often appeared live and well when he turned on the lights the next morning. Other studies have shown that the lateral line only enables fish to hear sounds that are at most a couple of body lengths from them.

5. In a river situation, the lateral line and inner ear system is probably not helpful for the trout to feed on items in the drift. One study demonstrated that the reactive distance of brook trout to drifting prey decreased as turbidity increased (Sweka and Hartman). I followed up with Dr. John Sweka from West Virginia University about brook trout continuing to feed in the drift at great turbidity. His response was that when the water became turbid, the fish no longer "drift feed" in the classic sense. They become more active and swim throughout the stream in search of prey. Although this switch in foraging strategies compensated for the decreased reactive distance, it was energetically costly and specific growth rates decreased under turbid conditions. This is not a condition conducive to growing big trout.

6. Charlie White authored nine books on marine life and recorded many fish species on video in both still- and moving-water environments over a period of more than ten years. His findings are thought provoking and his video series is a must-see for any serious angler. While most of White's research was on large piscivorous salmon in the Pacific Ocean, he also looked at many freshwater game fish, including rainbow trout, and much of what he learned about the behavior of fish is applicable to other trout.

7. Notes for Stillwaters:

   (1) 100'+ horizontal visibility for humans

   (2) Less than 10' horizontal visibility for humans

   (3) Less than 8' horizontal visibility for humans

   (4) Estimates provided by Paul Johnson, author of *The Scientific Angler* (1984). Johnson spent countless hours diving for and photographing fish in oceans and lakes.

   Notes for Moving Waters:

   (5) Estimates provided by Dr. Gary Grossman, Professor of Animal Ecology at the University of Georgia, School of Forest Resources and co-author of Barrett, J. D., G. D. Grossman, and J. Rosenfeld. 1992. Turbidity induced changes in reactive distance in rainbow trout (*Oncorhynchus mykiss*). *Trans. Am. Fish. Soc.* 121: 437–443.

8. During the day, the rods are extended on long stalks so that their sensitive parts are buried in a layer of pigmented epithelium. This epithelium shields the rods so that very little light reaches them from the sides, and the cones shield them from axially propagating light. At night the cones are extended out into the pigmented epithelium, and the rods are contracted back to where the cones were during the day. These processes are not instantaneous and take most of the dusk and dawn periods to complete.

9. A mature trout has three active color cones (red, blue, and green) that enable the fish to see these colors and combinations of them. Juvenile trout have a fourth ultraviolet light cone that is lost as the fish changes its food sources and/or matures (Douglas and Djamgoz). Trout have retinal sensitivities that are strong on the blue side and can differentiate between shades of blue that are slightly different.

10. There is little organic matter in oligotrophic waters so the light is scattered, making it look blue to us. When there is a lot of organic matter in the water, such as in a farm pond, the color green, a short wavelength is absorbed readily by this material and longer wavelengths (orange and red) are absorbed less, but they still don't penetrate that deep. This is because the algae and higher plants absorb all of the reds and blues during photosynthesis. This leaves the green wavelength that penetrates the deepest and reflects back to our eyes. The extreme end of the spectrum are bogs and "black water" areas where there is so much humic substances that all light is absorbed. Just before this extreme are typical muddy creeks where the water looks brown because we see some refraction on the red end of the spectrum. The red light penetration is still limited, as this color is a longer wavelength.

11. This data was contributed by Paul Johnson. Johnson notes that there are not abrupt changes in color as you reach a specific depth. Rather the color shift is subtle and progressive. He also notes that the degree of turbidity influences the depth at which these color shifts occur, and apart from relative ambient light intensity levels, there are marginal differences between horizontal versus vertical visibility. This assumes, however, homogeneity within the environment. If turbid stratification layers exist, significant differences can occur. The table should not be viewed as an absolute but rather, an approximation.
    (1) Estimates provided by Paul Johnson
    (2) 100′+ horizontal visible for humans
    (3) Less than 10′ horizontal visibility for humans
    (4) Less than 8′ horizontal visibility for humans

12. In another study, the reaction of the cutthroat trout to the sticklebacks was tested with varying degrees of light. The finding was that as light was reduced (less overall and red light) and all of the colors turned to black, the attacks on the sticklebacks declined (Moodie). The trout could still see the sticklebacks, but there were no strong contrasts in coloration to elicit a response.

13. Smell and taste are both forms of chemoreception. Chemicals in the water stimulate chemical receptors in or on different parts of the fish's body. Smelling is accomplished through the nostrils, much like humans. The taste buds of trout are found in many parts of the body, not just in the mouth, and they are often concentrated on the fins and tail. Whether it is called smell or taste simply depends on where the chemical receptors are located and how they are wired to the brain. While the fly fisher probably does not want the trout to swallow his or her presentation, the amount of time that the fly resides in the trout's mouth can be a determining factor in whether you are able to get a good hook-set.

14. Pure Fishing in Spirit Lake, Iowa is the umbrella organization for a number of angling and camping supply companies, including Berkley. In the lab at Pure Fishing they have dozens of

tanks with different types of fish where they conduct carefully controlled experiments to test the fish's reaction to new lures, scents, and lines. Paul Johnson, an alumnus of Pure Fishing, did much of his research while working there. They spent over a decade testing thousands of scents on trout, bass, walleye, pike, catfish, and other game fish to determine what the fish like (which they incorporate in the recipes for Power Bait). During the process, they also found what fish do not like.

15. Often people use the term circadian rhythm in place of daily rhythms. Only when animal rhythms are studied in artificial and constant conditions do they have an almost 24-hour cycle, described by the term "circadian." The rhythms are never circadian in a day/night condition.

16. Newman's total hours fished were 2,078 and total fish hooked were 3,915 for an average of 1.88 fish per hour (including days and hours skunked). During this period, he took a total of 369 feeding samples from rainbow trout killed, and the stomach contents were examined for the quantity and frequency of each type of invertebrate or prey fish.

17. This is easiest to see in a newborn human, in which (according to extensive evidence) conscious awareness of one's self has not yet emerged. Nonetheless, the baby's behavior enables it to feed as necessary in order to maintain adequate nutrition. It's easy to feed a baby if it hasn't been fed for some time, but when satiated the child won't eat. Some people with profound mental retardation have no capacity for conscious awareness, but they still get hungry, eat, and stop eating when satiated. There are multiple regulatory controls of vertebrate eating and they typically entail a combination of internal signals (of which we are unaware) that act directly on the brain. External stimulus factors also play a role, such as the presence of food (we suddenly become hungry because of insulin release in response to food odors), or learned associations between food and eating, as in eating at mealtimes whether we are hungry or not (Rose).

18. Most studies of trout find that their stomachs are more than half filled or that most stomach contents are fresh. Initially, the findings of these studies seem to suggest that trout do not feed until their stomachs are empty and then feed until they are satiated. However, food absorption takes place chiefly in the lower gut next to the stomach and in the pyloric caecae (Johnston). So although the stomach may be empty or full, this is not an indication of satiation. For carnivores, such as trout, that have periodic access to food sources, such as drifting invertebrates, this storage capacity is essential (Boujard and Leatherland).

19. There is a similar plausible hypothesis. A study about arctic char (a fish similar to brook trout) and brown trout showed that in certain Scandinavian lakes both had the same preferred diets of aquatic and terrestrial invertebrates. But during the summertime, the more dominant brown trout excluded the char from the littoral zone (the more productive area of the lake that receives light) and forced them to feed out in the lake on the less preferred zooplankton. Another study on Loch Leven in Scotland suggested that larger and more territorial brown trout that feed on benthic food items displaced the smaller trout upwards in the water column where there were fewer food items. To survive, these fish became more aggressive when feeding, making them more susceptible to anglers fishing on or near the water's surface (Thorpe). Thus, big trout can

bully their smaller comrades, creating areas that will have greater concentrations of big trout than others.

20. "Nylon" is the Dupont trade name for polyamide, although most people use the word nylon generically. There are many forms of nylon and there are few, if any, that haven't been experimented with for monofilament fishing line. Each type of nylon has its own characteristics (hardness, break strength, heat resistance) that are useful to the angler. Most of nylon monofilaments on the market are a combination of nylon 6 and nylon 66, with 85 percent of the former and 15 percent of the latter. The technical description is a nylon 6/66 co-polymer. The characteristics of a nylon 6/66 are good abrasion resistance, flexibility, clarity, surface hardness, and knot strength. Some resin manufacturers put in special additives to strengthen these attributes. The resin is one of the keys to how well your knots will perform or your line will handle under pressure. The process of transforming nylon from a pellet form to a monofilament also gives it special attributes.

BIBLIOGRAPHY

Adron, J.W., Grant, P.T., and Cowey, C.B. 1973. A system for the quantitative study of the learning capacity of rainbow trout and its application to the study of food preference and behavior. *Journal of Fish Biology.* 6, 625–636.

Ali, M.A., Ryder R.A., and Anctil, M. 1977. Photoreceptors and Visual Pigments as Related to Behavioral Responses and Preferred Habitats of Perches (*Perca* spp.) and Pikeperches (*Stizostedion* spp.) *Journal Fisheries Research Board of Canada.* 34: 1475–1480.

Ali, M.A., Boujard, T., and Gerkema, M. 1992. Terminology in biological rhythms. In Ali, M.A. (ed.). 1992. *Rhythms in Fishes.* Plenum Press.

Ali, M.A. 1992. *Rhythms in Fishes.* Plenum Press.

———. 1979. *Environmental Physiology of Fishes.* Plenum Press.

———. 1975. *Vision in Fishes: New Approaches in Research.* Plenum Press.

Anderson, Norman. 1966. Depressant Effect of Moonlight on Activity of Aquatic Insects. *Nature.* 209, 5020: 319–320.

Angradi, T.R. and Griffith, J.S. 1990. Diel feeding chronology and diet selection of rainbow trout (*Oncorhynchus mykiss*) in the Henry's Fork of the Snake River, Idaho. *Canadian Journal of Fisheries and Aquatic Science.* 47: 199–209.

Angstadt, J.D. and Moore, W.H. 1997. A circadian rhythm of swimming behavior in a predatory leech of the family Erpobdellidae, *American Midland Nature.* 137: 165–172.

Bachman, R.A. 1984. Foraging Behavior of Free-Ranging Wild and Hatchery Brown Trout in a Stream. *Transactions of the American Fisheries Society.* 113, 1–32.

Bagliniere, J.L. and Maisse, Gerard. 1999. *Biology and Ecology of the Brown and Sea Trout.* Praxis Publishing Ltd.

Balon, Eugene K. 1980. *Charrs: Salmonid Fishes of the Genus Salvelinus.* Dr. W. Junk bv Publishers.

Barnes, Robert D. 1987. *Invertebrate Zoology Fifth Edition.* CBS College Publishing.

Barrett, J.D., Grossman, G.D., and Rosenfeld, J. 1992. Turbidity induced changes in reactive distance in rainbow trout (*Oncorhynchus mykiss*). *Transactions of the American Fisheries Society.* 121, 437–443.

Barrett, B.A. and McKeown, B. 1988. Sustained exercise augments long-term starvation increases in plasma growth hormone in the steelhead trout, *Salmo gairdneri. Canadian Journal of Zoology.* 66: 853–855.

Barron, Terry. 1998. *Terry Barron's No-Nonsense Guide to Fly Fishing Pyramid Lake.* Sisters, OR: David Communications.

Batty, R.S., Blaxter, J.H.S., and Liddy, D.A. 1986. Herring filter feeding in the dark. *Marsh Biology.* 91: 371–376.

B.C. Outdoors. 2000. *Freshwater Fishing Directory and Atlas.* OP Publishing Ltd.

Beauchamp, D.A., Baldwin, C.M., Vogel, J.L., and Gubala, C.P. 1999. Estimating diel, depth-specific foraging opportunities with visual encounter rate model for pelagic piscivores. *Canadian Journal of Fisheries and Aquatic Science.* 56 (Suppl. 1) 128–139.

Becker, George C. 1983. *Fishes of Wisconsin.* Madison, Wisconsin. The University of Wisconsin Press.

Behnke, R.J. 2001. Telephone interviews and written correspondence while at Colorado State University.

Behnke, R.J. 1992. *Native Trout of Western North America.* American Fisheries Society Monograph 6.

Behnke, R.J. 1986. About Trout—Brown Trout. *Trout.* Winter.

Bell, Michael A. and Foster, Susan A. 1994. (eds.) *The Evolutionary Biology of the Three-spined Stickleback.* Oxford Science Publications.

Berners, Dame Juliana. 1496. *The Treatyse of Fysshynge with an Angle.* First printed in the *Boke of St. Albans.* (Second Edition). Westminster.

Beukema, J.J. 1970. Acquired hook-avoidance in the pike *Esox lucius* fish with artificial and natural baits. *Journal of Fish Biology.* 2, 155–160.

Black, E.C. 1957. Alternations in the blood level of lactic acid in certain salmonid fishes following muscular activity. I Kamloops trout, *Salmo gairdneri. Journal Fisheries Research Board of Canada.* 14, 117–134.

Black, E.C. 1957. Alternations in the blood level of lactic acid in certain salmonid fishes following muscular activity. II Lake trout, *Salvelinus namaychush. Journal Fisheries Research Board of Canada.* 14, 117–134.

Blaxter, J.H.S. 1976. The role of light in the vertical migration of fish. A review in Evans, G.C., Bainbridge, R., and Rakham, O. (eds.): Light as an ecological factor: II. Blackwell, London, Chapter 8.

Blaxter, J.H.S., Denton, E.J., and Gray, J.A.B. Acoustico-lateralis systems in clupeid fishes. In: Tavolga, W.N., Popper, A.N., Fay, R.R. (eds.) *Hearing and Sound Communication in Fishes.* Springer-Verlag.

Bleckman, H., Tittel, G., and Blubaum-Gronau, E. The Lateral Line System of Surface-Feeding Fish: Anatomy, Physiology, and Behavior. In: Coombs, S., Gorner P., and Munz, H. (eds.) 1989. *The Mechanosensory Lateral Line Neurobiology and Evolution.* Springer-Verlag. pp. 501–526.

Bolliet, V., Cheewasedtham, C., Houlihan, D. Gelineau, A., and Boujard, T. 2000. Effect of feeding time on digestibility, growth performance, and protein metabolism in the rainbow trout *Oncorhynchus mykiss:* interactions with dietary fat levels. *Aquatic Living Resource.* 13, (2) 107–1113.

Boney, A.D. 1975. *Phytoplankton.* Edward Arnold Limited.

Borger, Gary A. 1991. *Designing Trout Flies.* Tomorrow River Press.

————. 1995. *Presentation.* Tomorrow River Press.

Boujard, T. and Leatherland, J.F. 1992. Demand-feeding behavior and diel pattern of feeding activity in *Oncorhynchus mykiss* held under different photoperiod regimes. *Journal of Fish Biology.* 40, 535–544.

Boujard, T. 1999. Les Rythmes Circadiens D'Alimentation Chez Les Teleosteens. *Cybium,* 23 (1) 89–112.

Boujard, T., Gelineau, A., and Corraze, G. 1995. Time of a single daily meal influences growth performance in a rainbow trout, *Oncorhynchus mykiss* (Walbaum). *Aquaculture Research.* 26, 341–349.

Breck, J.E. 1993. Foraging theory and piscivorous fish: are forage fish just big zooplankton? *Transactions of the American Fisheries Society.* 122: 902–911.

Brett, J.R. 1971. Satiation time, appetite, and maximum food intake of sockeye salmon (*Oncorhynchus nerka*). *Journal of the Fisheries Research Board of Canada.* 28, 409–415.

Bronmark, Christer and Hansson, Lars-Anders. 1998. *The Biology of Lakes and Ponds.* Oxford University Press.

Brook Trout Subcommittee. 1997. *Status of Brook Trout prepared for the Lake Superior Technical Committee.* U.S. Fish and Wildlife Service and the Wisconsin Department of Natural Resources.

Brooks, Charles E. 1976. *Nymph Fishing for Larger Trout.* Nick Lyons Books/Winchester Press.

Bruhn, Karl. 1999. *Fly Fishing British Columbia: Masters Series Book 1.* Heritage House Publishing Company, Ltd.

Bruhn, Karl. 1992. *Best of B.C. Lake Fishing.* Whitecap Books.

Butler, Robert. Rogue Trout. In: Stolz, Judith and Schnell, Judith. (eds.) 1991. *Trout.* Stackpole Books.

Butler, R.L. and Hawthorne, V.M. 1968. The Reactions of Dominant Trout to Changes in Overhead Artificial Cover. *Transactions of the American Fisheries Society.* 97: 37–41.

Calabi, Silvio. 1990. *Trout & Salmon Of The World.* The Wellfleet Press.

Campbell, R.N. 1979. Ferox trout, *Salmo trutta* (L.), and charr, *Salvelinus alpinus.* (L.), in Scottish lochs. *Journal of Fish Biology.* 14: 1–29.

Carey, W.E. 1985. Comparative ontogeny of photobehavioral responses of charrs (Salvelinus species). *Environmental Biology of Fishes.* 12, No. 3. 189–200.

Carey, W.E. and Noakes, D.L.G. 1981. Development of photobehavioral responses in young rainbow trout, *Salmo gairdneri* Ricardson. *Journal of Fish Biology.* 19: 285–296.

Casselman, J.M. 1996. Age, growth, and environmental requirements of pike. In: Craig, John F. *Pike, Biology and Exploitation.* Chapman & Hall.

Chan, Brian. 2000–2001. Interviews via email.

Clapp, D.F., Clark, R.D., and Diane, J.S. 1990. Range, Activity, and Habitat of Large, Free-Ranging Brown Trout in a Michigan Stream. *Transactions of the American Fisheries Society.* 119: 1022–1034.

Colebrook, J.M. 1960. Some observations on zooplankton swarms in Windermere. *Journal of Animal Ecology*. 29: 241–242.

Combs, Trey. 1991. *Steelhead Fly Fishing*. The Lyons Press.

Contor, C.R. and J.S. Griffith. 1995. Nocturnal emergence of juvenile rainbow trout from winter concealment relative to light intensity. Hydrobiologia 299: 179–183.

Coombs, S., Gorner, P., and Munz, H. (eds.). 1989. *The Mechanosensory Lateral Line: Neurobiology and Evolution*. New York, NY: Springer-Verlag.

Corbet, P.S. 1958. Lunar periodicity of aquatic insects in Lake Victoria. *Nature*. 182: 330–331.

Cowan, C.A. and Peckarsky, B.L. 1994. Diel feeding and positioning periodicity of a grazing mayfly in a trout stream and a fishless stream. *Canadian Journal of Fisheries and Aquatic Science*. 51: 450–459.

Croton Watershed Chapter of Trout Unlimited. 1992. *A Fly Fisherman's Guide to Fishing the Croton Watershed in Westchester & Putnam Counties, New York*. Bedford Hills, New York: The Croton Watershed Chapter of Trout Unlimited.

Dawidowicz, P., Pijanowska, J., and Ciechomski, K. 1990. Vertical Migration of *Chaoborus* larvae is induced by the presence of fish. *Limnology and Oceanography*, 35, 1631–7.

Deeley, M.A. and Benfey, T.J. 1995. Learning ability of triploid brook trout. *Journal of Fish Biology*. 46: 905–907.

Diana, J.S., Hudson, J.P., and Clark, R.D. Jr. Seasonal and Daily Movements of Large Brown Trout in a Michigan Stream. Unpublished paper.

Douglas, R.H. 2001. Email communication.

Douglas, R.H. and Djamgoz, M.B.A. 1990. *The Visual System of Fish*. Chapman Hall.

Dunn, Denver McClain and Harp, George L. *Determining the Possible Limitations by Cottid Species on Brown Trout Populations in Bull Shoals Lake Cold Tailwater*. Arkansas Game and Fish Commission, Arkansas Project F-63. 56 pages.

Earnhardt, Tom. 2001. *Boats for Fishermen*. The Lyons Press.

Elliott, J.M. 1994. *Quantitative Ecology and the Brown Trout*. Oxford University Press.

Elliott, J.M. 1970. The diel activity patterns of caddis larvae (Trichoptera). *Journal of Zoology, London*. 160, 279–290.

Emery, A.R. 1973. Preliminary comparisons of day and night habits of freshwater fish in Ontario lakes. *Journal Fisheries Research Board of Canada*. 30: 761–774.

Enger, P.S., Kalmijn, A.D.J., and Sand O. Behavioral Investigations on the Functions of the Lateral Line and Inner Ear in Predation. In: Coombs, S., Gorner P., and Munz, H. (eds) 1989. *The Mechanosensory Lateral Line Neurobiology and Evolution*. Springer-Verlag. pp. 575–587.

Englund, Goran and Krupa, James. 2000. Habitat use by crayfish in stream pools: influence of predators, depth, and body size. *Freshwater Biology*. 43, 75–83.

Engle, Ed. 1991. *Fly Fishing the Tailwaters.* Stackpole.

Evans, David H. 1993. *The Physiology of Fishes.* CRC Press, Inc.

Fisheries Branch, B.C. Ministry of Environment. Unpublished data on rainbow trout in Quesnel Lake, B.C. tabulated by the Williams Lake field office.

Flick, Arthur. 1947. *Streamside Guide to Naturals and Their Imitations.* Putnam.

Flick, W.A. and Webster, D.A. 1976. Production of Wild, Domestic, and Interstrain Hybrids of Brook Trout (*Salvelinus fontinalis*) in Natural Ponds. *Journal Fisheries Research Board of Canada.* 33: 1525–1539.

Flick, W.A. 1977. Some observations, age, growth, food habits, and vulnerability of large brook trout (*Salvelinus Fontinalis*) from four Canadian lakes. *Naturaliste Canada.* 104: 353–359.

Garrell, Martin and Garell, Janet. 1978. Seeforellen, World's Largest Brown Trout. *Fly Fishing World.* July-August.

Garrett, J.W. and Bennett, D.H. 1995. Seasonal Movement of Adult Brown Trout Relative to Temperature in a Coolwater Reservoir. *Journal of Fisheries Management.* 15, 480–487.

Gelineau, A., Medale, F., and Boujard, T. 1998. Effect of feeding time on postprandial nitrogen excretion and energy expenditure in rainbow trout. *Journal of Fish Biology.* 52, 655–664.

George, D.G. and Edwards, R.W. 1976. The effect of wind on the distribution of chlorophyll and crustacean plankton in a shallow eutrophic reservoir. *Journal of Applied Ecology,* 13, 667–690.

Gerking, Shelby D. 1994. *Feeding Ecology of Fish.* Academic Press.

Gern, W.A., Greenhouse, S.S., Nervina, J.M., and Gasser P.J. The Rainbow Trout Pineal Organ: An Endocrine Photometer. In: Ali, M.A. 1992. (ed.). *Rhythms in Fishes.* Plenum Press.

Ghidalia, W. Structural and Biological Aspects of Pigments. In: Bliss, G. and Mantel, L. *The Biology of Crustacea. Integument, Pigments, and Hormonal Processes.* 1985. Academic Press.

Gibson, R.N. Lunar and Tidal Rhythms in Fish. In: Thorpe, J.E. 1978. (ed.) *Rhythmic Activity of Fishes.* Academic Press.

Ginetz, R.M. and Larkin, P.A. 1973. Choice of Colors of Food Items by Rainbow Trout (*Salmo gairdneri*). Journal of the Fisheries Research Board of Canada. 30: 229–234.

Gliwicz, Z.M. 1986. A Lunar Cycle in Zooplankton. *Ecology.* 67: (4) 883–897.

Gliwicz, Z.M. and Zachner A. 1992. Diel Migrations of Juvenile Fish—A Ghost of Predation Past or Present. *Archiv Fur Hydrobiologie.* 124: (4) 385–410.

Gliwicz, Z.M. 1999. Predictability of Seasonal and Diel Events in Tropical and Temperate Lakes and Reservoirs. *Theoretical Reservoir Ecology and its Applications.* 99–124.

Gliwicz, Z.M. 1986. Predation and the evolution of vertical migration in zooplankton. *Nature.* 320. 746–748.

Greenhalgh, Macolm. 1998. *The Complete Book of Fly Fishing, A Worldwide Guide to the Fish, the Waters, the Flies, and the Challenge.* Reed Consumer Books Limited.

Greer, Ron. 1995. *Ferox Trout And Artic Charr: A Predator, its Pursuit and its Prey.* Swan Hill Press.

Hafeez, M.A. and Quay, W.B. 1970. Pineal acetylserotonin methyltransferase activity in the teleost fishes *Hesperoleucus symmetricus* and *Salmo gairdneri,* with evidence. Comp. & Gen. Pharmacol. 1, 257–262.

Hafeez, M.A. 1970. Effect of melatonin on body coloration and spontaneous swimming activity in rainbow trout, *Salmo gairdneri.* Comp. Biochem. Physiol. 36: 639–656.

Halford, Frederic M. 1910. *Modern Development of the Dry Fly.* George Routledge and Sons, Limited.

Hanneman, W. Wm. 2001. *What Trout Actually See.* Hanneman Specialties.

Hannon, Doug and Carter, W. Horrace. 1980. *Doug Hannon's Field Guide to Bass Fishing.* Atlantic Publishing Co.

Hanych, D.A., Ross, M.R., Magnien, R.E., and Suggars, A.L. 1983. Nocturnal inshore movement of the mimic shiner (*Notropis volucellus*): a possible predator avoidance. *Canadian Journal of Fisheries and Aquatic Science.* 40: 888–894.

Hart, P.J.B. and Ison, S. 1991. The influence of prey size and abundance, and individual phenotype on prey choice by the three-spined stickleback, *Gasterosteus aculeatus* L. *Journal of Fish Biology.* 38: 359–372.

Hartland-Rowe, R. 1955. Lunar rhythm in the emergence of an ephemeropteran. *Nature* (London) 1976: 657.

Hastings, Michael. 1998. The brain, circadian rhythms, and clock genes. *Biomedical Journal.* 317. 1704–1707.

Hastings, M., Maywood, E.S., and Ebling, F.J.P. 1995. The role of the circadian system in photoperiodic time measurement in animals. NATO Advanced Studies Institute Series A. 277, 95–106.

Hauer, Richard F. and Lambert, Gary A. (eds.) 1996. *Methods in Stream Ecology.* Academic Press.

Heacox, Cecil E. 1974. *The Compleat Brown Trout.* Winchester Press.

Helfman, G.S. 1981. Twilight Activities and Temporal Structure in a Freshwater Fish Community. *Canadian Journal of Fisheries and Aquatic Science.* 38: 1405–1420.

Henderson, M.A. and Northcote, T.G. 1985. Visual prey detection and foraging in sympatric cutthroat trout (*Salmo clarki clarki*) and Dolly Varden (*Salvelinus malma*). *Canadian Journal of Fisheries and Aquatic Science.* 42, 785–790.

Henderson, N.E. 1963. Influence of Light and Temperature on the Reproductive Cycle of the Eastern Brook Trout, *Salvelinus fontinalis* (Mitchell). *Journal of the Fisheries Research Board of Canada.* 20 (4) 859–897.

Herter, George Leonard. 1971. *Minnows of North America and their Streamer Imitations.* Herter's, Inc.

Hickoff, Steve and Plumley, Rhey. 1999. *Flyfisher's Guide to Northern New England.* Wilderness Adventures Press.

Hills, John Waller. 1971. *A History of Fly Fishing for Trout.* New York: Freshet Press.

Howick, G.L. and O'Brien, W.J. 1983. Piscivorous Feeding Behavior of Largemouth Bass: An Experimental Analysis. *Transactions of the American Fisheries Society.* 112: 508–516.

Hudy, Mark. 1988. Brown Trout Population Structures in White River Tailwaters Currently Managed Under No Special Regulations. *Proceedings of the Brown Trout Workshop, Asheville, April 27–28, 1988.* 94–97.

Huntingford, F.A. and Torricelli, Patrizia. 1993. *Behavioral Ecology of Fishes.* Harwood Academic Publishers GmbH.

Huntingford, F.A., Wright P.J., and Tierney, J.F. Adaptive variation in antipredator behavior in three-spined stickleback. In: Bell, Michael A. and Foster, Susan A. 1994. (eds.) *The Evolutionary Biology of the Three-spined Stickleback.* Oxford Science Publications.

Hutchinson, G.E. 1967. *A Treatise on Limnology.* Vol. II. John Wiley & Sons, Inc.

Ibrahim, A.A. and Huntingford, F.A. 1989. Laboratory and field studies on diet choice in three-spined sticklebacks (*Gasterosteus aculeatus*) in relation to profitability and visual features of prey. *Journal of Fish Biology.* 34: 245–257.

Ibrahim, A.A. and Huntingford, F.A. 1989. The role of visual cues in prey selection in three-spined sticklebacks (*Gasterosteus aculeatus*). *Ethology,* 81. 265–272.

Ibrahim, A.A. and Huntingford, F.A. 1988. Foraging efficiency in relation to within-species variation in morpholoty in three-spined sticklebacks (*Gasterosteus aculeatus*). *Journal of Fish Biology.* 33: 823–824.

International Game Fish Association. 2001. *World Record Game Fishes.*

Irving, R.G. 1954. Ecology of the Cutthroat Trout in Henry's Lake, Idaho. *Transactions of the American Fisheries Society.* 84: 275–296.

Jaenicke, M.J. 1998. Survey of the Rainbow Trout Sport Fishery on the Nonvianuk and Alagnak River, 1996. Alaska Department of Fish and Wildlife, Fishery Data Series No. 98–13.

Jakobsen, P.J. and Johnsen, G.H. 1987. The influence of predation on horizontal distribution of zooplankton species. *Freshwater Biology.* 17: 501–507.

Jenkins, T.M., Jr. 1969. Night feeding of brown and rainbow trout in an experimental stream channel. *Journal Fisheries Research Board of Canada.* 26, 3275–3278.

Jenkins, T.M. 1969. Observations on Color Changes of Brown and Rainbow Trout (*Salmo trutta* and *S. gairdneri*) in Stream Habitats, with Description of an Unusual Color Pattern in Brown Trout. *Transactions of the American Fisheries Society.* No. 3, pp. 517–519.

Jennings, Preston J. 1935. *A Book of Trout Flies.* Crown Publishers.

Johnson, Daniel M., Petersen, Richard R., Lycan, D. Richard, Sweet, James W., Neuhaus, Mark E., and Schaedel, Andrew L. 1985. *Atlas of Oregon Lakes.* Oregon State University Press.

Johnson, Paul. 1984. *The Scientific Angler: Using the Latest Underwater Research to Improve Your Catch.* Charles Scribner's Sons.

Johnston, W.L. 1990. Role of brain serotonin in the control of food intake by rainbow trout, *Oncorhynchus mykiss.* Ph.D. Dissertation, Guelph, Ontario: University of Guelph.

Jude, David. 1987. Diet and Selection of Major Prey Species by Lake Michigan Salmonines, 1973–1982. *Transactions of the American Fisheries Society,* Volume 116, September 1987, Number 5

Kalmijn, A.J. Functional Evolution of Lateral Line and Inner Ear Sensory Systems In: Coombs, S., Gorner P., and Munz, H. (eds.) 1989. *The Mechanosensory Lateral Line Neurobiology and Evolution.* Springer-Verlag. pp. 188–215.

Karas, Nick. 1997. *Brook Trout.* The Lyons Press.

Kaufmann, Randall. 1998. *Fly Patterns of Umpqua Feather Merchants.* Umpqua Feather Merchants.

Kavaliers, Martin. The Pineal Organ and Circadian Rhythms of Fishes. In: Ali, M.A. 1979. *Environmental Physiology of Fishes.* Plenum Press.

Kelso, J.R.M. 1976. Diel Movement of Walleye, *Stizostedion vitreum vitreum,* in West Blue Lake, Manitoba, as determined by Ultrasonic Tracking. *Journal Fishery Research Board of Canada.* 33: 2070–2072.

Kelso, J.R.M. 1978. Diel rhythm in activity of walleye, *Stizostedion vitreum vitreum. Journal of Fish Biology.* 12: 593–599.

King, Verdun. 2001. Written correspondence while at the University of Cambridge.

Knight, John Alden. 1972. *Moon Up, Moon Down.* Solunar Sales Company.

Knopf, Robert. R. 1982. Diel Activity Habitat Observations and the Effect of Light Intensity on Radiotagged Largemouth Bass. Unpublished Master's Thesis from the Central Michigan University.

Kustich, Rick and Kustich, Jerry. 1999. *Fly Fishing for Great Lakes Steelhead: An Advanced Look at an Emerging Fishery.* West River Publishing.

L'Abee-Lund, J.H., Aass, P., and Saegrov, H. 1996. Prey orientation in piscivorous brown trout. *Journal of Fish Biology.* 48: 871–877.

LaFontaine, Gary. 1981. *Caddisflies.* Nick Lyons Books.

———. 1976. *Challenge of the Trout.* Mountain Press Publishing Company.

———. 1993. *Trout Flies: Proven Patterns.* Greycliff Publishing Co.

Lampert, W. and Sommer, U. 1997. *Limnoecology: The Ecology of Lakes and Streams.* Oxford University Press.

Lampert, W. 1993. Ultimate causes of diel vertical migration of zooplankton: new evidence for the predator-avoidance hypothesis. *Archiv fur Hydrobiologie Beiheft Ergebnisse der Limnologie,* 39, 79–88.

Leatherland, J.F., Farbridge, K.J., and Boujard, T. 1992. Lunar and Semi-Lunar Rhythms in Fishes. In: Ali, M.A. *Rhythms in Fishes.* Plenum Press.

Limeres, Rene and Pedersen, Gunnar. 1995. *Alaska Fishing.* Foghorn Press.

Loose, Carsten J. 1993. *Daphnia* diel vertical migration behavior: Response to vertebrate predator abundance. *Archiv fur Hydrobiologie Beiheft Ergebnisse der Limnologie,* 39, 29–36.

Lorman, J.G. 1975. Feeding and activity of the crayfish *Orconectes rusticus* in a northern Wisconsin lake. M.S. Thesis. University of Wisconsin, Madison. 56 p.

Luecke, C. and Wurtsbaugh, W. 1993. Effects of moon and daylight on hydroacoustic estimates of pelagic fish abundance. *Transactions of the American Fishery Society.* 122: 112–120.

Luecke, C. 1986. A change in the pattern of vertical migration of *Chaoborus flavicans* after the introduction of trout. *Journal of Plankton Research.* 8, 649–657.

Lythgoe, J.N. 1979. *The Ecology of Vision.* Oxford.

Marbury, Mary Orvis. 1988. *Favorite Flies And Their Histories.* The Wellfleet Press. Reprint.

Mason, J.W. and Hunt, R.L. 1967. Mortality of deeply hooked rainbow trout. *The Progressive Fish-Culturist.* April. 87–91.

McLennan, D.A. and McPhail, J.D. 1990. Experimental investigations of the significance of sexually dimorphic nuptial coloration in *Gasterosteus aculeatus* (L.): the relationship between male color and female behavior. *Canadian Journal of Zoology.* 68, 482–492.

McPhail, J.D. 1984. Ecology and evolution of sympatric sticklebacks (Gasterosteue): Morphological and genetic evidence for a species pair in Enos Lake, British Columbia. *Canadian Journal of Zoology.* 62, 1402–1408.

Meka, Julie. 2000. Telephone interview while conducting a radiotelemetry project on the Alagnak River in Alaska with the United States Geological Survey, Biological Division.

Milinski, M. 1984. A predator's cost of overwhelming the confusion-effect of swarming prey. *Animal Behavior.* 32: 1157–1162.

Milinski, M. and Heller, R. 1978. Influence of a predator on the optimal foraging behavior of sticklebacks (*Gasterosteus aculeatus* L.) *Nature* 275: 624–644.

Milinski, M. 1977. Do all members of a swarm suffer the same predation? *Zeitschrift fur Tierpsycholigie,* 37, 400–402.

Minard, R.E., Alexandersdottir, M., and Sonnichsen, S. 1992. Estimation of Abundance, Seasonal Distribution, and Size and Age Composition of Rainbow Trout in the Kvichak River, Alaska, 1986–1991. Alaska Department of Fish and Wildlife, Fishery Data Series No. 92–51.

Montgomery, J.C. 1989. Lateral Line Detection of Plantonic Prey. In: Coombs, S., Gorner P., and Munz, H. (eds.) *The Mechanosensory Lateral Line Neurobiology and Evolution.* Springer-Verlag. pp. 561–574.

Moodie, G.E.E. 1972. Predation, natural selection, and adaptation in an unusual three-spined stickleback. *Heredity.* 28, Part 2, 155–167.

Moodie, G.E.E. 2001. Email correspondence.

Moyle, P.B. and Cech, J.J. 1988. *Fishes: An Introduction to Ichthyology, Second Edition.* Prentice Hall.

National Freshwater Fishing Hall of Fame. 2001. *Official World and U.S.A. State Freshwater Angling Records.*

Needham, J.G. and Needham, P.R. 1938. *A Guide to the Study of Freshwater Biology.* Comstock.

Neill, W.E. 1990. Induced vertical migration in copepods as a defense against invertebrate predation. *Nature,* 345, 524–6.

Nielson, B.R. and Lentsch, L. 1988. Bonneville cutthroat trout in Bear Lake: status and management. American Fisheries Society Symposium. 4: 128–133.

Nilsson, N.A. and Northcote, T.G. 1981. Rainbow trout (*Salmo gairdneri*) and cut-throat trout (*S. clarki*) interactions in coastal British Columbia lakes. *Canadian Journal of Fisheries and Aquatic Science.* 38, 1228–1246.

Newman, Bob. 1998. *Fly Fishing Structure: The Flyfisher's Guide to Reading and Understanding the Water.* Sycamore Island Books.

Ohguchi, O. 1981. Prey density and selection against oddity by three-spined sticklebacks. *Advances in Ethology,* 23: 1–79.

Oregon Department of Fish and Wildlife (ODF&W). 2001. Telephone interview with Keith Braun.

Oregon Department of Fish and Wildlife (ODF&W). 1989. Life History of Rainbow Trout and Effects of Angling Regulations, Deschutes River, Oregon. Information Reports. Number 89–6.

Oregon Department of Fish and Wildlife (ODF&W). 1990. Age composition, spawning runs, and average length at age of rainbow trout sampled in Spring Creek, a tributary of the Williamson River, April and May 1990. Source: Progress Reports 1990.

Oregon Department of Fish and Wildlife (ODF&W). 1997. Unpublished data on growth rates of rainbow trout in Crane Prairie Reservoir, OR.

Oswald, R.L. 1978. The use of telemetry to study light synchronization with feeding and gill ventilation rates in *Salmo trutta. Journal of Fish Biology.* 13: 729–739.

Page, L.M. and Burr B.M. 1991. *Peterson Field Guides Freshwater Fishes.* Houghton Mifflin Company.

Palmer, John D. 1995. *The Biological Rhythms and Clocks of Intertidal Animals.* Oxford University Press.

Pearson, Alan. 1979. *Catching Big Trout.* Stanley Paul.

Pennak, R.W. 1978. *Freshwater Invertebrates of the United States,* 2nd Edition. Wiley-Interscience.

Phillips, Don. 2000. *The Technology of Fly Rods.* Frank Amato Publications, Inc.

Pickering, A.D., Pottinger, T.G., and Christie, P. (1982). Recovery of the brown trout, *Salmo Trutta L.,* from acute handling stress: a time-course study. *Journal of Fish Biology.* 20, 229–244.

Pitcher, Tony J. 1986. *The Behavior of Teleost Fishes.* The Johns Hopkins University Press.

Popper, A. 2001. Email correspondence.

Power, Geoffrey. The brook charr, *Salvelinus fontinalis.* In: Balon, Eugene K. *Charrs: Salmonid Fishes of the Genus Salvelinus.* 1980. Dr. W. Junk bv Publishers.

Prins, R., Rutemiller, R., and Carder, S. 1972. Molting of the crayfish *Orconectes immunis* (Hagen), in relation to temperature, photoperiod, and light intensity. *ASB Bull.* 19(2): 93.

Radakov, D.V. 1973. *Schooling in the Ecology of Fish.* John Wiley & Sons.

Randolph, John. 1994. Handling Fish. *Fly Fisherman* magazine. December.

Raymond, Steve. 1994. *Kamloops: An Angler's Study of the Kamloops Trout.* Frank Amato Publications.

Redfish Consulting Limited. 2001. *Kootenay Lake Rainbow Trout Survey Questionnaire Results.* Prepared for the Nelson Fisheries Branch, Province of British Columbia, Ministry of Environment, Lands and Parks.

Reimchen, T.E. 1991. Evolutionary attributes of headfirst prey manipulation and swallowing in piscivores. *Canadian Journal of Zoology.* 69: 2912–2916.

Reimchen, T.E. 1991. Trout foraging failures and the evolution of body size in sticklebacks. *Copeia* 1991: 1098–1104.

Reingold, Melvin. 1975. Effects of displacing, hooking, and releasing on migrating adult steelhead trout. *Transactions of the American Fishery Society.* 3, 458–460.

Richey, David. 1981. *Complete Guide to Lake Fishing: An Outdoor Life Book.* Crown Publishers Inc.

Richmond, Scott. 1994. *Fishing in Oregon's Cascade Lakes.* Flying Pencil Publications.

———. 1998. *Fishing in Oregon's Best Fly Waters.* Flying Pencil Publications.

Rickards, Denny. 1997. *Fly Fishing Stillwaters for Trophy Trout.* Stillwater Productions.

———. 1999. *Fly Fishing The West's Best Trophy Lakes.* Stillwater Productions.

Riehle, M.D. and Griffith, J.S. 1993. Changes in Habitat Use and Feeding Chronology of Juvenile Rainbow Trout (*Oncorhynchus mykiss*) in Fall and the Onset of Winter in Silver Creek, Idaho. *Canadian Journal of Fisheries and Aquatic Science.* 50: 2119–2118.

Ringler, N.H. 1979. Selective predation by drift-feeding brown trout. *Journal of the Fisheries Research Board of Canada.* 36: 392–403.

Ringler, N.H. 1985. Individual and temporal variation in prey switching by brown trout, *Salmo trutta. Copeia.* 1985: 918–926.

Robinson, Henry W. and Buchanan, Thomas M. 1984. *Fishes of Arkansas.* The University of Arkansas Press.

Rose, J.D. Do Fish Feel Pain? Printed version of the luncheon address at the Trout Unlimited Wild Trout VII Conference.

Rose, J.D. 2001. Email correspondence.

Rosenbauer, Tom. 1988. *Reading Trout Streams, An Orvis Guide.* Lyons and Burford, Publishers.

Ryder, R.A. 1977. Effects of Ambient Light Variations on Behavior of Yearling, Subadult, and Adult Walleye (*Stizostedion vitreum vitreum*). *Journal Fishery Research Board of Canada.* 34: 1481–1491.

Sanchez-Vazquez, F.J. and Tabata, M. Circadian rhythms of demand-feeding and locomotor activity in rainbow trout. *Journal of Fish Biology.* 52: 255–267.

Sawyer, Roy T. 1986. *Leech Biology and Behavior Volumes I–III.* Clarendon Press.

Schisler, G.J. and Bergersen, E.P. 1996. Postrelease Hooking Mortality of Rainbow Trout Caught on Scented Baits. *North American Journal of Fisheries Management.* 16, 570–578.

Schollmeyer, Jim. 1995. *Hatch Guide for Lakes: Naturals and Their Imitations for Stillwater Trout Fishing.* Frank Amato Publications, Inc.

Schram, F.R. 1986. *Crustacea.* Oxford University Press.

Schullery, Paul. 1987. *American Fly Fishing: A History.* Lyons and Burford Publishers.

Scott, W.B. and Crossman, E.J. 1998. *Freshwater Fishes of Canada.* Galt House Publications, Ltd.

Semler, D.E. 1971. Some aspects of adaption in a polymorphism for breeding colours in the three-spined stickleback (*Gasterosteus aculeatus*). *Journal of Zoology, London.* 165, 291–302.

Shewey, John. 1998. *Oregon Blue Ribbon Fly Fishing Guide.* Frank Amato Publications, Inc.

Sigler, William F. and Sigler, John W. 1996. *Fishes of Utah: A Natural History.* University of Utah Press.

Smith, J.R. and L.J. Weber. 1976. The regulation of day-night changes in hydroxyindole-O-methyltransferase activity in the pineal gland of steelhead trout (*Salmo gairdneri*). *Canadian Journal Zoology* 54: 1530–1534.

Smith, Scott E. 1999. *Ontario Blue Ribbon Fly Fishing.* Guide. Frank Amato Publications, Inc.

Sosin, Mark. 1982. Brown Trout Breakthrough. *Sports Afield.* February.

Sosin, Mark and Clark, John. 1973. *Through the Fish's Eye: An Angler's Guide to Gamefish Behavior.* Book Division, Times Mirror Magazines, Inc.

Spieler, Richard E. Feeding-Entrained Circadian Rhythms in Fishes. In: Ali, M.A. 1992. (ed.). *Rhythms in Fishes.* Plenum Press.

Stein, R.A. and Magnuson, J.J. 1976. Behavioral response of crayfish to a fish predator. *Ecology.* 57, 751–761.

Stolz, Judith and Schnell, Judith. (eds.) 1991. *Trout.* Stackpole Books.

Sweka, J.A. and Hartman, K.L. 2001. Influence of turbidity on brook trout reactive distance and foraging success. *Transactions of the American Fisheries Society.* 130: 138–146.

Sweka, J.A. and Hartman, K.L. 2001. Effects of turbidity on prey consumption and growth in brook trout and implications for biogenetics modeling. *Canadian Journal of Fisheries and Aquatic Sciences.* 59(2): 386–393.

Swift, D.R. 1974. Activity Cycles in Brown Trout. *Journal of the Fisheries Research Board of Canada.* 21: 133–138.

Swisher, Doug and Richards, Carl. 2001. *Selective Trout.* Lyons Press.

Tallman, W.G. 1932. Part of a Ton of Trout: A Pyramid Lake Catch. *The Sierra Sportsman.* July. p. 7.

Taylor, A.H. 1978. An Analysis of the Trout Fishing at Eye Brook—A Eutrophic Reservoir. *Journal of Animal Ecology.* 47, 407–423.

Teeny, Jim. 1996. *The Teeny Technique For Salmon & Steelhead.* Odysseus Editions.

Teeny, Jim. *Catching More Steelhead—Breaking Tradition.* Scientific Anglers.

Thorpe, J.E. 1978. *Rhythmic Activity of Fishes.* Academic Press.

———. 1973. The movements of brown trout, *Salmo trutta* (L.) in Loch Leven, Kinross, Scotland. *Journal of Fish Biology.* 6, 153–180.

Tinbergen, N. 1948. Social Releasers and the Experimental Method Required for their Study. *Wilson Bulletin.* 60, no. 1: 5–51.

Tinbergen, N. 1951. *The Study of Instinct.* Oxford University Press.

Trotter, Patrick C. 1987. *Cutthroat.* Colorado Associated University Press.

Turner, A.M. and Mittelbach, G.G. 1990. Predator avoidance and community structure: interactions among piscivores, plantivores, and plankton. *Ecology.* 71: 2241–2254.

University of North Carolina at Chapel Hill. 1998. Major Discovery: Scientists Find Eye Pigment Controls Circadian Rhythms.

Veniard, John. 1970. *Reservoir and Lake Flies.* St. Martin's Press.

Videler, John J. 1993. *Fish Swimming.* Chapman & Hall.

Vidergar, D.T. 2000. Population Estimates, Food Habits, and Estimates of Consumption of Selected Predatory Fishes in Lake Pend Oreille, Idaho. 2000. Unpublished Master's Thesis from the University of Idaho.

Vinyard, G.L. and O'Brien, J.W. 1996. Effects of Light and Turbidity on the Reactive Distance of Bluegill (*Lepomis macrochirus*). *Journal Fisheries Research Board of Canada.* 33: 2845–2849.

Vogel, L.J. and Beauchamp, D.A. 1999. Effects of light, prey size, and turbidity on reaction distances of lake trout (*Salvelinus namaycush*) to salmonid prey. *Canadian Journal of Fisheries and Aquatic Science.* 56: 1293–1297.

Wallace, J.B. and Anderson, N.H. Habitat, Life History, and Behavioral Adaptions of Aquatic Insects. In, Merritt, R.W. and Cummins, K.W. 1996. *An Introduction to the Aquatic Insects of North America.* Kendall/Hunt Publishing Company.

Waszczuk, Henry and Labignan, Italo. 1996. *In Quest of Big Fish.* Key Porter Books. Ltd.

Waters, Thomas F. 2000. *Wildstream: A Natural History of a Free Flowing River.* Riparian Press.

Watson, John. 1899. *The English Lake District Fisheries.* Lawrence and Bullen, Ltd.

Watson, Rupert. 1999. *Salmon, Trout, and Charr of the World: A Fisherman's Natural History.* Swan Hill Press.

Webb, P.W. 1982. Avoidance Responses of Fathead Minnow to Strikes by Four Teleost Predators. *Journal of Comparative Physiology.* 147:371–378.

Wedemeyer, G. 1976. Physiological response of juvenile coho salmon (*Oncorhynchus kisutch*) and rainbow trout (*Salmo gairdneri*) to handling and crowding stress in intensive fish culture. *Journal of the Fisheries Research Board of Canada.* 33, 2699–2702.

Wetzel, R.G. 2001. *Limnology: Lake and River Ecosystems, Third Edition.* Academic Press.

White, Charlie. 1992. *Hatchet Lake Northern Pike, Hatchet Lake Walleye. (Tape #8)* Cabin Fever Entertainment, Inc.

———. 1992. *Light and Color, How Game Fish Feed. (Tape #9)* Cabin Fever Entertainment, Inc.

———. 1992. *Shearwater Coho & Chum, Sound and Vibration. (Tape #14)* Cabin Fever Entertainment, Inc.

———. 1992. *The Ultimate Lure.* Cabin Fever Entertainment, Inc.

———. 1992. *Why Fish Strike . . . Why They Don't.* Cabin Fever Entertainment, Inc.

Whitlock, Dave. 1982. *Dave Whitlock's Guide to Aquatic Trout Foods.* Lyons and Burford Publishers.

Whitney, R.R. 1969. Schooling of Fishes Relative to Available Light. *Transactions of the American Fisheries Society.* 3: 497–504.

Willers, W.B. 1981. *Trout Biology, An Angler's Guide.* The University of Wisconsin Press.

Williams, Mark D. 1996. *Trout Fishing Sourcebook.* Menasha Ridge Press.

Windell, J.T., Kitchell, J.F., Norris, D.O., and Foltz, J.W. 1976. Temperature and rate of gastric evacuation by rainbow trout, *Salmo gairdneri*. *Transactions of the American Fisheries Society*. 105, 712–7.

Wright, Steve 1995. *Ozark Trout Tales: A Fishing Guide for the White River System*. White River Chronicle.

Wurtsbaugh, W. and Li, H. 1985. Diel migrations of zooplanktivorous fish (*Menidia beryllina*) in relation to the distribution of its prey in a large eutrophic lake. *Limnology Oceanography*. 30: 565–576.

Young, M.K. 1996. Light Sets the Molecular Controls of Circadian Rhythms. Publication from the Laboratory of Genetics at the Rockefeller University.

Young, M.K., Rader, R.B., and Belish, T.A. 1997. Influence of macroinvertebrate drift and light on the activity and movement of Colorado River cutthroat trout. *Transactions of the American Fisheries Society*. 126: 428–437.

Young, M.K. 1999. Summer diel-activity and movement of adult brown trout in high-elevation streams in Wyoming, U.S.A. *Journal of Fish Biology*. 54: 181–189.

Zachmann, A., Knijff, S.C.M., Ali, M.A., and Anctil, M. 1992. Effects of photoperiod and different intensities of light exposure on melatonin levels in the blood, pineal organ, and retina of the brook trout (*Salvelinus fontinalis Mitchill*). *Canadian Journal Zoology*. 70: 25–29.

INDEX